PARALLEL
CITIES

PARALLEL
CITIES

THE MULTILEVEL METROPOLIS

Andrew Blauvelt
Editor

THE MULTILEVEL METROPOLIS

PARALLEL CITIES:

Jennifer Yoos
Vincent James

PARALLEL CITIES:

Parallel Cities: The Multilevel Metropolis is edited by Andrew Blauvelt written by Jennifer Yoos and Vincent James, and published by the Walker Art Center, Minneapolis.

Support is provided by a grant from the Andrew W. Mellon Foundation in support of Walker Art Center publications.

First Edition ©2016 Walker Art Center

All rights reserved under pan-American copyright conventions. No part of this publication may be reproduced or utilized in any form or by any means without permission in writing from the publisher. Inquiries should be addressed to: Publications Director, Walker Art Center, 1750 Hennepin Avenue, Minneapolis, MN 55403.

Every reasonable attempt has been made to identify owners of copyright. Errors or omissions will be corrected in subsequent editions.

Available through D.A.P./Distributed Art Publishers, 155 Sixth Avenue, New York, NY 10013.
www.artbook.com

Library of Congress Cataloging-in-Publication Data

Names: Yoos, Jennifer, author. / James, Vincent, author. / Blauvelt, Andrew, 1964- editor.
Title: Parallel cities : the multilevel metropolis.
Description: First Edition. | Minneapolis : Walker Art Center, 2016. | "Parallel Cities: The Multilevel Metropolis is edited by Andrew Blauvelt written by Jennifer Yoos and Vincent James, and published by the Walker Art Center, Minneapolis." | Includes bibliographical references and index.
Identifiers: LCCN 2016012931 | ISBN 9781935963127 (pbk.)
Subjects: LCSH: Skywalks. | Architecture--Human factors. | City planning.
Classification: LCC NA9074 .Y66 2016 | DDC 711/.4--dc23
LC record available at http://lccn.loc.gov/2016012931

Senior Curator, Design, Research, and Publishing: Andrew Blauvelt
Design Director: Emmet Byrne
Designer: Alex DeArmond
Editor: Kathleen McLean
Curatorial Research Assistant: Anna Renken
Senior Imaging Specialist: Greg Beckel
Design Studio Manager: Ashley Duffalo
Indexer: Candace Hyatt

Printed by Die Keure, Belgium

Typeface: Agipo

Papers: MultiOffset (cover and jacket), Munken Pure (text)

Cover:
A.   Athelstan Spilhaus and R. Buckminster Fuller, Minnesota Experimental City (MXC), 1969–1973, drawing by Krishnan Narayanan, 1971 master of architecture, Courtesy Northwest Architectural Archives, University of Minnesota Libraries (page 100)
B.   El Lissitzky and Mart Stam, Wolkenbügel, Moscow, 1923–1924, View toward the Kremlin, 1925, Collection Van Abbemuseum, Eindhoven, the Netherlands (page 34)
C.   Ludwig Hilberseimer, Highrise City (Hochhausstadt): Perspective view, North-South Street, 1924, Gift of George E. Danforth, 1983, The Art Institute of Chicago   Photo ©The Art Institute of Chicago (page 72)
D.   Harold Hanen, +15 Plan, Calgary, Canada, from "A Development Plan for Downtown," *Architecture Canada* (November/December 1966), Courtesy Royal Architectural Institute of Canada (RAIC) Image courtesy University of Minnesota Libraries (page 105)
E.   Regional Plan Association, Access Tree Diagram, Urban Design Manhattan, 1969, Courtesy Regional Plan Association (page 108)
F.   Guy Debord with Asger Jorn, The Naked City, 1957, Courtesy Musée d'Art Moderne et Contemporain de Strasbourg, Cabinet d'Art Graphique   Photo: Musées de Strasbourg, M. Bertola ©BNF, dpt Manuscripts, Fonds Guy Debord (page 81)
G.   Le Corbusier, Ilot Insalubre No. 6, presented at CIAM 5, Paris, 1936 ©FLC/ADAGP, Paris/Artists Rights Society (ARS), New York 2016 (page 60)

Appendix: Unless otherwise noted, all photos are courtesy VJAA.

FOREWORD

This book is the result of decades of research about cities, in particular the multilevel condition of "skyways," the covered, elevated footbridges that crisscross the downtowns of Minneapolis and St. Paul. For many visitors and residents, these architectural oddities are a core part of the Twin Cities' urban identity and experience. In 2001, the Walker hosted an artist-in-residence project with Catherine Opie in which her series of photographs of the city's skyways and ice-fishing houses resulted in an exhibition and accompanying catalogue showcasing these iconic structures and distinctively Minnesotan experiences. However, architects Vincent James and Jennifer Yoos reveal that our skyway systems, while seemingly unique to Minnesota, are part of a much larger and complicated history about the dream of building an elevated city. The story they put forth in this groundbreaking study spans the world and travels through time, taking us from the rooftop passages of the ancient city of Ghadames to the gliding escalators of contemporary Hong Kong.

I am pleased that this institution could publish new scholarship on such an unexplored topic, bringing to fruition the results of five years of work with former Walker senior curator of architecture and design Andrew Blauvelt. As he notes in his preface, the Walker has had a long engagement with the topic, including its 1985 national conference on skyways. As a contemporary arts center, the Walker is intensely interested in the forces that shape our cities and our lives. The built environment has also been a topic of recent Walker exhibitions, programs, and initiatives in which we have partnered with other civic entities to help forge conversations and spur action. Our collaborations over the past five years with the Minneapolis Parks Foundation on the Next Generation of Parks to the Hennepin Theatre Trust on the development of the new West Downtown Cultural District along Hennepin Avenue from the Walker to the Mississippi River.

This book is the culmination of passionate research by Vince and Jennifer, who are the founding principals of the award-winning Minneapolis-based architectural practice VJAA. Their projects have become touchstones to the Walker and its community of friends and patrons—from the stunning Dayton residence on Lake of the Isles to the beautiful Minneapolis Rowing Club along the banks of the Mississippi River. They also took part in a charrette at the Walker several years ago to help us envision and make tangible our idea for an "open field"—outdoor spaces to engage audiences through the arts. As part of the winning proposal, their team's resulting design for a grove of trees, a reassertion of our Vineland Place entry, and a new "front yard" created a communal space with a great social vibe for visitors. These elements, intended to be temporary, would become important concepts in the more permanent reimagining of our campus. Six years later, the lessons of Open Field can be gleaned in the Walker's new entry pavilion on Vineland Place—currently under construction and scheduled to reopen in late 2016—which together with the rehabilitation of the Minneapolis Sculpture Garden in 2017 will establish a new heart and social hub for the entire nineteen-acre campus.

I would like to acknowledge not only Vince and Jennifer's important scholarly contributions to the past and future of urban design represented by this publication, but also their commitment and contributions to the built environment of the Twin Cities and beyond. I am also grateful to Andrew, now director of the Cranbrook Art Museum in Bloomfield Hills, Michigan, for his eighteen years as curator and design director at the Walker. During his nearly two decades here, he created many rich platforms for scholarship, dialogue, and public debate around design and urban planning. This timely and comprehensive publication, which he helped conceptualize and edit, is no exception.

Olga Viso
Executive Director, Walker Art Center

ACKNOWL-EDGMENTS

We are grateful to the Walker Art Center for supporting a concept as challenging and open-ended as *Parallel Cities* and to the Graham Foundation for Advanced Studies in the Fine Arts for its initial generous research grant in 2000. We are also grateful to Andrew Blauvelt for the past five years of continuous collaboration, provocation, insight, and commitment. Without him, this book would not have been possible.

Over the course of this complex fifteen-year research project, we have engaged a wide group of institutions and individuals who have advised us in our work or supported the project in various ways. We would particularly like to thank the Harvard Loeb Fellowship and Graduate School of Design, the MIT School of Architecture and Planning and its exhibitions program, the University of Minnesota School of Architecture, the University of Arkansas Fay Jones School of Architecture, and the Illinois Institute of Technology's College of Architecture. We are also appreciative of and grateful to the following individuals for their ongoing support: Nader Tehrani, Marlon Blackwell, Steven Holl, Thomas Fisher, John Ronan, James Stockard, Interboro (Georgeen Theodore, Daniel D'Oca, and Tobias Armborst), Abby Bussel, and a special thanks to our business partner, Nathan Knutson.

As architects—not scholars or historians—we pursued this project while maintaining our practice. Our research began with the trajectory of an idea that grew to engage many disciplines beyond our abilities as architects to address. We are appreciative of the generosity and advice of a number of scholars; these conversations have continually reshaped and inspired our work. We are especially grateful to Hashim Sarkis (MIT), Margaret Crawford (Berkeley), Eric Mumford (Washington University), Brent Ryan (MIT), Laurent Gutierrez and Valérie Portefaix (Map Office and Hong Kong Polytechnic University), and Robert McCarter (Washington University) for specific expertise. We would like to thank members of our office who contributed to the project, particularly collaborators Dzenita Hadziomerovic and Jeff Niematz, who developed the graphic analysis of existing cities.

We are obliged to a number of archives and individuals for access to original materials and information, including the Francis Loeb Library, Harvard University; the Northwest Architectural Archives and Cheryll Fong, the University of Minnesota; the Briscoe Center for American History, the University of Texas-Austin; the City of Calgary Archives; the Hong Kong Department of Transport; and the Minnesota Historical Society. We are also thankful for the insights gained from the following professionals: W. C. Chan, senior engineer, Transport Department, Hong Kong; Ron

Ference, +15 coordinator; Ofer Manor, Jerusalem city architect; and Weiwen Huang, former director, Department of Urban and Architecture Design, Shenzhen Municipal Planning Bureau, and main organizer, Shenzhen & Hong Kong Bi-City Biennale of Urbanism/Architecture.

At the Walker Art Center, early picture research was undertaken by Kathie Smith and later completed by Anna Renken, who ably sourced and obtained the numerous image rights necessary for this publication. Meredith Kessler promoted this project in the media in concert with our colleagues at D.A.P./Distributed Art Publishers, New York. We are grateful to Alex DeArmond for the beautiful design of this book and to his sensitive and inventive handling of its content, and our sincere thanks to design director Emmet Byrne, image specialist Greg Beckel, and publications manager Ashley Duffalo in the Walker's design studio for handling the myriad details for the preparation, printing, and distribution of the publication. Kathleen McLean and Andrew Blauvelt patiently edited the publication through several drafts and we are appreciative of their insightful contributions and the rigor of their edits and commentary.

Above all, we would like to thank Odette James and our families for their endless support and encouragement.

Jennifer Yoos and Vincent James

PREFACE

In 1985 the Walker Art Center and the University of Minnesota hosted a conference on pedestrian systems—skyways, tunnels, and streets.[1] An unusual topic for a museum perhaps, but not for the Walker, which had established itself as a participant and cultural leader in the civic life of Minneapolis. In the context of the museum's earlier efforts—such as its focus on the rehabilitation of Hennepin Avenue, a major thoroughfare that had fallen into decline in the 1960s, or in shaping the architecture of the city's downtown and emerging skyline—the subject appeared to be a logical choice.[2] The city itself would be a natural location for such a conference, as its elevated network of footbridges, dubbed the Minneapolis Skyway System, represented one of the most extensive in the world and, since its inception in 1962, has connected most major buildings in the downtown core.[3]

The conference was an interdisciplinary gathering featuring a diverse range of figures: architectural historian Colin Rowe; architecture critic for the *Dallas Morning News* David Dillon; urban geographer Judith Martin, a professor at the University of Minnesota; Donald Sinclair, coordinator for Calgary's +15 Skywalk system; Anthony Bouza, Minneapolis chief of police; and representatives from various urban planning departments around the country. This range of participants would signal the more sweeping concerns of its organizers as they tackled not only expected questions about architectural and urban design but also the social and political implications of creating, in effect, a parallel city some twenty feet above the existing one—a system that connects mostly privately-owned buildings through publicly accessible pathways. As Walker design curator Mickey Friedman summarized it, the primary questions revolved around issues of who gets to decide how such a system is deployed, designed, maintained, used, and accessed, and, of course, its impact on existing street life.[4] The conference did not resolve such issues but it did foreground concerns about the relationship between private property and public space—issues that have only grown more pronounced since the 1980s. This book does not resolve such issues either, but rather lays out the history of an idea of the multilevel city and its use of elevated pedestrian networks that has captivated the public imagination for centuries. While their discussion at the conference was limited to North American cities, the explorations in this publication extend further afield as new typologies have emerged in Asia and the Middle East, for instance.

Minneapolis and its twin city of St. Paul have adopted extensive systems of second-level footbridges for their respective downtowns, although each differs in implementation and history (see chapter 4). Now, a half-century later, these systems still elicit either praise or condemnation from hometown and out-of-town critics alike. Users and residents primarily cite the system's convenience—and their ability to walk across downtown without a coat in the city's formidable winter climate. Detractors point to the utilitarian banality of these "human gerbil tubes" that often have no design relationship to the buildings they connect and the displacement of street life to a world hovering just above the "real city." In these feelings, Minnesotans are not alone. One can find such sentiments—as well as many others—in multilevel cities and networks around the world.

These systems inherently seem to impose a set of conundrums for architects, planners, and policy-makers. Aesthetic issues could be resolved at their inception when skyways can be conceived and designed as a whole, typically as a blank slate. Such an opportunity might exist in a new or "instant city" in China, for example, or in the reconstruction of part of a city after its destruction, for instance in postwar London, or in the reuse of existing but abandoned infrastructure, like the High Line, an elevated section of railway turned park in New York. The displacement of street life might be beneficial in the context of mitigating congestion on city streets, such as those in Hong Kong or Mumbai. In smaller, less densely populated cities, the dispersal of people onto multiple levels hastens the impression of deserted streets at grade. Some systems present themselves as coherent and cohesively designed networks (such as the picture of modern efficiency and the product of authoritarian planning seen in the film *Metropolis)*, while others appear as an ad hoc assemblage of infrastructural sprawl or as a jumble of uncontrollable ductwork (not unlike the byproduct of dysfunctional bureaucracy portrayed in the movie *Brazil*). Although almost always public-facing in appearance and by access, such systems mimic the conditions of public streets but are governed by different codes of conduct, and their terms of use are prescribed by private interests. Such networks, the authors argue, tend to be self-perpetuating once established, a surreptitious form of urbanism that transforms entire cities with little direct public consent or engagement.

What these varying contexts suggest is that the concept of a multilevel city and its attendant network of elevated (and below grade) pedestrian pathways is not a universally transferable idea. What works well in one condition may fail in another, so adaptation and negotiation of such systems is key. Despite this rather obvious disclaimer, the concept of the multilevel city, particularly its elevated pedestrian networks, is an architectural trope that has migrated across the world and

throughout history. It is an idea that has evolved over time, taking on the sociopolitical context of incessant reinventions. As the authors relate, the modern concept of the multilevel city can be traced from its roots by social utopian thinkers at the time of the French Revolution in the eighteenth century to the Soviet Revolution in the twentieth century. In these contexts, architecture was called upon to reform rather than reflect social divisions. It has also been the by-product of a rational approach to modern city planning governed by traffic-flow efficiencies, public sanitation needs, and pedestrian safety concerns. In these situations it is deployed as a bureaucratic tool of functionalism to ameliorate the conditions of industrialization. It has been proffered as a surrogate of the city street itself—a space of varied programs and mixed uses for all citizens and thus a symbol of democratic access and individual autonomy. Conversely, it has been intentionally and unintentionally employed to separate populations and to segregate people. It has been used to shore up failing downtowns and for the mallification of discrete businesses—creating an endless corridor of consumption. By turns utopic and dystopian, epic and banal, the multilevel city with its elevated pedestrian networks reveals itself in distinct guises. Yoos and James offer the reader an unusual and insightful chronicle of these visionary transformations and prosaic instantiations.

In their excavation of this unique history of an architectural concept, they reveal a tangled network of connections among visionary architects, resourceful bureaucrats, passionate proselytizers, and utopian dreamers. They map the flow of ideas as they migrate from country to country and register their transformations in different social, cultural, and political contexts. This type of research and criticism goes against the grain of much architectural history. It requires bypassing contemporary preoccupations with architectural auteurism, whereby ideas arrive without historical acknowledgment while also foregoing the compartmentalization of architectural history into conveniently delimited time periods. It also requires an engagement with a subject that quite frankly is ignored or disparaged by architects. At first glance, explicating a history of "skyways" is decidedly unfashionable—like suggesting a history about highways or moving sidewalks. This kind of reaction reveals the infrastructural bias of the topic. Utilitarian, functional, and pardon the pun, pedestrian—terms like "skyway," "skywalk," and "pedway" conjure an image of relentlessly bleak environments, or in the words of anthropologist Marc Augé, "nonplaces"—the space of transience created by supermodernity. It is therefore surprising to find in this historical reconstitution of such a typology the remnants of exciting, visionary expressions about the future metropolis and the persistence of the multilevel city as a favorite meme. Because the topic is at its core about the production of space, the political contexts that gave rise to such forms as well as the social impact of multilevel urbanism cannot be ignored.

This process of Yoos and James's research and discovery was neither self-evident nor easy. As busy practitioners, they doggedly pursued their interests intermittently over many years—sifting through city archives and planning documents, conducting numerous site visits to such systems around the world, and exploring the topic with their students, with whom they debated the issues to further the discourse. We are truly grateful for their efforts. The following chronicle offers to the reader the fruits of their labor—a journey not unlike traversing the elevated city itself: a different perspective on a familiar scene, a fluid landscape with unexpected connections and surprise detours. Like the systems they map in the appendix of this book, the story of the multilevel city and its elevated pedestrian networks is perpetually incomplete, always awaiting the next connection.

Andrew Blauvelt

1. See Mildred Friedman, ed., "Skyways," in *Design Quarterly* no. 129 (Minneapolis: Walker Art Center, 1985) for an issue dedicated to the topics undertaken at the conference.
2. See Denise Scott Brown, ed., "Hennepin Avenue," in *Design Quarterly* no. 117 (Minneapolis: Walker Art Center, 1982) and Rem Koolhaas, ed., "City Center Profile," in *Design Quarterly* no. 125 (Minneapolis: Walker Art Center, 1984).
3. The first skyway footbridge was opened in 1962 and the system eventually grew to encompass 69 blocks of downtown Minneapolis, covering more than seven miles of walkways.
4. Friedman, *Design Quarterly* no. 129, 2–3.

INTRODUCTION

In his etymology of the word "street," Joseph Rykwert[1] described its origin in the simple path, followed by the well-trodden trail that gained symbolic importance through territorialization. The significance of the path of movement can be found in almost all cultures and is an essential characteristic of human settlements and cities. But more importantly, the origin of the street as a "free" and public sphere mediating the "private" interior domains of the city is built into our culturally defined understanding of the street as a true social space.

For Rykwert the street becomes a social institution of particular importance to urbanization through its paving—the capital investment made for its maintenance as a viable space of movement and social intercourse in the city. However, with its proliferation into many capital-intensive infrastructural layers, the street as "free space" has been problematized. Rykwert's succinct conceptual framework enables us to see why this is of such critical importance to the contemporary city, where the practical and symbolic role of the street in urban life has become increasingly complex.

We have structured this book to make connections between things that are typically separated in contemporary discourses on architecture and urban planning: theory and practice, form and function, and the ideal and the real. In discussions about cities, these topics are often set in opposition rather than integrated within a dialectical relationship. In *Parallel Cities*, we attempt to trace an idea—multilevel pedestrian urbanism—spanning centuries across individual authors, stylistic periods, and political economies. We investigate both the idealized and failed versions of an idea that has been a source of inspiration for visionaries hoping to perfect society and a source of trepidation for critics who fear the destruction of the social institution of the street.

In *Parallel Cities* we also examine the many ways in which the idea of the multilevel city has been invented and reinvented by diverse thinkers, motivated by a wide variety of concerns for the city as the locus of day-to-day life, human aspirations, and conflict. We believe it is critical to examine these issues from multiple perspectives and in multiple contexts, particularly because proposals for multilevel cities have recurred throughout history but always seem to be perceived as new and radical. Given the rapidly evolving forms of three-dimensional urbanization, a comprehensive critical discourse on this new urban reality seems overdue.

Toward this goal, we are less interested in the stylistic characteristics or formal ideologies that typically come to define these urban proposals, however important they may be. We propose, rather, an assessment of how these models facilitate or constrain our understanding of urban morphogenesis, and how the multilevel metropolis might evolve over an extended period of time. The socio-spatial implications of this phenomenon, including its experiential possibilities, are of critical concern for those interested in theorizing these still nascent urban forms.

Visionary projects for the multilevel city and their varied histories are intertwined with the socio-political and economic circumstances that fostered their development. Emerging from the urban turmoil of nineteenth-century Europe, the "city as a project" became an ongoing preoccupation of architects and urbanists throughout the twentieth century.[2] Encountering new and overwhelming urban problems of congestion, pollution, and civil unrest resulting largely from population growth and industrialization, architects believed that a modern planning discipline incorporating architecture and urban design could transform and modernize the city. Through the lens of social betterment, early twentieth-century architects considered buildings not only as individual objects, but also as interdependent components of larger urban systems defined principally by infrastructure. With this redefinition, the future of the street fell under the auspices of municipal governments and other authorities concerned with the livability and efficiency of cities.

In the mid-twentieth century, Team 10 and other architects and urbanists concerned with the functionalist banality of modernist cities would attempt to resuscitate the street as a social institution. The promotion of grade-separated pedestrian systems was one of the principal outcomes of this initiative. Despite their typically utilitarian forms, these systems were conceived and promoted by European architects who migrated to leading universities and urban planning departments in the United States and Canada. The extent to which these architects and urban designers and their American protégés successfully put into practice their form of urbanism in major North American cities, where they continue to flourish unnoticed, is one of the marvels of this unexamined history.

Since the 1980s, the notion that architects and urbanists working collectively would improve the public realm has largely given way to a distinctly different kind of urbanism. The dominance of neoliberal economics and the radicalization of the architect as author shifted the focus of urban development away from the concept of public space and toward the quasi-public spaces of private development. The multilevel urbanisms resulting from concentrated private capital are distinctly different from their social utopian predecessors. This shift

has potentially dramatic implications for the nature of social space in the twenty-first century.

While the urbanisms resulting from the privatization of public space are significantly changing the social, spatial, and economic character of cities, the project of the multilevel city has not been abandoned. It has simply been reinvented and redeployed in the service of neoliberal urbanization. Under these circumstances the discipline of architecture has changed, too. It seems that contemporary architectural practices tend to selectively ignore, or reinvent, the discipline's avant-garde history in individually branded projects, thus avoiding larger urban questions represented in the body of experimental work that has been developed over time. Because the contemporary preoccupation with the aesthetic and marketplace branding of individual building commissions tends to reinforce hermetic practices, a broader debate capable of contextualizing this work is absent. For this reason, among others, architecture as a discipline has become estranged from discourses on the evolving forms of the city as a social apparatus as well an as open field for political expression.[3]

Since the 1990s the proliferation of proposals for elevated pedestrian spaces reveals a renewed interest in multilevel urban space. Many of the most interesting and provocative projects suggest both the positive and negative possibilities of these new urban prototypes. In recent ventures we see bridges stretched taut between multiple buildings in Steven Holl's high-wire act, the Linked Hybrid project (2009) in Beijing. In MVRDV's proposal for Seoul called the Cloud (2011) and the group's recent proposal for a financial center in the Bund in Shanghai (2015), high-rise towers are grafted together by pixelating the building module to form a bridge of housing and public space. Other projects such as Holl's Vanke Center (2009) in Shenzhen link multiple buildings and programs into elaborate city-scaled lattices. Urban retail complexes by Zaha Hadid Architects, Foreign Office Architects, and Future Systems weave layered bands of horizontal circulation, extending interiorized commercial space to an urban scale. Elsewhere, planners and architects propose elevated green walkways raised above the street, hoping to repeat the success of James Corner Field Operations and Diller Scofidio + Renfro's High Line in New York (2009–2014).

While architects of such high-profile projects knowingly or unknowingly reference the concepts of an earlier avant-garde, such as "social condensers," "floating cities," and "horizontal skyscrapers," they often ignore the systemic, bureaucratic, and commonplace forms of multilevel pedestrian networks that have been developing continuously since the 1960s in cities around the world.

Although these existing built systems offer a wealth of information on the positive and negative effects of these urbanisms, they have received little or no critical attention from the design professions.

Why have of the most radical ongoing experiments in urban planning and design been largely ignored or gone unnoticed? What does the success of such incremental methods of growth suggest for large-scale urban transformation? What do these systems offer the city as a social and political apparatus? What are the opportunities and risks of deliberately deploying these new urban forms on a large scale?

Elevated pedestrian systems are almost always understood in reference to the original grade-level street and the social space of the city. Such systems have delaminated the street into its constituent programmatic parts, extrapolating it into three dimensions. Has the density and complexity of modern cities made it impossible for the many uses of the street to simultaneously occupy a single plane? Despite the variety of urban schemes, one thing stands out: the historic street is the progenitor of the multilevel pedestrian city. But the question has to be asked: will this continue to be true?

Having been for centuries the idée fixe of architects and urban reformers with radically different social, political, and economic agendas, the idea of the multilevel city has demonstrated an astonishing resiliency. Whether characterized in some cases by relatively open urban networks and in others by circumscribed urban enclaves in the sky, we believe that these urbanisms represent the likely forms of future high-density cities. The ongoing transformation of the contemporary metropolis into complex three-dimensional pedestrian spaces should provoke architects and urban planners interested in the social, functional, and experiential life of the city to critically reassess the history of the multilevel city and the ongoing experiments taking place around the world.

Jennifer Yoos and Vincent James

1.   Joseph Rykwert, "The Street: The Use of Its History," in Stanford Anderson, *On Streets* (Cambridge: MIT Press, 1986).
2.   As Pier Vittorio Aureli describes it in his book *City as a Project* (Berlin: Ruby Press, 2013).
3.   Bernardo Secchi, "Three Stories for the XXth Century," presented at the II International PhD Seminar on Urbanism, Barcelona, June 27, 2005, published in *Planum.net: The European Journal of Planning*.

The Phalanx has no outside streets or open road-ways exposed to the elements. All the portions of the central edifice can be traversed by means of a wide gallery which runs along the second floor of the whole building. At each extremity of this spacious corridor there are elevated passages, supported by columns, and also attractive underground passages which connect all the parts of the Phalanx and the adjoining buildings. Thus everything is linked by a series of passage-ways which are sheltered, elegant, and comfortable in winter thanks to the help of heaters and ventilators.

The street-galleries are a mode of internal communication which would alone be sufficient to inspire disdain for the palaces and great cities of civilization. Once a man has seen the street-galleries of a Phalanx, he will look upon the most elegant civilized palace as a place of exile, a residence worthy of fools who, after three thousand years of architectural studies, have not yet learned how to build themselves healthy and comfortable lodgings. In civilization we can only conceive of luxury in the simple mode; we have no conception of the compound or collective forms of luxury...

— Charles Fourier, "Street-Galleries" in *The Utopian City*, 1822

1. VISIONARY CITIES/ VERTIGINOUS METROPOLIS

1. VISIONARY CITIES/ VERTIGINOUS METROPOLIS

1. Jonathan Beecher, *Charles Fourier: The Visionary and His World* (Berkeley: University of California Press, 1986), 243–250.
2. Lukasz Stanek, *Henri Lefebvre on Space: Architecture, Urban Research, and the Production of Theory* (Minneapolis: University of Minnesota Press, 2011), 176–179.
3. Anthony Vidler, *Scenes of the Street* (New York: Monacelli Press, 2011), 47–50.

Emerging from the social and political change unleashed by the French Revolution, numerous utopian proposals in the nineteenth century would seek to radically transform society through new and socially liberating architectural and urban forms. In an attempt to transcend both the social limitations of individually articulated and programmed buildings and the maladies of the existing streets, socialist reformers proposed interconnected networks of interior space as a new form of the city. At the heart of this project was the belief that a radical transformation of the built environment would inevitably lead to social emancipation and the restructuring of society. While taking on a number of architectural guises, the spatial characteristics of these urban utopias consistently included second-level public gathering spaces, typically linked together with bridges spanning the streets.

One of the inventors and leading theorists of this social-utopian project was Charles Fourier, an eccentric reformer who spent his life developing and promoting a new form of communitarian society based on pleasure and the liberation of individual passions and creativity. Highly critical of the compartmentalized spaces of traditional architecture, Fourier saw class struggle and revolution as the inevitable negative result of the suppression of basic human desires and the lack of spatial proximity and connectivity.

In 1790, shortly after the French Revolution, Fourier visited the Palais-Royal, the site of the first Parisian arcades that had been newly redesigned as a public entertainment complex (1784). At the palace he witnessed what he saw as a grand social experiment within the mixing spaces of an urban-scaled architectural interior designed for public gatherings, shopping, and entertainment. The Palais-Royal complex included arcades, theaters, cafés and salons, political forums, and gardens for strolling, people-watching, and other informal activities. Inspired by this new socio-spatial invention, Fourier believed that if these new spaces were extended to the scale, such activities of the city would take place not in the public street but in these grand domestic interiors, fusing architecture and civic space.

In the 1820s, just as the Palais-Royal had been repurposed as a more liberal and egalitarian space of political and social exchange, Fourier began to develop his plan for what he called the Phalanstère, a prototype for a quasi-urban building complex designed around a carefully scripted community of one thousand six hundred twenty individuals. The design was focused in particular on the arcadelike *rue corridor*, or street-gallery, situated on the level above the ground floor, like the *bel étage* of the aristocratic palaces, only now serving the desires and needs of the communitarians. When all of the comforts and conveniences of the palace were made available to a cross section of the classes, Fourier believed social interaction and cohesion would be the natural result.[1]

These elevated and interconnected street-galleries were Fourier's principal spatial invention, suggesting a new kind of urbanism and a key to what he described as "an architecture of association."[2] Circulating through the splendid, climate-controlled grand mixing chambers, the communitarians would enjoy the leveling effects of shared comfort and convenience, arguably two of the most fundamental of behavioral factors underlying urban morphogenesis. A belief in the ability of architectural form to facilitate social behavior was fundamental to Fourier's communitarian vision. That view would influence architects, urbanists, and sociologists interested in multilevel cities well into the twentieth century.[3] Fourier's socialist project would be first carried forward by his followers and become a lasting symbol of socially driven urban spatialities, albeit one with ever-shifting implications.

Proselyte Victor Considerant advocated that Fourier's ideas be constructed at an urban scale in the latest cast-iron-and-glass building methods linking architectural and technological innovation on the socialist agenda:

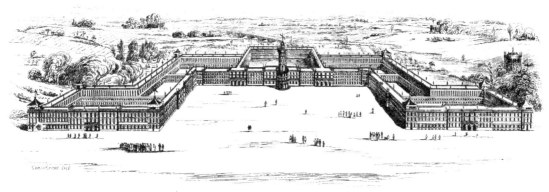

A

B

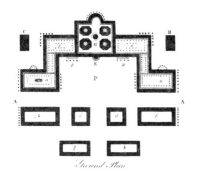

C

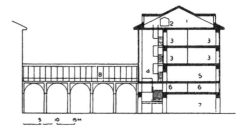

1 Loft with rooms for guests
2 Reservoirs
3 Private Rooms
4 *Rue Intérieure*
5 Assembly rooms
6 Mezzanine, with accom-
   modation for children
7 Ground floor with space
   for vehicles
8 Covered footbridge
   (*rue corridor*)

A.   Charles Fourier, Etching
from Phalanstère, Courtesy Albert
Brisbane, *Social Destiny of Man,
or, Association and Reorganization
of Industry* (Philadelphia: C. F.
Stollmeyer, 1840)
B.   Charles Fourier, Plan from
Phalanstère, Courtesy Albert
Brisbane, *Social Destiny of Man,
or, Association and Reorganization
of Industry* (Philadelphia: C. F.
Stollmeyer, 1840)
C.   Charles Fourier, Phalanstère,
diagram of footbridges
4.   Victor Considerant,
*Considerations Sociale sur la
Architectonique* (Paris: Les libraires
du Palais-Royal, 1834), 63.
5.   Vidler, *Scenes of the Street*,
49–50.

The gallery street is certainly one of the most characteristic organs of social architecture. It serves for great feasts and special gatherings. Adorned with flowers like the most beautiful glass-houses, decorated with the richest products of art and industry, the galleries and salons of the Phalanstéries provide splendid permanent exhibitions for the artists of Harmony. It is probable that they will be constructed entirely of glass.

Sometimes outside, sometimes inside the palace, sometimes widening out to form a wide rotunda, an atrium flooded with light, projecting its corridors across the courtyards on columns or light suspension bridges to join together the two parallel faces of the building, finally branching out to the great white stairways and opening up wide and sumptuous communication throughout.[4]

Fourier's Phalanstère was not intended as an end in itself but as a prototype of social architecture organized around grand interior spaces, a predecessor in a series of urban prototypes that would change society. After his death in 1837, other prominent nineteenth-century social reformers such as Robert Owen promoted the idea of communal architecture, inspiring the construction of hundreds of model towns around the world.[5] Fourier's optimistic concept of a socio-scientific utopia that could be integrated with industry was adapted to a range of other projects and conceptually expanded by nineteenth-century

– Etching of Charles Fourier's "garantiste" city, attributed to Jean-Baptiste André Godin
6. Peter Wolf, "Urban Redevelopment 19th-Century Style: Older, Bolder Ideas for Today," in *Design Quarterly* no. 85, Urban Redevelopment: 19th-Century Vision, 20th-Century Version (1972): 3–17.

reformers. Fourier's acceptance of individual property rights and his rejection of strict social egalitarianism also appealed to industrialists such as Jean-Baptiste André Godin, who built a communal Familistère (Social Palace) (1856–1859) to house a cast-iron stove manufacturing factory and residential housing complex that would ultimately be managed by its worker-residents.

Borie and Moilin: Social Utopias for Paris

The transformation of Paris by Baron von Haussmann during the Second Empire would inspire subsequent plans from radical utopian socialists. Motivated in part by a critical assessment of the broad boulevards and the loss of intimacy, the new schemes for interconnected multilevel urban spaces and social interiors were proposed by visionaries building on the work of Charles Fourier. Although the value of Haussmann's modernization of the city's infrastructure was not lost on these authors, multilevel urbanisms seemed to offer similar infrastructural advantages while providing an antidote to the impersonal expanses of the emerging cosmopolitan city.

In 1865, Henri Jules Borie, a Parisian civil engineer, published four prototypes for the reconstruction of Paris. In his plans, massive ten-story, mixed-use building complexes were organized in orthogonal patterns corresponding to a new geometric street grid. Elevated glass-covered bridges and street galleries interconnected the blocks on the fifth level, spanning the ground-level and glass-enclosed spaces, including winter gardens, exposition halls, and markets.[6] Residential apartments were incorporated into the mixed-use urban fabric, including commercial space, civic amenities, and cultural institutions. Borie was essentially proposing reproducing virtually all of the functions of the city in a three-dimensional matrix. Called Aérodromes, these urban complexes were to be superimposed on the existing fabric of Paris through a series of incremental erasures in rundown neighborhoods, presaging Le Corbusier's grand tabula rasa of Plan Voisin (1925) and also the mixed-use housing blocks

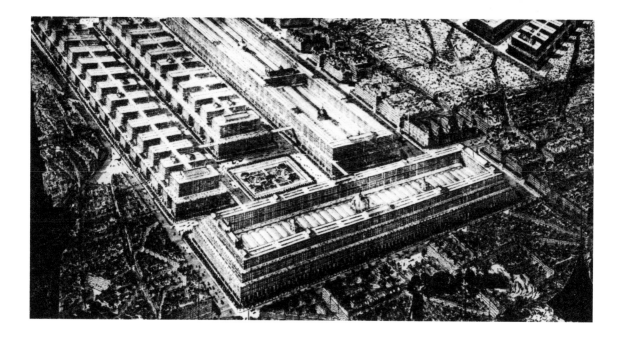

— Henri Jules Borie, High-rise dwelling units (Aérodromes), Paris, 1865, Courtesy Walker Art Center Archives
7. David Harvey, *Paris, Capital of Modernity* (London: Routledge, 2005), 283.
8. Peter Wolf, *Eugène Hénard and the Beginning of Urbanism in Paris 1900–1914* (The Hague, Netherlands: ANDO, 1968), 233.

during the postwar period of the twentieth century. Socially, Borie's plan for implementation attempted to achieve mixed-income housing like that of Charles Fourier, with the project to be publically built and units either sold or rented by the city of Paris.

Other proposals were even more ambitious. In 1869, Jules-Antoine Moilin, a writer and doctor specializing in respiratory diseases, proposed a scheme for Paris as radical as Haussmann's but completely different. Building on the work of Fourier, Considerant, and Borie, Moilin proposed the transformation of Paris into a multilevel interiorized city. In his book *Paris in the Year 2000*, Moilin described in detail the future metropolis. Instead of Haussmann's massive new boulevards, Moilin proposed an elevated pedestrian fabric throughout the city. One of the most innovative aspects of the scheme was the wholesale appropriation of the existing second level to create a continuous pedestrian concourse. Paris would be hollowed out and relined with palatial interiors or *rue galeries* connected with enclosed bridges forming a weatherproof, luxurious, upper-level pedestrian network throughout the city.[7] Moilin's plan would have altered Paris in its entirety, devouring the historic fabric and disregarding the formal and spatial logic of more traditional buildings. In adapting to the irregularities of existing building alignments with ramps and stairs, Moilin's vision of a new kind of parasitic urbanism would prove prescient and remarkably accurate to the realities of the pedestrian systems built across North America more than one hundred years later. Rejecting the idea of Borie's publically financed superblocks, Moilin predicted that *Paris in the Year 2000* would be achieved through revolution and the wholesale annexation of private property throughout the city. It was a scheme that would have required absolute authoritarian control for implementation. However, this question of public versus private development, ownership, and control of elevated pedestrian systems would remain a persistent problem for governments and private developers implementing the various forms of multilevel urbanism.[8]

The Layered Street
_____

Although unrealized, Moilin's vision of a sectional readaptation of Paris would later inspire the urban plans of Eugène Hénard as the city became more of a

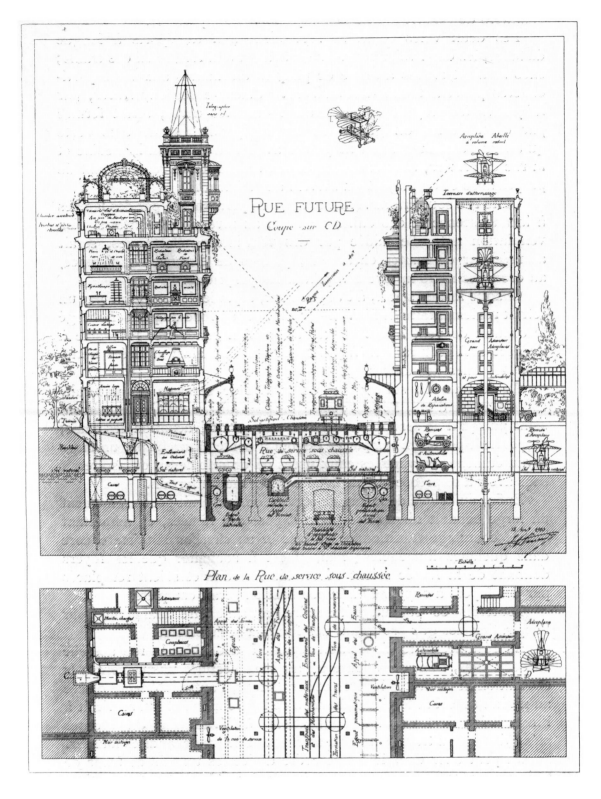

– Eugène Hénard, *Cities of the Future*, Paris, 1910, Courtesy University of Minnesota Libraries

9. Paul Rabinow, *French Modern: Norms and Forms of the Social Environment* (Cambridge: MIT Press, 1989), 251–257.
10. Ibid., 213.
11. Peter Wolf, "City Structuring and Social Sense, 19th- and 20th-Century Urbanism," in *Perspecta* vol. 13/14 (1971): 220–233.

scientific and engineering problem. Instead of proposals for the interiorization of the city as a panacea for the social and economic problems of mid-nineteenth-century Paris, at the turn of the century a new approach to the renovation of the city was being developed. As Paris grew in density, the separation of pedestrians from motorized transportation became a preoccupation, as did the engineering of utilities and sanitation systems.

In the early twentieth century, Paris had enormous problems with congestion. The city had experienced rapid population growth and industrialization between 1851 and 1900, while the net area of open space had decreased by half due to speculation driven by Haussmann's plans. Overcrowding and inadequate housing led to renewed concerns for health and hygiene in areas that had not yet been modernized. From 1905 to 1914, there was a renewal of French reformist socialism in Paris amid political conflict, with both the left and the right sharing interests in urban transformation. While London and Berlin moved ahead of Paris in enacting policies supporting urban planning, Paris benefited from the continuation of an ongoing dialogue around social reform. Moving away from the revolutionary zeal of earlier movements and social utopian schemes, the new reformers shifted their tactics to detailed analysis and site-specific strategies for the city.

With the growing influence of sociology and anthropology, the Musée Social was established in 1894, a privately funded organization to consolidate information around "the social question." It rapidly evolved into a private research group, or think-tank, to consider the topic of urbanism in the public interest. In 1908 the Musée Social formed a committee to address the problems of the city framed around the topic of hygiene. It was divided into two groups, one for design and one for implementation. Eugène Hénard, a long-term city architect, led the design section to investigate problems and develop planning strategies. These were later compiled as his *Études sur le transformation de Paris* (1903–1914).

The urbanisms that materialized under the leadership of Hénard began with a dissection of the city street into its multiple functions. The separation of pedestrian circulation from vehicles had become a central preoccupation as cities like Paris grew in density. By articulating in section the individual functions of the street, a wide range of possibilities for the modern city emerged.[9] The complex relationships between pedestrian and vehicular circulation, mechanical conveyance, sanitation, and the distribution of utilities could be logically engineered. While the dream of the multilevel city continued, it became less fantastical and more rational as the modern metropolis was engineered as a three-dimensional design problem.

Hénard's interest in sociology and scientific method resulted in the first statistical study of traffic and its impact on the city. The modeling was detailed, dividing data by types of traffic and time of day, and he compared his analysis with other cities exhibiting similar traffic but less congestion. His design methodology focused on patterns, flows, and devices, while also applying the provisional implementation strategies of Haussmann.[10]

While Hénard's multilevel urban proposals were never directly enacted, he quickly became an important international figure. Because his designs were prototypical, they had the ability to be applied in other cities with similar concerns. Although radical in their implications for urban development, the prototypes were promoted in pragmatic terms. Hénard also invented the *Ville-Pilotis* (city on stilts), rooftop landing pads for "aeroplanes of the bee-type," and the first traffic-flow diagrams for Paris. Hénard's ideas had significant influence on architects and planners, most notably Le Corbusier.[11] This included the important concept of "urbanisme" that was broadly framed as the interconnection of different urban programs, the continuity of the urban fabric in plan and section, and the importance of flows—movement patterns that shape the city.

12. Royal Institute of British Architects, Town Planning Conference London, October 10–15, 1910, *Transactions* (London: The Royal Institute of British Architects, 1911): 345–367.
13. Patrick Abercrombie, "Paris: Some Influences That Have Shaped Its Growth," *The Town Planning Review*, vol. 2, no. 4 (Liverpool: Liverpool University Press, 1912), 309–320.
14. Kenneth Frampton, "The Evolution of Housing Concepts: 1870–1970," in *Another Chance for Housing: Low-Rise Alternatives* (New York: Museum of Modern Art, 1973), 5.
15. Eve Blau, *The Architecture of Red Vienna* (Cambridge: MIT Press, 1999), 300–301.

Shortly after the enactment of the British Town Planning Bill of 1909, Hénard presented the lecture "Cities of the Future" at the Royal Institute of British Architects London Town Planning Conference in 1910.[12] This was the first international conference on urban design. The following year, future London County Council planner Patrick Abercrombie published a paper on the urban strategies of Paris and the techniques of Hénard in *Town Planning Review*.[13] Around this time, the formal study and practice of urban planning began uniting infrastructure and architecture in an integrated approach to urbanization. The multilevel street schemes presented at the London Town Planning Conference in 1910 further crystalized into a set of urban design strategies as other cities struggled with similar issues of health, housing, and circulation.

From the period of the Musée Social in Paris and Hénard's set-back street model (1903–1912), called the *boulevard à redans*, new collective forms of social housing were proposed, including some with "surrogate streets" that elevated pedestrians safely above the congested and polluted streets. Aside from the early Familistère of Jean-Baptiste André Godin with its large, enclosed central courts ringed by open corridors, there are very few examples of similar social housing schemes designed or built before the 1950s. Basing their work on Hénard's, Henri Sauvage and Charles Sarazin further developed the housing spatial typology, creating a range of technically innovative set-back building forms with elevated circulation decks. In Amsterdam, Michiel Brinkman employed similar raised decks in his Justus Van Effen Housing Complex project in Rotterdam (1919–1921), treating it not only as a connection between units but as a way to create access from the ground floor to the upper levels, thereby displacing the street.[14] Adolf Loos, who was director of Socialist/Public Housing for Vienna from 1919 to 1924, continued to experiment with this typology in his unbuilt Terrassenhaus project (1923).[15] As these remnant dreams of socialist utopian housing complexes with interconnected communal living spaces began to fade they were replaced by an interest in larger urban systems and infrastructure.

The Vertiginous Cities of Corbett, Ferriss, and Hood

Crisscrossed with elevated streets and bridges, the soaring vertiginous images of New York City, the burgeoning capitalist utopia of the early twentieth century, have almost become a cliché of visionary urbanism. But through their dramatic illustrations, Harvey Wiley Corbett, Hugh Ferriss, and Raymond Hood conveyed the thrilling three-dimensional city with its densely layered streets and constant motion. The ease and efficiency of such a city was evident in the stratified layers of mode-separated transportation, spacious elevated sidewalks, moving walkways, spiraling escalators, vehicles, and underground trains—even mooring masts for dirigibles on the spires of skyscrapers. This was a functional city of spectacular scale and dizzying height made possible by the technological innovations of the industrial age and the creative power of capital. It was also a city of leisure with pedestrian promenades and arcaded storefronts, a cosmopolitan city of pleasure, sociability, and commerce. On the elevated sidewalks high above the noise of vehicular traffic, a new urban gentility had been achieved.

The high-rise development of New York in the 1920s was the beginning of an international intoxication with the spectacle of the vertically oriented city and the power of laissez-faire capital to rapidly transform it. As pointed out by historian Jean Louis Cohen, New York was at the epicenter of this radical new form of urbanism that would have lasting consequences on the form of cities globally. But he also points out that there was, in reality, a feedback loop between ideas being generated in the United States and those emanating from the European avant-garde. The result was an accelerated process of

– Harvey Wiley Corbett, *The Wonderful City You May Live to See*, 1925, Courtesy Avery Architectural and Fine Arts Library, Columbia University

– William R. Leigh, "Great City of
the Future," *Cosmopolitan* (November
1908), Courtesy the Skyscraper
Museum

appropriation, reinvention, and application. The promotion and dissemination
of these ideas was dependent on a loose network of individuals, each pursu-
ing their individual ideas for the multilevel city.

The most influential advocate for this form of vertical urbanism was
Corbett. Having attended the École nationale supérieure des Beaux-Arts, he
completed his education in 1900 and moved to New York, where he began his
lifelong obsession with the multilevel city. Following the international publication of Hénard's multilevel propositions, Corbett began to promote similar but
more ambitious versions of traffic separation in the 1920s, which he adapted

A. Moses King, "King's Dreams
of New York," *King's Views of New
York*, 1900, Courtesy the Skyscraper
Museum
B. Hugh Ferriss, Overhead
traffic-ways, New York City, in *The
Metropolis of Tomorrow* (1929),
Courtesy Ellen Moon

to the verticality of the skyscraper city but in images reminiscent of Antonio Sant'Elia. Corbett's urban forms embraced New York's verticality as a kinesthetic experience. Conceiving of the city as a three-dimensional apparatus to manage flows, he fused the pragmatic imperatives of efficiency and convenience with the poetic drama of the vertiginous city.

Infrastructure had long been seen as a three-dimensional problem in New York City. Grand Central Station by Reed & Stern and Warren & Wetmore (1903–1913) was a significant example of a complex three-dimensional mixture of architecture and infrastructure. But what captured the public imagination most after the turn of the century were the fantastical images of the synthesized vertiginous city. The most notable early renderings were published as *Moses King's Views of New York*, using Charles Lamb's *Air-streets* (1908). Other images of the multilevel metropolis appeared in newspapers and popular magazines such as *Scientific American*, including the most famous by collaborators Corbett, Ferriss, and Hood. Even dystopian depictions of the multilevel city as the dark armature of the urban metabolism, like the film set for Fritz Lang's *Metropolis* (1927), had the capacity to capture the public imagination.

The concept of a city that was zoned sectionally continued to be the subject of much speculation between 1913 and 1930 in New York. Corbett reimagined the city around its vertical axis and the social space of the street, taking on a role similar to that of Hénard. He used nearly identical implementation strategies and methods of public promotion and education, and acted independently of government as chair of the Regional Plan of New York's studies on traffic segregation. Collaborating with architects Raymond Hood and Hugh Ferriss, he proposed futuristic multilevel systems that integrated modern transportation into dense pedestrian urban environments.

A.   Fritz Lang, Film still from
Metropolis, Germany, 1927, Courtesy
UFA/Photofest ©UFA
B.   Harvey Wiley Corbett, Proposal
for elevated walkways in New
York City, 1923, Courtesy Avery
Architectural and Fine Arts Library,
Columbia University

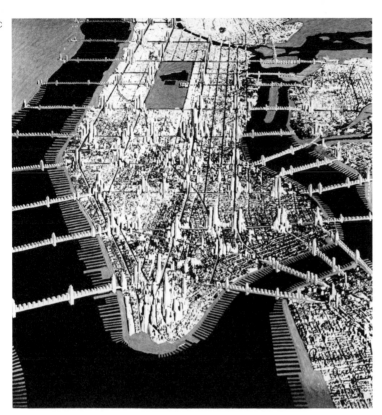

C

D

D.   Raymond Hood, Skyscraper Bridges, New York City, 1929 (detail), Collection Jennifer Reed, Trientje Hood Reed Estate
C.   Raymond Hood, Proposal for Manhattan of 1950, 1925 (drawing over aerial photograph), Courtesy Jennifer Reed

16.   Hugh Ferriss, *The Metropolis of Tomorrow* (New York: Dover Publications, 2005), 65.
17.   Fredric Jameson, "The Brick and the Balloon: Architecture, Idealism and Land Speculation," in *New Left Review* I/228 (March–April 1998), 14.

In 1929, Hugh Ferriss published *Metropolis of Tomorrow*, which proposed "Overhead Traffic Ways." Reversing typical proposals for the sectional layering of pedestrians above vehicles and based on his illustrations for Corbett's studies, he created viaducts for automobiles and pedways above the street, which were to be accommodated in the set-backs of Manhattan's skyscrapers.[16] That same year Raymond Hood proposed a series of "skyscraper bridges" over the East River and the Hudson River that would serve as separate communities, each with a mix of apartments, offices, stores, hotels, and theaters. Hood realized that with the increasing density of the city the division between buildings and infrastructure would begin to disappear.

Aspects of all of these projects can be found in Rockefeller Center (1931–1940). Designed in a collaborative process over a six-year period, the final project synthesized the diverse visions of Raymond Hood, Hugh Ferriss, and Harvey Wiley Corbett. An earlier, unrealized version of the project layered underground tunnels and subways, pathways, and elevated hanging gardens interconnected with walkways and bridges. Rockefeller Center has been described by Fredric Jameson as the pinnacle of the formation of the urban enclave typology, a place immersed within the city but distinctly separate from it.[17] It is a city within a city, the opposite of the cosmopolitan intent of the original multilevel Manhattan proposals.

The Ideal and the Real: Multilevel Urbanisms after the Russian Revolution

The next stage of cultural development will encompass all aspects of life: human productivity and creativity, the most precious faculties of man.... One of our utopian ideas is the desire to overcome the limitations of the substructure, of the earthbound. We have developed this idea in a series of proposals (sky-hooks, stadium grandstands, Paris garage).... It is the task of technology to make sure that all

A.   Lazar Khidekel, Design for a city on pilotis, 1925, Courtesy the Lazar Khidekel Family Archives and Collection ©All rights reserved
B.   Georgy Krutikov, City of the Future (evolution of architectural principles in urban planning and organization of the home), developed residential complex "labor commune," 1928 ©State Shchusev Museum, Moscow
18.   Richard Stites, *Revolutionary Dreams: Utopian Vision and Experimental Life in the Russian Revolution* (Cambridge: Oxford University Press, 1991) 23–27, 45, 168. Fourierism had been taught in Russia since the 1840s—Nicholas Chernyshevsky's Fourierist novel, *What Is to Be Done?* (1863) depicts a glass palace enclosing a commune with elevated galleries and social rooms based on the Phalanstere. The book became very popular after the Revolution, rivaling Karl Marx's *Das Kapital*. Many socialist utopian classics were reissued at that time, including Fourier's *Phalanstère* (10 editions from 1917 to 1926), and Thomas Moore's *Utopia* as well as works by Robert Owen, Étienne Cabet, Claude Henry de Rouvroy, and Comte de Sant-Simon. To replace the Tsarist statues destroyed by the new order, monuments were constructed to honor the socialist utopians and included many representations of Western socialist utopians such as Owen, Saint-Simon, and Fourier.

these elementary volumes that produce new relationships and tensions in space will be structurally safe…. The idea of the conquest of the substructure, the earthbound, can be extended even further and calls for the conquest of gravity as such. It demands floating structures, a physical-dynamic architecture.

—El Lissitzky, *An Architecture of World Revolution*, 1929

Concurrent with the elevated urban proposals for the capitalist city, a more communal vision of the multilevel city emerged in the Soviet Union in the early twentieth century. With the formation of the Soviet state following the October Revolution of 1917, the *communa* (commune) or *dom communa* (communal dwelling) became central preoccupations in the development of urban systems for a new society. At its onset, Soviet architects derived the program of their work from the French socialist utopians, especially Fourier, including their descriptions of communal spaces.[18] Unlike Fourier, however, they adopted the Marxist goal that redefined private as public. The revolutionary furor of the future city was spread through the literary descriptions of writers like Émile Zola, Moilin, Jules Verne, Gustave Kahn, and Nikolay Chernyschevsky. From the beginning, the work was experimental, radical, and utopian.

The avant-garde began to view elements of Soviet architecture as "tools of social changes" or *sotsialnye kondensatory* (social condensers), and inevitably focused on reimagining the socio-spatial concepts proposed by the French socialist utopians. The social condenser used circulation and overlapping programs to foster community interaction and was seen as a means to achieve social cohesion through appropriate forms of architecture and urban design. The Soviet government furthered this experimentation and promotion

A

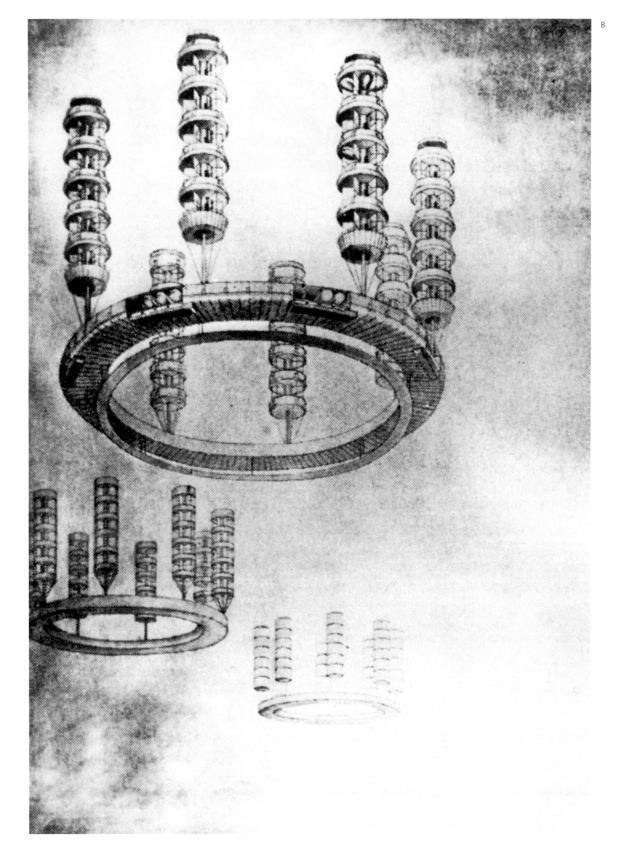

A.   Georgy Krutikov, City of the Future (evolution of architectural principles in urban planning and organization of the home), developed residential complex "labor commune," Option 3, 1928 ©State Shchusev Museum, Moscow
B.   Konstantin Melnikov, Entry for an office for the Leningradskaja Pravda, Moscow, 1924, Courtesy Architectural Collections and Productions, Faculty of Architecture and the Built Environment, TU Delft, the Netherlands, with thanks to Robert Nottrot   Photo: H. Schouten and H. Kruze
19.   Catherine Cooke, *Russian Avant-Garde Theories of Art, Architecture and the City* (London: Academy Editions, 1995), 23–90, 191.
20.   Stites, *Revolutionary Dreams*, 200–203, 209.
21.   Selim O. Khan-Magomedov, *Pioneers of Soviet Architecture: The Search for New Solutions in the 1920s and 1930s* (New York: Rizzoli, 1987), 341, 345–348

B

through a series of competitions, beginning with housing as its first priority. While much of this work was never built, it was integral to the development and promotion of new architectural practices and a culture of research-based design. Beginning simultaneously with the small scale of the communal residence and larger urban systems, the theorization of social and collective space resulted in the reimagining of buildings and cities and the invention of a new collective spatial typology.[19] While there were ideological differences, for example in determining appropriate formal vocabularies and their underlying theoretical basis or between advocating for urbanism or disurbanism, the branches of the movement were unified around the essential concept of the communal, which was enabled through elevated space and circulation. More precisely, the Association of New Architects (ASNOVA) practiced an aesthetic rationalism that advocated a nonurban redistribution of the population groups and the Organization of Contemporary Architects (OSA) advocated a technical, functional rationalism, but both agreed upon the concept of the social condenser.

Alexander Rodchenko pursued some of these earliest speculative forms. He believed that in the future buildings would be experienced from within and above by inhabitants of skyscrapers or from the air by travelers. Thus the aerial view would become the basis of the new architectural and urban forms: "All kinds of walkways and cantilevered roofs, light as bridges, all transparent and highly interesting from the aesthetic point of view."[20] Rodchenko proposed his idea of an aerial city in 1920. His urban vision would be defined by a new "upper zone," with aerial transport providing circulation.

The work of ASNOVA built on contemporary ideas about the psychology of perception.[21] Rodchenko, Lissitzky, Konstantin Melnikov, and others were interested in movement and the expressive forms of the skyscraper-metropolis as well as aspects of social function. Their views eventually evolved to incorporate aspects of both. ASNOVA's formal logic was spatial, and grew out of the arts-based faculty at Vkhutemas, which was the leading architecture and design school in Moscow. With a multidisciplinary program like the

A. El Lissitzky and Mart Stam, Wolkenbügel, Moscow, 1923–1924, View toward the Kremlin, 1925, Collection Van Abbemuseum, Eindhoven, the Netherlands Photo Peter Cox, Eindhoven, the Netherlands ©2016 Artists Rights Society (ARS), New York
B. Map showing eight proposed Wolkenbügel on the Boulevard Ring of Moscow, circa 1925 ©2016 Artists Rights Society (ARS), New York
C. Axonometric, circa 1925 ©2016 Artists Rights Society (ARS), New York
D. View toward Strastnoj Boulevard, 1925, Collection Van Abbemuseum, Eindhoven, the Netherlands Photo Peter Cox, Eindhoven, the Netherlands ©2016 Artists Rights Society (ARS), New York

A

B
C
D

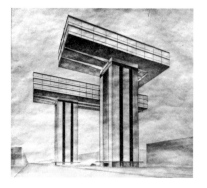

– Konstantin Melnikov, Paris
Mutilevel car park project for
1,000 cars, Paris, 1925, Courtesy
Architectural Collections and
Productions, Faculty of Architecture
and the Built Environment, TU Delft,
the Netherlands, with thanks to
Robert Nottrot Photo: H. Schouten
and H. Kruze
22. Khan-Magomedov, *Pioneers of
Soviet Architecture*, 277–310.
23. Manfredo Tafuri, *The Sphere and
the Labyrinth* (Cambridge: MIT Press,
1990), 151.

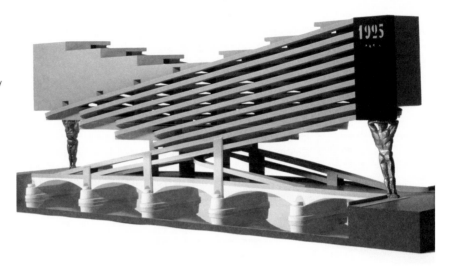

Bauhaus, its pedagogy was driven by investigations that were aligned with international movements in art such as Cubism, Futurism, and Dada.

From this perspective, the abstract and utopian forms of the elevated path of communal living became an analog for the experience of flight, speed, and lightness. Its evolution aligned with the desire to make architecture weightless and floating. Wildly experimental projects such as Georgy Krutikov's Flying City (1928) or those of Suprematist painter and architect Lazar Khidekel's Aerial Cities (1928) literally elevated the social space of the inhabitant and the physical form of the city while creating a universally accessible space enabling social equity. One of the earliest fantastical projects, Anton Lavinsky's City on Springs (1923), proposed an entire pedestrian street system elevated above traffic. Buildings would be lifted high above the city to create acoustic and visual separations from the layers of traffic and people moving below. Buildings would be equipped with mechanisms that could rotate the structures so that all units would receive equal sun exposure. Khidekel's Flying City (1922–1929) was a series of studies that looked at an elevated horizontal city hovering above the ground plane. While a student at the Vkhutemas, Krutikov first proposed his Flying City, in which he imagined that the ground plane would be cleared of buildings and used for work or recreation. The residential buildings of the city would be elevated above, and a communal ring would be used to dock mobile cabins—the main transport between the two realms.

Experimental work was also done abroad, such as Melnikov's work in Paris, or through collaborations with European architects, such as Lissitzky working with Mart Stam. Their Wolkenbügel (Cloud-Hanger) project (1923–1924) for Moscow proposed a network of horizontal buildings supported by vertical circulation cores that would connect to the subway, street level, and future air traffic above. Using the similar logic of buildings elevated above the roadway, Melnikov proposed a prototypical parking garage for Paris in 1925, hovering above transport and the existing bridges crossing the Seine and connected to street traffic with ramps.[22] Manfredo Tafuri criticized this early avant-garde work for its inability to engage the city on its own terms as a "communication machine." Instead of focusing on the larger condition of the city, they focused instead on the "microcosm of the object."[23]

The excitement over the future metropolis and popular interest in its promised vertiginous experience migrated to Moscow and fueled the

A.   Moisei Ginzburg and Ignatii
Milinis, Narkomfin Building, Moscow,
1930, Courtesy Victor Buchli
Photo: D. Arkin, 1935
B.   Moisei Ginzburg and G.A.
Zundblat, Proposed site plan,
Narkomfin Building, drawing by
Victor Buchli after the original (1990),
Courtesy Victor Buchli
24. Anatole Kopp, *Town and
Revolution: Soviet Architecture and
City Planning 1917–35* (London:
Thames and Hudson, 1967), 129–155.
25. Stites, *Revolutionary Dreams*,
198.

Constructivists' interest in American technology, its industrial processes, and the construction of a skyscraper-based city. In 1926, the architecture magazine *Sovremennaya architektura* (1926–1930) focused its first issue on the topic of the city. It published reviews of Le Corbusier's 1924 book *Urbanisme* (*City of Tomorrow*) and on Erich Mendelsohn's 1929 *Amerika*, featuring detailed material on Corbett's work in New York City and his Regional Plan. Reviewers critiqued the projects from a Soviet perspective, arguing that these vertical and capitalist forms of the metropolis "impeded the horizontal" and the ability for urban connectivity and unimpeded flow.[24] "*Amerika*," said Lissitzky, "had turned the European horizontal corridor into a vertical lift shaft." The skyscraper typology of the American metropolis had defined a discontinuous spatial form that was oriented skyward with disconnected floor plates vertically connected by elevator shafts located remotely from the street. During this period, early ideas of clusters of buildings evolved to accommodate more continuous elevated infrastructure and created only a more pragmatic form of an elevated urbanism.

The Real

The concept of the social condenser would become an integral part of a shared architectural vocabulary expressing the socialist ambitions for a new society and the city of the future. Formalized and promoted by the newly formed OSA, which was based out of the more technically oriented Moscow State Technical University (MVTU), the concept was theorized by members such as the Vesnin brothers (Leonid, Victor, and Alexander), Ivan Leonidov, Rodchenko, and Moisei Ginzburg, their focus was on the social-functional. Roman Khiger, the editor of *Sovremennaya architektura*, founded by the Vesnins and Ginzburg, described the architect's responsibility to see the city as a social condenser with the potential to "alter radically the structure of human life—productive, social, and personal."[25] This was, presumably, not to be the responsibility of the government, but rather the result of individual, collective, and shared experimentation by architects, designers, and planners.

A

B
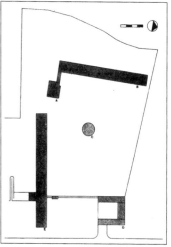

A.   Gosprom Building, 1929, World
War II Eastern campaign, 1942,
Courtesy DPA Picture-Alliance/
AFP DPA–Zentralbild Beliner Verlag
Archiv
B.   Seafrimov, Felger, and Kravets,
Plan and views of the House of
Industry (Gosprom) in Kharkov,
1925–1928, S. O. Khan-Magomedov,
*Pioneers of Soviet Architecture: The
Search for New Solutions in the 1920s
and 1930s* (New York: Rizzoli, 1987)

A

B

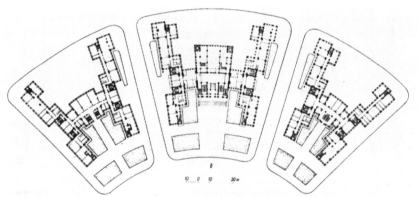

A.   Vesnin Brothers,
Narkomtiazhprom proposal for
Moscow, 1933–1934, Courtesy NVO/
Wikimedia Commons
B.   Theo van Doesburg, Circulation
City (Cité de Circulation), 1929,
Collection Met Nieuwe Instituut,
donation Van Moorsel
C.   Frederick Kiesler, Sketch for
Horizontal Skyscraper, Paris, 1925
26. Commonalities also included
the creating of internationally influ-
ential cultural programs that were
the beginnings of modernism—the
Bauhaus was founded in 1919 and
the Russian State Art and Technical
College (Vkhutemas) was founded
in 1920.

The social condenser as a means to encourage collective living and social interaction became the ongoing project of both ASNOVA and OSA.[26] From 1922 on, Ginzburg and others formally studied the social condenser typology at the residential scale. Nikolai Ladovsky proposed the interiorized and interconnected Communal House (1920) and Melnikov developed an early model of this typology of communal housing employing interconnected and interiorized bridges (1922). Prototypes were tested at Vkhutemas and through design competitions, resulting in a government-led research group headed by Ginzburg beginning in 1928. The group focused on a series of community housing types that explored collective living patterns, incorporating social condensers through interconnecting bridges and communal spaces, while minimizing cost and area. A series of the most efficient, Type F, were developed and constructed by different subgroups under Ginzburg, exploring various configurations and program combinations, which included the Narkomfin Housing project (1929) built by Ginzburg and Ignatii Milinis.

At Vkhutemas the same linking elements were also promoted by ASNOVA members such as El Lissitzky. Students of both programs developed proposals for more public projects with a social agenda. The work took on the form of collective research into emerging typologies of worker's clubs, communal dwellings, skyscraper complexes, factories, markets, and new governmental facilities. Ideas for the social condensers were also spread through national government-sponsored competitions for similar facilities such as factories, the cultural Palaces of Labor, and the governmental House of Soviets. The results were widely promoted. The Gosprom building applied the social condenser at a municipal level. Designed in 1925 by Ukrainian Constructivist architects Sergei Serafimov, Samuel Kravets, and Mark Felger, it was built in 1929 in the city of Kharkov, serving to imprint the capitol with a new interconnected multilevel architecture that was distinctly Soviet.

To Berlin and Beyond: The Migration of the Elevated City

Underlying the reemergence of the social utopian project for the city and renewed connections between the cities of Moscow, Berlin, Vienna, and Amsterdam were the political shifts that happened in Europe after World War I: the 1917 October Revolution in Russia (Red October); the Social Democrats taking power in Vienna in 1918 (Red Vienna); the 1919 Socialist Revolution in Germany (Weimar Republic); and the formation of Amsterdam's

A

B

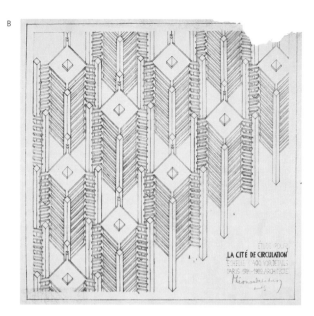

C

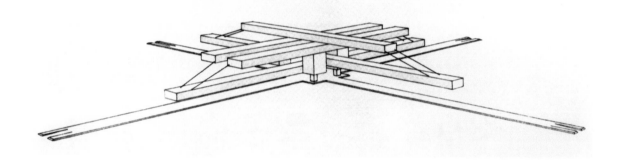

27. El Lissitzky developed collaborations with prominent members who were part of the Dutch de Stijl movement between 1922 and 1925, including Theo van Doesberg (1922–1923), Frederick Kiesler, and Mart Stam, and had close ties with the Bauhaus (through László Moholy-Nagy). Collaboratively, they formed and promoted an international form of Soviet Constructivism centered on Germany, which expanded to Switzerland, Poland, Hungary, and Czechoslovakia.
28. A number of groups were formed around this interest in an international form of Constructivism. Der Ring was viewed as the avant-garde counterpart of OSA in Berlin; its members included Erich Mendelsohn, Ernst May, Arthur Korn, Ludwig Mies van der Rohe, Walter Gropius, and Ludwig Hilberseimer. These connections were also part of the early formation of CIAM until the dissolution of the social and artistic experiment of Constructivism by Stalin in 1932.
29. Tafuri, *The Sphere and the Labyrinth*, 120.

social-democratic municipal government in 1919. Even though cities like Vienna and Amsterdam were under conservative rule, the leadership and local architects pursued social change through urban design speculations. In this context, the parallel work of the Constructivists held great interest.[27]

In 1921 El Lissitzky took a position as the Soviet cultural ambassador to Weimar Germany. Along with Berthold Lubetkin and Constructivist artist Naum Gabo, he traveled to Germany and organized the *Erste Russische Kunstausstellung* (*First Russian Art Exhibition*). Responsible for promoting Soviet art and culture, he prepared and promoted emerging ideas in Soviet architecture and urbanism through the design of exhibitions and publications.[28]

There were many connections between architects in the Soviet Union during the Constructivist period (1920–1930) and those in Berlin and other emerging socialist cities in Europe.[29] A number of parallel movements in these new socialist democratic states started to rethink buildings and their relationship to cities and promoted new forms of social housing. These movements also saw design in a shared way, as a tool for building a new society and a modern life. The most recognized project to arise from these collaborations was the aforementioned Wolkenbügel by Lissitzky and Stam. Multilevel urban projects were explored by others in this association at around the same time, including Frederick Kiesler's Horizontal Skyscraper (1925), Theo van Doesburg's Circulation City (1924), and Ludwig Hilberseimer's Highrise City (1929).

– Berthold Lubetkin, Avtostroy, "The First Socialist Town," *Architectural Review* (May 1932), Architectural Press Archive/RIBA Library Photographs Collection
30. Ibid., 151–159.
31. Ernst May's work was of great interest to the Soviets in their ambitions for the rapid construction of new cities. In 1925 he was appointed as head of public housing and planning for the city of Frankfurt. His aim was to promote social renewal through rationality and functionality with the idea that transforming architecture would cause societal reform. Over the next five years, he built fifteen thousand units of modern housing; achieved by reducing buildings to their essentials and using systemized methods of construction.

The City Project for the Future

Concurrent to this loosely experimental work during the 1920s and 1930s was the development of the Sotsgorod, or socialist cities for the future. Focused on rapid industrialization centered in Siberia, these urban schemes used communal housing components as the key feature. In 1918, building on a series of plans influenced by the concept of Ebenezer Howard's Garden City (1898), architect Boris Sakulin created a scientific and highly rational redesign of Moscow based on data discarding the underlying romanticism of the greenbelt city. The plan was both spatial and economic. Described by Lenin as a "bureaucratic utopia," it consisted of two parts: a complex mathematical mapping titled the Influence Chart and a report entitled "City of the Future." The Influence Chart was both economic and spatial, distributing industry, transportation, and housing. This scientific and data-driven attitude toward planning put the impetus on each individual project to create a true socialist city and define a field of aggregated parts for experimentation.[30]

Because of the interest in industrialization and the ideology of disurbanism, the Soviet focus was on building new industrial cities in undeveloped areas, referred to as the first Five Year Plan. The linear city was studied as a model for these new towns by Nicolay Milyutin, based on a nineteenth-century linear city scheme by Arturo Sora y Mata in Spain. To achieve their ambitious goals of design and construction for the Sotsgorod and other urban industrialization and mass housing projects in their Five Year Plan, they imported

nearly a thousand architects from newly socialist governments such as the Weimar Republic, Red Vienna, the Netherlands, and France, including Ernst May, Hannes Meyer (Bauhaus Brigade), Arthur Korn, Mart Stam, André Lurçat, Le Corbusier, and Erich Mendelsohn.[31]

May and his group of collaborators moved to Moscow in 1930 to begin work. Over the next three years they developed plans for twenty new Sotsgorod cities, including the Linear City of Magnitogorsk and the town of Avtostroy, the

– Le Corbusier, Centrosoyuz building, Moscow, 1928 (constructed 1933) ©Ricard Pare

32. Peter Serenyil, "Le Corbusier, Fourier, and the Monastery of Ema," *The Art Bulletin*, vol. 49, no. 4 (December 1967): 277–286.

33. Although Stanislaw Moos suggests that Le Corbusier didn't mention Fourier until the 1950s and his political interests are often speculated on as being oriented toward Sant-Simon.

"Detroit of Moscow." The master plans incorporated the interconnected communal house types developed by the Soviet government and Ginzburg.

The Lyricism of Motion: Le Corbusier's Moscow Laboratory

Like Charles Fourier, Le Corbusier believed that humanity would have to entirely remake its urban environment in order to reform society. Connecting Le Corbusier to ideas about the communal, Peter Serenyi furthers this connection between Fourier and Le Corbusier, finding parallel concepts, techniques, and methodologies. He makes the argument that these ideas were initially transferred to Le Corbusier through his introduction to Tony Garnier in 1908.[32] However, as a Swiss architect working in France, he would have been exposed to a range of socialist utopian proposals for the multilevel city as well as reinterpretations of Fourier, from Garnier to Borie and Hénard.[33] Through his work with August Perret, Le Courbusier would also have also been familiar with his schemes for New York–style towers interconnected with bridges (1922). However, Le Corbusier's initial concepts of *rue intereure* were limited to forms similar to the precedents of these other proposals. Only after his visit to Moscow in 1928 would they be transformed into more "lyrical" architectural concepts.

This influence was reciprocal. Le Corbusier's ideas had long been studied by the Constructivists. They drew from Le Corbusier's *Urbanisme*, which included the work of Hénard and elevated transit in New York, and

A.   Richard Neutra, Rush City
Reformed, 1925–1930 ©Dion Neutra,
Architect, Courtesy Richard and
Dion Neutra Papers, Department of
Special Collections, Charles E. Young
Research Library, UCLA
B.   Le Corbusier, Palace of Soviets,
Moscow, 1932 ©FLC/ADAGP, Paris/
Artists Rights Society (ARS), New
York 2016

A

B

34. Kenneth Frampton, *Modern Architecture: A Critical History* (New York: Thames & Hudson, 1992), 179.
35. Jean-Louis Cohen, *Le Corbusier and the Mystique of the USSR: Theories and Projects for Moscow 1928–1936* (Princeton: Princeton University Press, 1992), 116–118.

his own initial scheme for three million inhabitants. In 1925, an exhibition of Soviet work was held in Paris at the Grand Palais, presenting the urban work of Melnikov, Rodchenko, Vladimir Tatlin, and the Vesnin brothers to a Parisian audience. However, the application of the elevated and interiorized pedestrian street (*rue corridor*) was not yet present in his work and appeared clearly only after his first visit to Moscow, where he furthered his connections with the Vesnins and Ginzburg.[34] While Le Corbusier had already been clearly interested in the work of the Constructivists from the mid-1920s, and the Soviets had become familiar with his early work from writers and promoters such as El Lissitzky, it wasn't until 1928 that he developed a direct connection to Moscow.

In summer 1928 Le Corbusier was invited to participate in a competition for the design of the headquarters of the *Centrosoyuz* (People's Cooperatives) (1928–1936) in Moscow. While there, he further studied the work of the Constructivists, and in this context completed the first drawings for the project. Le Corbusier's organization and formal expression resonated with his Soviet competitors to the degree that they advocated for his selection over their own. He received the commission and returned to Paris along with Nikolai Kolli, a Soviet architect who had studied at Vkhutemas and also worked with Viktor Vesnin. Kolli continued to work on the project in Paris until 1933, when he returned to Moscow.

In the Soviet capital Le Corbusier rediscovered an idea from his colleagues at CIAM that he had previously dismissed—particularly in the work of Richard Neutra and Hilberseimer—the elevated pedestrian street. But during his Moscow trip, Le Corbusier also became fascinated with Ginzburg's social condenser project and the soon-to-be-constructed Narkomfin building. He brought a set of drawings back to Paris. He also studied the linear city of Milyutin. This work directly influenced the Centrosoyuz along with other subsequent projects that employed elevated interior streets. After his exposure to Moscow, his work exhibited a shift from a rationalist obsession with the machine and Taylorist principles to a more social and experiential use of technology. A spatially expressive use of circulation elements can be seen interiorized in projects such as the Centrosoyuz and the Ville Savoye (1929).[35]

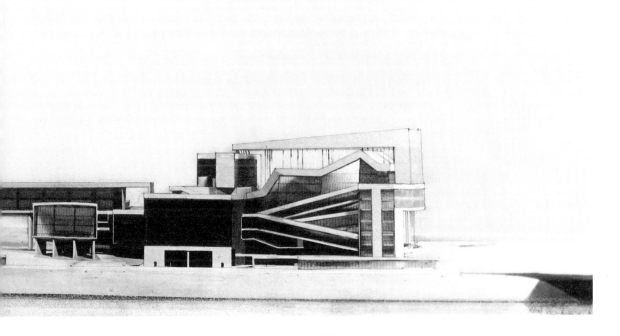

36. Ibid., 116–117, 137–153.
37. Frederick Starr, "Le Corbusier and the USRR," *Cahiers du monde russe et soviétique*, vol. 21. no. 2. (April–June 1980): 209–221.
38. Ibid., 209–221.
39. Claudia Quiring et al., eds., *Ernst May 1886–1970* (Munich: Prestel, 2011), 158–180.

As Le Corbusier commented after his first visit to Moscow in 1928:

I thought I would encounter my typical adversaries in Moscow— the creators of "Constructivism." This opinion was grounded in the recent attitudes of German architects who, for some time now, have been proclaiming the eminently utilitarian principles of the Neue Sachlichkeit (new objectivity, included Ernst May, Hilberseimer, early Bauhaus).... Yet in Moscow I found, not spiritual antagonists, but fervent adherents to what I consider fundamental to human works: the lofty intentions that raise these works above their utilitarian function, and which confer upon them the lyricism that brings us joy.... I say that Constructivism, which denotes a revolutionary intention, is in reality the vehicle of an intensely lyrical intent, one that is potentially transcendent. It reveals with fervor the exhilarating prospect of a future. My feeling is that what interests all these Russians is in fact a poetic idea.[36]

In 1930 Le Corbusier was invited to review the Green Cities competition, giving him the opportunity to look closely at a range of urban proposals for transforming Moscow into a new collective society. After reviewing proposals by Ginzburg, Vesnin, Melnikov, and others, he put forward his own ideas for the socialist transformation of the city. Weeks later, along with other leaders, he was invited to submit ideas for the redevelopment of Moscow in the form of a questionnaire and "as many proposals" as he wished. Le Corbusier followed up with a sixty-six-page report and twenty-one pages of drawings.

Similar to the strategy of May's Sotsgorod cities, Le Corbusier developed a rational zoning strategy that used the interlinked Soviet housing prototypes, particularly Ginzburg's.[37] His urban plan for the city employed a variation of the Soviet social condenser in the form of a network of streets in the air with rooftop walkways to connect a zone of stepped or set-back housing. Although his proposals were criticized by many Soviets, Le Corbusier hoped that eventually they would reconsider and adopt his design. In the interim, he continued to develop the project as the Response to Moscow and promoted it widely, including it at the CIAM III meeting in Brussels (1930), a predecessor to the highly anticipated CIAM IV in Moscow.

In the interest of making his scheme more universally applicable, he later scaled back his expansive design for Moscow as Ville Radieuse (Radiant City).[38] As Stalin ended Constructivism, and thus government support for modernist building, Le Corbusier, May, and the other Europeans fell out of favor and were largely forced out of the country by 1933.[39] These projects, meant to be a test of the true transformability of the city, would not be realized; political factors foreclosed on their completion.

The Centrosoyuz was successfully completed in 1936, despite Stalin's increasing antagonism toward modernism and Le Corbusier's loss of the Palace of Soviet's Competition in 1933. The ramping circulation of the project's interior street was realized as a poetic interpretation of its social purpose. The *rue corridor* concept was later incorporated into the Habitation Unité (1947–1952), a successful attempt to realize the final housing block of the Radiant City. Serenyi describes this later project as a culmination of Le Corbusier's journey toward a truly social architecture. The similarities between the Phalanstère and Habitation Unité are notable in many ways in their quantitative organization, including the number of inhabitants and apartments, the desire to support the varying needs of an intentionally diverse community, and the balancing of individual and collective space. Through Le Corbusier and other early modernists, the unrealized elevated visions of Fourier, the social utopians of the eighteenth century, and the multilevel experimentation of the Soviets were integrated into a new modern architecture.

The inhabitants would blow up the cat-walks: This is a picture of anti-reason itself, of error, of thoughtlessness. Madness. And all the solutions come to the same thing: separation of traffic according to speed. The pedestrian, from now on, will be confined to raised walks built up above the street, while traffic lanes remain at their present ground level. Madness.

— Le Corbusier, *Ville Radieuse* (*The Radiant City*), 1928

2. THE LONDON CRUCIBLE AND THE SOCIALIST DIASPORA

2. THE LONDON CRUCIBLE AND THE SOCIALIST DIASPORA

1. Kenneth Frampton, "The English Crucible, CIAM: Team 10, The English Context," conference, TU Delft, 2001. Accessed July 10, 2013, www.team10online.org/research /papers/delft1/frampton.pdf

While it would appear that the radical urbanisms of the avant-garde Constructivist project concluded with the rise of Stalinism and Socialist Realism in the East and modernism in the West, some of its key conceptual interests and spatial strategies continued in other places. The socialist utopian ideas fueling the experimentation of the early Constructivists shifted to other cities undergoing political transformation—from post-revolutionary socialist countries to recently democratized nations rebuilding postindustrial cities for a new century. Émigrés from the Soviet Union and the Weimar Republic in Germany acted as couriers for the urban and architectural concepts, and, in most cases, continued the trajectory of their previous work within their new social and political contexts.

For this reason it is fascinating to trace the migration and transformation of multilevel urban concepts across national and ideological borders and across many periods and authors. The spread and evolution of these utopian urban ideas occurred through the direct and indirect connections among architects who had widely varying and often conflicting agendas. This was particularly true in the case of London. Multilevel cities were promoted from the 1930s through the early 1950s by the Congrès Internationale d'Architecture Moderne (CIAM, or International Congress of Modern Architecture), a group of twenty-eight architects, and its cofounder Le Corbusier. However, the "catwalk-like" form of the elevated city that began to be built in the United Kingdom in the early 1950s and further developed in North American and Asian cities from the early 1960s is clearly distinct from the three-dimensional urban concepts of Le Corbusier that organized pedestrian movement on grade level or on an elevated podium with vehicular traffic positioned either above or below, respectively. Examples are his project for Ville Contemporaine (1922), Rio de Janeiro (1929), or Plan Obus, Algiers (1932), where he elevates the highway above the floating city. This unique form of the multilevel city would emerge in the United Kingdom prior to the introduction of CIAM modernism and as a result of recent émigrés from post-revolutionary socialist countries.

Kenneth Frampton writes about the period of Team 10, a subset of members that challenged the orthodoxy of CIAM's urban approach, calling the postwar London period a crucible—the melding together of many disparate ideas after the Blitz (1940–1941).[1] But from another perspective, the crucible formed much earlier during the interwar period (1919–1939), with architects immigrating to England from post-revolutionary socialist countries and the resulting formation of the Modern Architectural Research (MARS) Group in England.

While London's experimental urbanisms were also influenced by earlier provocations—such as Le Corbusier's Ville Contemporaine (1922) and Plan Voisin (1925), the work of Antonio Sant'Elia, Harvey Wiley Corbett's studies of New York, and Ludwig Hilberseimer's Highrise City (1924)—its particular form of multilevel urbanism was primarily driven by an idea that was centered on the social and the communal. Although the ambitions of many postwar London planners also included modernist preoccupations with efficiency and productivity, these urban experiments were chiefly intended to make cities more livable, healthy, and equitable through improved "communications." In other words, the quality of life in a city would be fostered through human contacts—social, intellectual, and commercial. While CIAM and its proponents of modern architecture were also interested in a new multilevel form of the city, they had a more apolitical view of the future metropolis. On the one hand, we principally see the idea of separating pedestrians and vehicular street traffic to solve the practical problems of congestion. On the other, the elevated pedestrian street becomes an urban-scaled social condenser interconnecting public pedestrian spaces and buildings to support communal living and thereby transform the old social orders.

– Le Corbusier, Proposal for "earthscrapers," Rio de Janeiro, 1929 ©FLC/ADAGP, Paris/Artists Rights Society (ARS), New York 2016

2. Dennis Sharp, "Concept and Interpretation: The aims and principles of the MARS Plan for London," *Perspecta* 13 (1971): 164–65.

3. Alan Powers, ed., *Modern Britain 1929–1939* (London: Design Museum, 1999), 24–26.

Interwar Modernism in London

The bringing together of post–World War I émigré architects in London paralleled the introduction of modern architecture to the country and led to the founding of the first MARS Group in 1933. The new model for collective design research was principally organized to promote progressive design ideas and to connect the British avant-garde with the growing modernist movement emerging in Europe and the USSR.[2] Its formation was built upon an existing social network within the English avant-garde, including the Heretics Club, the Hampstead Circle, and the English Constructivists. Although formed as the UK representative of CIAM, in its earliest stages the MARS Group was structured as more of a supporting network for already affiliated and like-minded collaborators. Initially, these groups had evolved out of the multi-disciplinary Hampstead Circle, which included visual artists, writers, scientists, and architects.[3] Noteworthy members included Constructivists László Moholy-Nagy, Naum Gabo, and engineer Ove Arup; British architects Leslie Martin and Maxwell Fry; and expatriate architects such as Serge Chermayeff and Berthold Lubetkin from Russia and Erno Goldfinger (namesake of the James Bond villain) from Hungary. Martin edited *Circle*, a journal of British Constructivism, published in 1937 with Nicholson and Gabo, which presented work by artists and architects like Lubetkin, El Lissitzky, and Erich Mendelsohn, as well as the CIAM architects and critic Lewis Mumford.

The earliest form of the MARS Group carried forward the idea that was later expressed so aptly by Le Corbusier in Moscow and in his proposal for Rio de Janeiro as the "lyricism and poetry of technology." The MARS Group aimed to reform society through the synthesis of art and science with architecture, and newly emerging disciplines such as urban planning. In the first issue of

A. Berthold Lubetkin, the Sverdlovsk Central Bureau, Ural District, "The First Socialist Town," *Architectural Review* (May 1932), Courtesy Architectural Press Archive/ RIBA Library Photographs Collection

B. Berthold Lubetkin, the Commune House, Armenia, *Architectural Review* (May 1932), Courtesy Architectural Press Archive/ RIBA Library Photographs Collection

4. John R. Gold, *The Experience of Modernism: Modern Architects and the Future City, 1928–1953* (London: Taylor & Francis, 1997), 89, 93.

5. Tatton-Brown built on this influence and carried forward a passion about Soviet ideas of architecture and urbanism throughout his career. See Jonathan Hughes, "Hospital-City," in *Architectural History*, vol. 40 (1997): 266–288.

6. Stan Allen and Hal Foster, "A Conversation with Kenneth Frampton," in *October* 10 (New York: Columbia University, 2003) 35–58.

7. Liverpool University under Charles Reilly was the earliest architecture school to promote modernism, combining ideas of Lewis Mumford and the work of Le Corbusier. The Architectural Association followed in 1935 and also incorporated Town Planning and sociologic factors. In addition to faculty such as Patrick Abercrombie, Liverpool's students included Maxwell Fry, Percy Johnson-Marshall, Arthur Ling, and Gordon Stephenson.

8. Iain Jackson and Jessica Holland, *The Architecture of Edwin Maxwell Fry and Jane Drew: Twentieth Century* (Liverpool: Ashgate Publishing, 2014), 68–69.

Circle, Martin critiqued the adoption of the modernist style without a larger social and technical agenda—arguing for a new synthesis through the lens of art. This very distinct orientation of the early MARS Group resulted from the direct ties of émigrés and their involvement in Soviet town planning and architecture as well as the International Constructivism/Functionalism movement that was based in Weimar Berlin.[4]

Architects with an interest in Soviet and Socialist postrevolutionary ideas about urbanism dominated this founding group of MARS, including Russian Constructivist Lubetkin, who began his firm, Tecton, in London in 1931. Led informally by a few early figures—Lubetkin, Wells Coates, Chermayeff, and Fry—the founding members of the MARS Group had an important impact due to their international connections.

In England the MARS Group strengthened the growing influence of CIAM and Le Corbusier while also taking a different trajectory in their development of new urban forms. The first CIAM representative in the UK was William Tatton-Brown, a graduate of the Architectural Association (AA) in London and member of Tecton. His involvement in CIAM originated with architect André Lurçat, his former employer and a Soviet expatriate practicing in Paris, who held lectures and events to promote Constructivist theory and Marxist ideas among his staff. During Tatton-Brown's employ, Lurçat was working in Moscow and collaborating with Moisei Ginzburg and others on the design of new Soviet cities.[5] Weimar Berlin architect Arthur Korn, who was a close friend of Ludwig Hilberseimer joined the MARS Group in 1938. Korn, along with Alison and Peter Smithson, subsequently taught both Cedric Price and Peter Cook of Archigram at the AA.[6] As the MARS Group grew, other significant British architects joined, including Denys Lasdun, a partner in Tecton (later the lead architect for the Southbank Centre); Peter Moro, also of Tecton (and Martin's collaborator on the Royal Festival Hall), and Percy Johnson-Marshall.[7] Interested in carrying forward their new ideas for British urbanism, Fry invited Martin and former colleague William Holford (future planner of London's thirty-mile Pedway scheme) from Liverpool to join the group in 1936 and carry these ideas to the universities where they were teaching.[8]

Tecton and the Theory of Contacts

Britain's emergence as a significant force in the modern movement coincided with the planning of the CIAM 4 congress in 1933 (part of a series of events and congresses beginning with CIAM I in 1928 and ending with CIAM XI in 1959). It also coincided with the beginning of the Great Depression and massive unemployment of architects. Although CIAM 4 was rerouted from Moscow to Marseilles/Athens because of political problems, thousands of architects from

A

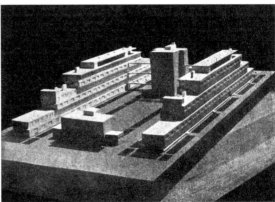

B

– Skinner, Bailey & Lubetkin, Golden Lane housing competition entry, 1952, RIBA Library Photographs Collection

9. Andrew Higgott, *Mediating Modernism: Architectural Cultures in Britain* (London: Taylor & Francis, 2007), 38.

10. Berthold Lubetkin, "The Builders," in *Architectural Review*, vol. IXXI (May 1932): 213.

11. John Gold, *The Experience of Modernism: Modern Architects and the Future City 1928–1953* (London: Taylor & Francis, 1997), 145–146.

England and Germany were being prepared during the preceding months to work in Russia on the Five Year Plan, effectively planting a seed of interest in Soviet architecture and planning during an economic recession. With the expectation that British architects would soon be working in Russia and that the MARS Group would be attending CIAM 4 in Moscow, a special issue of *Architectural Review* on Russia was published in May 1932.[9] This preceded by two years the groundbreaking and influential publication of European modernist architecture in the same journal in 1934.[10]

Architectural Review's special issue featured a large section by Lubetkin. His article was intended to introduce British architects to the various factions of Constructivist architecture and planning and the social agenda underlying their forms. Numerous projects were published, including a number of plans featuring the Constructivist concept of the social condenser. Many of these designs took the form of elevated and enclosed walkways interconnecting buildings, a precursor for many contemporary systems in North America and Asia. Designs also included Ginzburg's prototypical Narkomfin Housing project (1928–1932), which featured a continuous internalized street with linking bridge elements; a commune in Armenia with elevated connectors; projects by Lubetkin's teacher and employer, Konstantin Melnikov, with large volumetric social condensers linking buildings; and two newly constructed socialist cities planned by Ernst May, a German architect working in Russia—Avtostoy, with its elevated pedestrian bridges, and the planned linear city of Magnitogorsk, featuring elevated streets interconnecting housing blocks designed by Leonidov.[11]

As a member and early founder of the MARS Group, Lubetkin continued to bring forward Constructivist concepts to a wider professional audience. This experimentation and political activism can be found within the diversity of his practice, the frequent presentations and publications on Soviet architecture

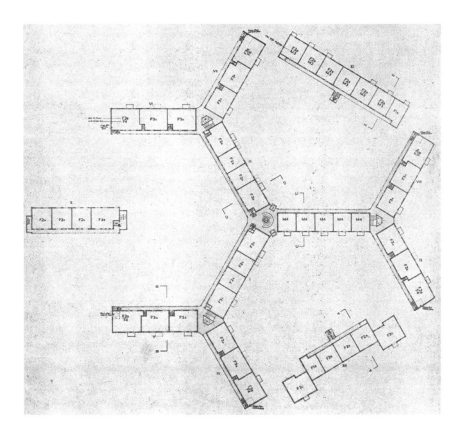

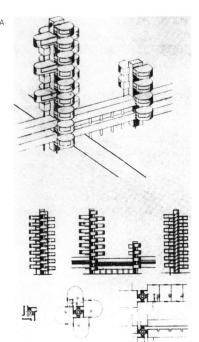

A. Representative social condenser work produced by students at the Vkhutemas during Lubetkin's tenure. Trifon Varentsov, Design for dwellings with cantilevered standardized dwelling units, Moscow, 1928
B. Lovopra team (Baranov, Krivitsky, and others), Model of competition design for housing commune, Leningrad, 1930
12. Aileen Tatton-Brown and William E. Tatton-Brown, "Three-Dimensional Town Planning, Parts 1 and 2," in *Architectural Review* 90 (1941) and 91 (1942).

in the decades of the 1930s and 1950s, and his ongoing engagement with architectural students and recent graduates of the AA. Aside from the critical success of his practice, Lubetkin was an important interwar figure promoting modern architecture in the UK. He had emigrated from Moscow to Weimar Berlin, then to Paris, and eventually London. Throughout his career, he had an ongoing interest in both the dynamic sculptural forms and the social effects of modern architecture. In the many projects of Tecton and their followers, there is a distinctive articulation and expression of linear, circular, and vertical social spaces interwoven with circulation.

Lubetkin had been educated at the Vkhutemas, a state art and technical school in Moscow, where he was taught by Melnikov, the Vesnins, Ginzburg, and Rodchenko. The influence of Melnikov and ASNOVA and his pursuit of new forms of socialist architecture and urbanism, particularly the use of social condensers found in the Narkomfkin project and in the work of Ginzburg and the OSA group, can be seen throughout Lubetkin's career and in the work of many architects coming out of Tecton. He left school before graduating, traveling and assisting Lissitzky and then working for May and Bruno Taut in Germany and then Melnikov and Auguste Perret in Paris.[12] Lubetkin's selection of European firms was intentional as he deliberately built a knowledge base that would be helpful to him when he returned to the USSR to continue the Constructivist project. Essential to these interests in social transformation were urban planning (Taut and May), new materials (Perret), and modern housing (May).

With the rise of Stalin and the demise of Constructivism in the early 1930s, Lubetkin decided to remain in London. His later work there, while often described as an example of early modernism in style and construction methods, can be seen as an extension of the social ideals and forms of the Constructivist project. Connections can also be seen between his work and that of his individual mentors or teachers, such as Lissitzky's development of a "gravity-free" architecture, Malevich and Leonidov's interests in "megastructural" interpretations of urban systems, or Ginzburg's functionalist reframing of the social condenser.

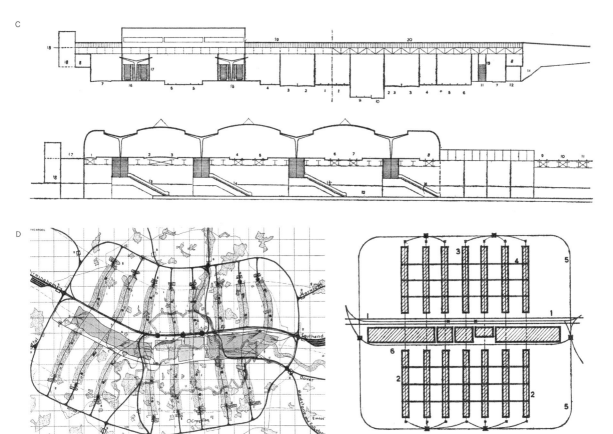

C. Arthur Korn, MARS Group, Three diagrams of the MARS Plan for London, *Architectural Review* (June 1942)
D. Master Plan for London based on research carried out by the Town Planning Committee of the MARS Group, 1942, Courtesy RIBA Library Photographs Collection

The MARS Plan for London

In the 1930s, a nascent form of the modern elevated city began to emerge among a small group of socially motivated architects in London. The urban speculations and multilevel concepts of Tecton for the borough of Finsbury, the three-dimensional town planning of the Tatton-Browns, and later the MARS Plan for London were evidence of the evolving interest in the multilevel city. Over time, the closely-knit group of designers influenced the ideas and implementation of numerous urban projects premised on the idea of social communications expanded to the scale of the city. The tenure of these early avant-gardists in the Planning Techniques Office (PTO) of the Ministry of Town and County Planning at the London County Council (LCC) after World War II and the consequent appearance of spectacular and experimental urban ideas in the 1950s, directly influenced the subsequent and widespread proliferation and deployment of elevated pedestrian systems in the 1960s.

The Town Planning Committee was an important subset of the MARS Group, shaping its two biggest achievements: the *New Architecture* exhibition in 1938 and their utopian Plan for London in 1942. Both of these projects marked the beginning of experiments with multilevel circulation networks that would influence the architectural culture of London over the next thirty years, directing the future forms of the international multilevel city.

While many key members of the MARS Group, particularly British architects Wells Coates and F.R.S. Yorke, were more aligned with the principles of CIAM and architects such as Le Corbusier, Marcel Breuer, and Walter Gropius, the Town Planning Committee's key members and the MARS Plan's central authors were architects with direct connections to Soviet models of urbanism.

– William and Aileen Tatton-Brown, Concept for pedestrian deck, *Architectural Review* (1941, 1942)

13. Tatton-Brown worked on several important schemes, including the winning entry in a competition to design working-class flats, the planning study, and the health center for Finsbury, and he was job architect for Highpoint 2 flats in Highgate.

14. An unusual perspective on Lubetkin's work can be found in William Curtis's 1974 article, "Berthold Lubetkin: or Socialist Architecture of the Diaspora." Rather than attributing Lubetkin's work to Le Corbusier, he describes how this work is representative of a utopian social ideal for architecture.

15. John R. Gold, "The MARS Plans for London, 1933–1942: Plurality and Experimentation in the City Plans of the Early British Modern Movement," in *The Town Planning Review*, vol. 66, no. 3 (July 1995): 252–253.

16. Lionel Esher, *The Rebuilding of England 1940–1980: A Broken Wave* (London: Penguin Books, 1981), 45–55.

17. Nicholas R. Fyfe, *Images of the Street: Planning, Identity, and Control in Public Space* (London and New York: Routledge, 1998), 52–53.

18. While the Tatton-Browns had connections to CIAM and Le Corbusier, their political interests in these ideas were parallel to those of Ginzburg and the Narkomfin Housing project, a culminating example of a collective research-based process intended to arrive at the most appropriate form for a standard Soviet residential and communal prototype. Described by Kenneth Frampton as the "*dom-kommuna*," its pursuit as collective research was the "optimum socio-architectural form that preoccupied the Soviet avant-garde throughout the twenties."

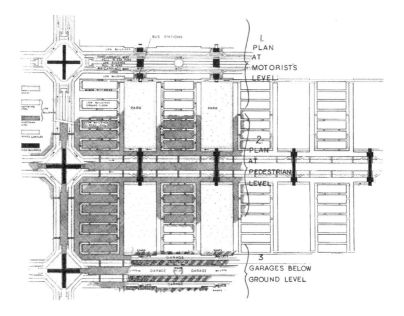

Other members of the Town Planning Committee were indirectly influenced by urban and architectural design strategies developed in the Soviet Union.

The first appearance of the elevated city that was found in the MARS Plan and popularized in 1960s London as the elevated street came from the MARS Group Town Planning Committee initially headed by William Tatton-Brown.[13] He began the MARS Plan for London in 1936 (with Aileen Tatton-Brown of Tecton) and continued its development as part of the MARS Group's presentation to CIAM in 1937.[14] Tatton-Brown, who was also working at Tecton, [15] published a conceptual study based on this work as a two-part series titled "Three-Dimensional Town Planning" in *Architectural Review* (1941–1942).

The Tatton-Browns developed their initial ideas in the form of elevated walkways and later promoted them through *Architectural Review* in the post-Blitz series.[16] An essential part of this planning was the concept of communications constructed as a means of facilitating human contacts.[17] Shared circulation nodes would create areas of intersection offering the potential for otherwise dispersed social communities to interact.[18] Within the historic city

19.   Peter Coe and Malcolm Reading, *Lubetkin and Tecton: Architecture and Social Commitment: A Critical Study* (London: Arts Council of Great Britain and the University of Bristol, 1981), 65, 167–169, 190.
20.   Eric Mumford, *The CIAM Discourse on Urbanism, 1928–1960* (Cambridge: MIT Press, 2000), 122.
21.   John Gold, *The Experience of Modernism: Modern Architects and the Future City 1928–1953* (London: Taylor & Francis, 1997), 89. Maxwell Fy had worked with Thomas Adam's firm in New York City, consulting on the Regional Plan (1929–1931).
22.   Mumford, *The CIAM Discourse on Urbanism*, 98, 122.
23.   Arthur Korn, Maxwell Fry, and Dennis Sharp, "MARS Plan for London," in *Perspecta*, vol. 13/14 (1971): 163–173.

of London, they attempted to integrate the new with the old by creating separate levels for shopping and leisure, positioning housing and offices above automobile traffic. The Tatton-Browns were also interested in creating an elevated pedestrian level using regulatory strategies. The idea was to implement a comprehensive multilevel pedestrian system incrementally based on a designed set of components.[19] This *Architectural Review* article was widely distributed and likely influenced Tatton-Brown's decision to join the LCC's Planning Techniques Office under Arthur Ling and William Holford after World War II.

The work of the Tatton-Browns was conceptually underpinned by Tecton's concurrent planning for the socialist borough of Finsbury and its ideas for social condensers. The Finsbury Plan also influenced later multilevel urban projects such as the Royal Festival Hall and the National Theatre and Southbank Centre development (1953). Lubetkin saw the body of work in Finsbury as his manifesto—a radical rethinking of and a new socialist urban reconstruction for the entire area after slum clearance, intended to encompass healthcare, housing, and education.

At the beginning of World War II, the master plan was reduced in scope and their work refocused on the design of a large underground complex to be used as an air-raid shelter. The underground bomb shelters were spiral-shaped social structures that reflected Lubetkin's interest in the spiral urban forms of Melnikov, and are a precursor for many of Tecton's later social condenser models—including the most compelling examples in the Bevan Court and the Dorset Estate projects in Finsbury. The Finsbury Plan, although never completed, did realize the Health Center, which featured a social condenser (similar to the Palace of Soviets) uniting two wings of the building. After the war, Tecton completed a series of public housing schemes (1943–1957) for Finsbury, including the Priory Green and Spa Green Estates, including elements of social condensers that were reduced in scale and impact from their prewar ambitions.[20] While the original grand visions of Finsbury were unrealized, the project resulted in a number of productive partnerships. In addition to architects who would carry the ambitions forward such as Tatton-Brown (1934–1938) and Moro and Lasdun, collaborators included engineer Ove Arup and physicist John Desmond Bernal.

As the MARS Group grew, it became more preoccupied with stylistic issues and less socially and politically oriented. Lubetkin dismissed those sharing this aesthetic focus as "The Flat Roof Club" and created a splinter group, the Architect's and Technician's Organization (ATO) in response. More radically left wing than the MARS Group, the ATO was formed by many members of Tecton and several MARS members sharing Lubetkin's commitment to socialist principles and their poetic expression. The ATO formed a parallel town-planning group in 1936 that produced urban projects largely based on Tecton's previous work, including the Worker's Flats venture at Finsbury. Other Tecton members interested in Soviet planning joined, including Serge Chermayeff, Erno Goldfinger, and eventually Percy Johnson-Marshall and Arthur Ling. In 1937, Arthur Korn, an acquaintance of Lubetkin, arrived in London and joined ATO. He worked with Lubetkin on an urban planning concept that was exhibited at the Olympia Exhibition Hall that same year.[21]

ATO dissolved in 1938; and Korn took over leadership of the MARS Town Planning Group that same year and was joined by Maxwell Fry, Ling, and engineer Felix Samuely.[22] Other members of this new group included Thomas Sharp, Hugh Casson, Johnson-Marshall, Gordon Shand, Goldfinger, and Peter Shepheard. Unlike the larger MARS Group, all of these architects were connected by their shared communist beliefs, which allowed them to imagine the radical transformation of a city into a completely new and publically constructed modern form. Korn, a refugee from Weimar Germany, had worked with Ernst May and Mart Stam in the USSR to design Soviet cities.[23]

– László Moholy-Nagy, Kinetic Construction System, 1922–1928, Courtesy Theaterwissenschaftliche Sammlung, University of Cologne ©2016 Artists Rights Society (ARS), New York/VG Bild-Kunst, Bonn

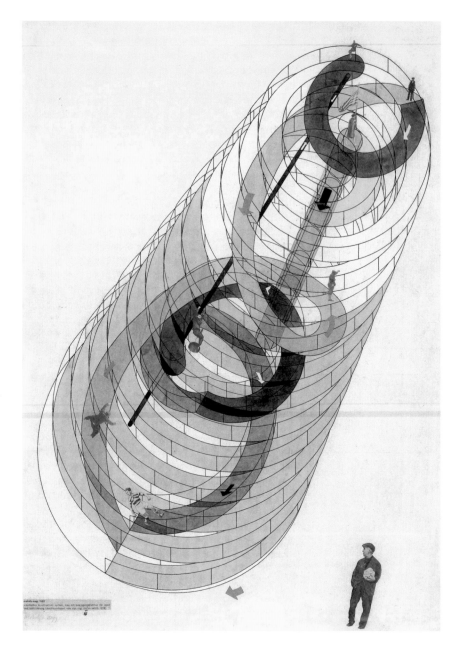

Collectively, the MARS Town Planning Group continued emphasizing linear city principles derived from Korn's work on the Magnitogorsk and Avtostoy projects and from Soviet urbanists such as Nikolay Milyutin and Moisei Ginzburg, among others. This very different trajectory of Soviet architecture was more rigid in its functionalist planning principles than that of Lubetkin and Tecton. While Lubetkin's social experiments in communal forms drew from his mentors Melnikov and Lissitzky and their linking of art, science, and human experience, Korn's approach was more aligned with the systematized functionalist strategies of May and Ginzburg and their interest in applying a uniform prototype.

The third key member was Arthur Ling, who had studied under Patrick Abercrombie and would later author the book *Soviet Cities*. Ling and his interests in Soviet architecture were focused on traffic control and the distribution

A.   Tecton, Bevin Court, Holford
Place, Finsbury, London, 1953–1954,
Courtesy Conway Library, Courtauld
Institute of Art, London
B.   Skinner, Bailey & Lubetkin,
Dorset Estate, Bethnal Green,
London, 1957, RIBA Library
Photographs Collection

24.   Kenneth Frampton, *The English
Crucible*.
25.   John R. Gold, "The MARS Plans
for London, 1933–1942: Plurality and
Experimentation in the City Plans of
the Early British Modern Movement,"
in *The Town Planning Review*, vol. 66,
no. 3 (July 1995): 243–267.
26.   Arthur Korn, Maxwell Fry, and
Dennis Sharp, "The MARS Group
Plan of London," in *Perspecta*, vol. 13
(1971): 163–173.
27.   John R. Gold, "The Mars Plans
for London," 252–253.
28.   John R. Gold, "Toward the
Functional City? MARS, CIAM and
the London Plans, 1933–1942," in
T. Deckker, ed., *The Modern City
Revisited* (London, Routledge, 2000),
81–99.

of population. Notably, socialist cities in the USSR under Stalin emphasized functionalism over the individual artistic experimentation of the early Constructivists. Tatton-Brown continued to work on this new linear city version of the MARS Plan, but he was frustrated by the new conceptual direction, particularly its dependence on railroads, as he believed that the automobile was critical to any future urban form.

The distinct form of these architectural ideas in the early MARS Group was a product of mixing different disciplines with architecture—and the emerging idea of architectural design as a collaborative form of research. This process enabled these concepts to spread and evolve among diverse authors with very different outcomes. Members of the MARS Group did not necessarily agree on a final product, and various members of its Town Planning Committee furthered the work independently of each other. Interdisciplinary research underpinned the practices of many early MARS members—particularly those who were also aligned with the work of biologist, sociologist, and planner Patrick Geddes, including William Holford, who led the technocratic PTO, and architects such as Leslie Martin, who was later influential in the field of computational design as a professor at Cambridge University.

Like the earlier plan, the new MARS Plan for London (1939–1942) was socialist and utopian in nature.[24] While none of the plans or design work was done for authorized groups or for clients, it was undertaken with the intent of influencing the future of the city.[25] Korn later described it as a polemical diagram that was conceived in terms of movement and assumed separation of different modes of traffic along its linear projections.[26] At intervals, multi-level interchanges allowed pedestrians to negotiate different levels of traffic. These interchanges were seen as a critical opportunity to create communal space.[27] Both versions of the MARS Plan for London—while differing in their urban form (clusters versus the linear city) and their emphasis on automobiles (Tatton-Brown) versus trains (Korn and Ling)—shared the idea of elevated pedestrian systems.[28]

A key shared concept was the theory of contacts and the desire to mix different populations. This theory shifted the intention of the elevated street from an infrastructural tool to relieve congestion toward a more complex form of three-dimensional public space that emphasized social mixing.

– Leslie Martin and Peter Moro, Royal Festival Hall, Festival of Britain, Southbank, London, 1949–1951, Courtesy John Maltby/RIBA Library Photographs Collection

29. Sarah Walford, "Architecture in Tension: An Examination of the Position of the Architect in the Private and Public Sectors, Focusing on the Training and Careers of Sir Basil Spence (1907–1976) and Sir Donald Gibson (1908–1991)" (PhD diss., University of Warwick, 2009).

30. John R. Gold, *The Practice of Modernism: Modern Architecture and Urban Transformation, 1954–1972* (London and New York, Routledge, 2007), 89.

Significant multilevel public projects constructed after the Blitz, such as the Barbican Estate, the Royal Festival Hall at Southbank Centre, and the City of London Pedway (an extensive planned network of elevated walkways in central London) actually began with these early 1930s utopian experiments of the interwar period. As they evolved and the British modernists became more connected to CIAM, the ideological rivalries of the past would reemerge as a struggle to define the social utopian city in terms of functionalism or in terms of lyricism, to use Le Corbusier's distinction.

The first comprehensive test of these ideas was developed in the town of Coventry just as England was entering World War II in 1939. In 1940 an exhibition entitled *Coventry Tomorrow* was curated by its city architect Donald Gibson along with colleague Johnson-Marshall of the MARS Group. The exhibition introduced proposals for modernized pedestrianized city centers, including the MARS Plan. Johnson-Marshall led the prewar team for Coventry, constructing the first model of elevated systems after the MARS Plan. He would later collaborate on the replanning of Burma with Tatton-Brown during World War II.[29] This varied prewar work became a model for multilevel pedestrianized city centers in several British new towns and influenced comprehensive development areas after the war.[30]

Postwar London

In London the Town Planning Committee was first formed in 1949. At that time there was a confluence of factors that made the possibility of a radical new urban form seem tangible. After the devastation of the London Blitz there was a willing government looking to rebuild the city and a public that had been recently introduced to new urban ideas in popular culture—from the futuristic depictions of the city to the real, multilevel demonstration projects at the Festival of Britain (1951) promoting British advances in technology, architecture, design, and art. There were also modern architects who had been speculating on the

– Patrick Abercrombie, "bubble diagram," from the County of London Plan, 1943, illustrated by by Arthur Ling and D. K. Johnson, Courtesy London Metropolitan Archives

possibility of recreating London as a modern city since the end of World War I, well before the possibility ever existed.

Through a large-scale, government-led reconstruction effort that incorporated the visions of this smaller group of modern architects, the reconstruction of London as a modern city began in earnest. While seemingly regional in its implications, this more socially-oriented version of a new multilevel urbanism would in fact initiate a global transformation of cities over the next fifty years. Although not fully resolved, the principles underlying the radical social experimentation of the multilevel MARS Plan remained influential in the ongoing work by the City of London Department of Architecture and Town Planning. Plans to reconstruct the city's bombed-out sites and create new towns around the perimeter gained momentum with the passage of the Town Planning Act of 1947 and the emergence of the UK's first elected socialist government. The Abercrombie Plan for London (1944) and the advisory Barlow Report (1940) set into place a plan for large-scale comprehensive change along with a bureaucratic structure for incremental implementation in the areas most affected by the Blitz. Through these initiatives an organization was created to interpret the widely accepted plan. It included a structure for oversight and guidance led by MARS Plan co-author Arthur Ling as chief planning officer of the LCC Ministry of Town Planning Office, and the PTO for design research and the creation of the approved planning strategies.

The PTO and the LCC were staffed with a large group of architects interested in new Soviet cities as a unique model of scientific and research-driven design and most importantly, their technocratic implementation strategies. In addition, other allies of the MARS Group promoted the radical idea

– C. H. Holden and W. G. Holford, Two views of reconstruction in the City of London, 1947, Illustration by Gordon Cullen ©City of London Corporation (London Metropolitan Archives)

31. Stephen V. Ward, "Gordon Stephenson and the 'Galaxy of Talent:' Planning for Postwar Reconstruction in Britain 1942–1947," in *The Town Planning Review* 83 (3), 2012.

32. Mark Crinson and Jules Lubbock, *Architecture—Art or Profession? Three Hundred Years of Architectural Education in Britain* (Manchester: Manchester University Press, 1994), 108.

33. Shortly after completing this work with Arthur Korn, Arthur Ling visited the Soviet Union in 1939, wrote a book on Soviet cities, and became the chairman of the Architecture and Town Planning committee for the Anglo-Soviet Friendship Society concurrently with his leadership of the LCC. Other members included William Holford, Charles Holden, Donald Gibson, and Percy Johnson-Marshall.

34. Arthur Ling, *Planning and Building in the USSR* (London: Bantam Books, 1943).

35. Sir Peter Hall describes this group and their membership in the Anglo-Soviet Friendship Society, the ATO, and the Communist Party in *Cities of Tomorrow: An Intellectual History of Urban Planning and Design* (London: Wiley-Blackwell, 2002), 255–256. Elevated city planners who were members included Holford (30-Mile Pedway), Ling (Chairman), Donald Gibson (Coventry), Johnson-Marshall (Southbank), Thomas Sharp (Exeter Phoenix), Graeme Shankland (Hook and Liverpool), William Tatton-Brown (MARS), Peter Shepheard (Stevenage), and Gordon Stephenson (Stevenage).

36. Michael Hebbert, "The City of London Walkway Experiment," in *Journal of the American Planning Association* 59, vol. 4 (1993): 433–450.

of an elevated pedestrian system from within the city government. By the end of World War II the LCC Ministry of Town Planning's PTO was reconstituted with the same members of the MARS Group Town Planning committee: William Tatton-Brown, Percy Johnson-Marshall, Thomas Sharp, Hugh Casson, Peter Shepheard, and a few others, including Gordon Stephenson and Myles Wright, who had been working with William Holford on previous projects, and Colin Buchanan (*Traffic in Towns*, 1963).[31] While not a member of the MARS Town Planning Group, Stephenson had been employed by Le Corbusier (1930–1932), concurrent with the Palace of Soviets and Plan Obus, Algiers projects, and he had also worked for Harvey Wiley Corbett in New York.[32] These architects all were also proposing elevated pedestrian systems in new towns (Gibson, Stephenson, Ling, and Sharp) and in other urban areas (Holford, Ling, Johnson-Marshall, Tatton-Brown).[33]

Ling was the strongest advocate for adopting Soviet urban design strategies for reconstruction. After developing an interest in Soviet town planning during a visit to Moscow in 1939, he authored a book and a series of articles heralding the USSR's success in such endeavors.[34] Johnson-Marshall held similar beliefs and promoted public architecture as a realization of his communist ideals throughout his career. Because of these associations, there was an ideological and often utopian attitude underpinning the work that also continued the concerns and ideas of the MARS Group's Town Planning Committee.[35]

The PTO was tasked with developing new three-dimensional strategies to guide the design of new towns in London and the Comprehensive Development Areas, those places most impacted by the Blitz. A small group of data-driven researchers studied traffic and building massing. The team's work was summarized in a master plan (May 1947) that included a section called "Pedestrian Ways," which identified strategies and opportunities for multilevel foot traffic separation in central London. The systems were designed as implementation policies for modernist infrastructure and were illustrated in ways that reinforced associations with traditional streets. The City of London Corporation supported the proposals and the LCC acquired the land and developed strategies to implement in the Comprehensive Development Areas.

The PTO members would guide work in these areas. Among them were Hugh Casson, who directed the architecture for the Festival of Britain, and Percy Johnson-Marshall as chief planning officer for the London reconstruction areas, including the Southbank Centre and the Barbican Estate from 1946 to 1959.[36] With the passage of the Town Planning Act of 1947 and the emergence of the UK's first elected socialist government, these demonstration

A.   Chamberlin, Powell and Bon,
Barbican Centre, London, 1959–1982,
Courtesy John Maltby/RIBA Library
Photographs Collection
B.   London County Council
Special Works Group Architects,
including Warren Chalk and Ron
Herron, Southbank Centre, London,
1963–1968, Courtesy Wars/Wikimedia
Commons
C.   London County Council Special
Works Architects, Pedway System
at the Barbican Tube System Station
and the Barbican Estate, London

projects would eventually grow into a more radical plan for the thirty-mile London Pedway. They also provided the impetus for a broad range of seemingly disparate but ongoing experiments with interconnected multilevel projects over the next twenty years in new towns such as Coventry, Exeter, and Stevenage, which added elevated systems in commercial cores completed in the 1960s.

While much is made about the importation of modernism through CIAM, less is known about the exportation of a distinctly British set of ideas that developed prior to the famous urban proposals of Alison and Peter Smithson. While the British arrived late to CIAM and contributed little until CIAM 5, postwar international interest in the MARS Group, CIAM 6, and the LCC's reconstruction after the Blitz led to two CIAM conferences being held in England. CIAM began the search for likely cities to implement their new urban strategies. By the end of World War II, it appeared that the country in which these ideas were most likely to be employed was the UK, where the large membership of the MARS Group worked in tandem with political structures that supported reconstruction. Le Corbusier, Sigfried Giedion, and Josep Lluís Sert, the new president of CIAM,

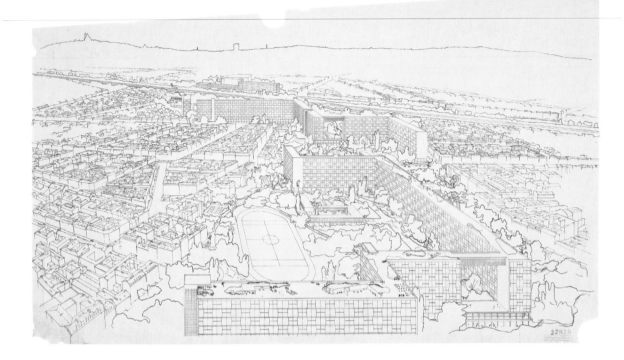

– Le Corbusier, Ilot Insalubre No. 6, presented at CIAM 5, Paris, 1936 ©FLC/ADAGP, Paris/Artists Rights Society (ARS), New York 2016

37. Emmanuel Marmaras, *Planning London for the Post-War Era 1945–60* (Heidelberg, Germany: Springer, 2015), 181, 191–193.

38. Madges Bacon, "Sert's Evolving Concept of the Urban Core," in Josep Lluís Sert, *The Architect of Urban Design 1953–1969*, Eric Mumford, ed. (New Haven: Yale University Press, 2008), 90–102.

39. Eric Mumford, *The CIAM Discourse on Urbanism*, 202–219.

40. Barry Curtis, "The Heart of the City," in *Non-Plan: Essays on Freedom, Participation and Change in Modern Architecture and Urbanism*, Jonathan Hughes and Simon Sadler, eds. (London, Architectural Press, 2000), 56.

41. Marmaras, *Planning London for the Post-War Era*, 326–327.

42. These areas had been developing since 1947, but in 1952 the Labor Government lost power to the conservatives and the developments shifted from publicly designed, financed, and constructed projects to those led by private developers under the design oversight of the LCC architecture department. Both the Southbank and Barbican projects were affected by this change, although master plans had already been completed that required multilevel pedestrian circulation.

wanted to mobilize this group without giving over too much control, and advocated for postwar CIAM sessions to be held in the UK.

Arthur Ling presented the outcomes of the new planning legislation at CIAM 6 in Bridgwater (1947). The session on urbanism was co-chaired by Le Corbusier and Ling and included a presentation by William Holford on the emerging prescriptive functionalism of the PTO.[37] The overall work exhibited began to suggest a new relevance for the multilevel city in its nascent stage in London. This included Le Corbusier's Plan for Reconstruction of Sant-Die (1945) with its nodal figures of pedestrian bridges interconnecting volumes,[38] and Wiener and Sert's (Town Planning Associates) plan for Cidade de Motores, Brazil (1944–1947), with its elevated form taking a different trajectory featuring a continuous elevated podium and voids forming courtyards.[39] While both of these examples are multilevel typologies, their spatial and formal logic differed from the form of multilevel systems evolving in England. Le Corbusier's earlier proposals using elevated connectors prior to CIAM 6 (Ilot Insalubré [1936] and Sant-Die) were never intended as a continuous urban network but similarly as a set of convenient multilevel bridge linkages.

By 1951, CIAM 8, "The Heart of the City," was held concurrently with the Festival of Britain, which was the first multilevel development site to apply the new principles of the PTO through the design arm of the LCC, led by chief architect Leslie Martin. The initial work by the LCC on the Southbank Centre development was presented by Ling,[40] who discussed the multilevel Royal Festival Hall (1948–1951) as well as the site's use of elevated platforms and bridges. Other multilevel test sites were toured by CIAM members, including Stevenage New Town (1950) with its first elevated bridge. Further projects presented included the multilevel plans for the reconstruction of Coventry, Sert and Wiener's civic centers for Chimbote and Lima, Peru, which also employed elevated podium structures with courtyards, and the Bogota Master Plan collaboration using Le Corbusier's 7V model of traffic separation.[41] Ling led the presentation on urbanism, and Holford delivered "The Commercial Core of London" on the Central Reconstruction Areas.[42]

A.   London County Council Special
Works Groups Architects, including
Archigram's Warren Chalk and Ron
Herron, Southbank Centre, London,
1963–1968, Courtesy Southbank
Centre Archive
B.   Leslie Martin, Sketch of 1953
Southbank scheme, Courtesy London
Metropolitan Archives

A

B

Following CIAM 8, the earlier podium form of the multilevel city of Le Corbusier and Sert evolved into a multilevel urbanism that bore similarities to the MARS Group and early PTO and LCC schemes. The Bogota Master Plan (1949–1953) developed further by Sert employed continuous platforms and bridges similar to the systems proposed by the Tatton-Browns in 1942. Inexplicably, Ling's work was not included in Sert's publication of the proceedings of CIAM 8, despite his coeditor Jacqueline Tyrwhitt's membership in the MARS Group. The impact of CIAM 8 was internationally significant, signaling the beginning of involvement in CIAM by the Japanese, led by Kenzo Tange, and the United States, two countries that would greatly influence the international construction of pedestrianized city centers in the postwar period. The

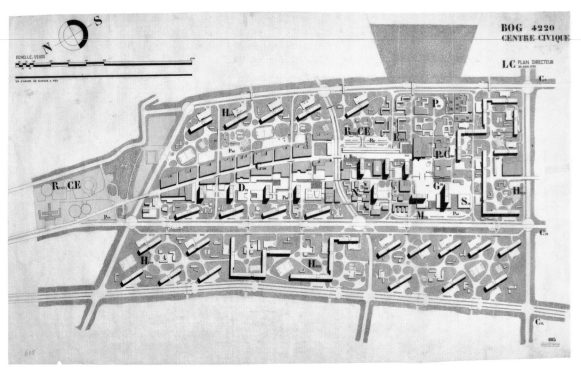

A. Le Corbusier, Centre Civique Plan, Bogota Master Plan without Bridges, 1950 ©FLC/ADAGP, Paris/ Artists Rights Society (ARS), New York 2016
B. Wiener and Sert, Town Planning Associates, Bogota Masterplan, 1949–1950, presented at CIAM 8 (hosted by MARS) with elevated city center system, Courtesy the Frances Loeb Library, Harvard University Graduate School of Design

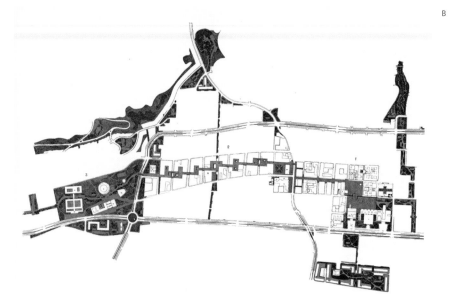

more human scale of urban work presented in CIAM 8 was part of a new trajectory for CIAM. This influence can be seen in the evolution of projects that led to the new multilevel city form introduced at CIAM 9 in the work of Alison and Peter Smithson. Interestingly, this emphasis on the human scale can be traced to early work in post–World War I London where connections were first made between ideas emerging in the British design culture and an international dialogue about the new form of the modern city.

43. The Percy Johnson-Marshall Collection Archives, University of Edinburgh.
44. Simon Sadler, *Archigram: Architecture without Architecture* (Cambridge: MIT Press, 2005), 74.
45. David Douglas-James, "Ad Classics: Royal National Theatre/ Denys Lasdun," in ArchDaily, September 8, 2015, accessed March 1, 2016, http://www.archdaily.com /772979/ad.classics-royal.national -theatre-denys-lasdun.

While Kenneth Frampton has identified the unacknowledged influence of Russian Constructivism on British modernism in elements such as the Skylon and Dome used at the Festival of Britain, the influence of Constructivism can also be seen in many other respects. Led by Ling and Johnson-Marshall as part of a larger and more permanent redevelopment of the Southbank and directed by architects Hugh Casson and Leslie Martin, the Festival of Britain could be viewed as a design laboratory for the multilevel city, and its public popularity a validation of this new approach to urban space.

The area that would eventually host the Southbank Centre offered an opportunity to test these new forms on a large scale. Ling and Johnson-Marshall hired MARS colleagues to develop the elevated work and arranged design competitions for adjacent areas. As large urban-scaled systems, these prototypes quickly evolved into more radical forms. Martin, designed the central Royal Festival Hall (1949–1951) with its multilevel circulation along with Peter Moro from the LCC, and as LCC chief architect he designed the first master plan of elevated walkways on the Southbank Centre. The project employs upper-level promenades and other pedestrian networks for "intercommunication" to allow connections between buildings.[43] Widely acknowledged as being influenced by Lubetkin at Finsbury, the Festival of Britain development and its successor, the Southbank Centre, were the first significant expression of a set of ideas around elevated social space that eventually spread to other areas of the world. Unlike the later work by William Holford in Paternoster Square and the early multilevel schemes in the New Towns, the arrangement appeared to be more informal, organic, and less rigidly organized.

Concurrent with some of their more experimental work, future Archigram members Warren Chalk, Dennis Crompton, and Ron Herron were employed by the LCC and specifically designed the multilevel pedestrian system of the Southbank Centre—a complex of cultural projects interconnected by elevated plazas and walkways built on the site of the Festival of Britain along the Southbank of the Thames. It included the Royal Festival Hall, the Hayward Gallery (1968), and the National Theatre (1976). Chalk described the multilevel movement strategies: "The original concept of the building (complex) was to produce an anonymous pile, subservient to a series of pedestrian walkways, a sort of Mappin Terrace [the artificial habitat mound at the London Zoo] for people instead of goats."[44] The Hayward Gallery at the Southbank was designed by the same team of LCC architects following Martin's departure in 1956. Denys Lasdun described the next phase of the Southbank project in social terms after he took over work on the multilevel National Theatre. Its architecture was an urban landscape of "strata" that organized social space.[45] The Southbank area was a successful testing ground for these ideas, and its initial elevated pedestrian circulation strategies (aka "deck-access systems" or "streets in the sky") were used to structure a series of design competitions for other critical areas. Organized by Ling and Johnson-Marshall to promote this new form of multilevel urbanism, they included: Piccadilly Circus (1961), which received a commendation for Peter Cook; Elephant and Castle (1951–1956), won by MARS Plan colleague Erno Goldfinger; and the Golden Lane Housing competition (1951) and the Barbican Estate project, both won by Chamberlin, Powell, and Bon. Both the Southbank Centre and the Barbican were seen as applications of this new form of urbanism and were designed and overseen by the LCC, eventually expanding and transforming both banks of the River Thames with projects featuring elevated pedestrian networks. In 1955, plans were drawn up for the Barbican and Paternoster Square developments that included towers, podiums, and walkways. The projects were again led by Johnson-Marshall and Ling with chief planning consultant Holford. Between 1954 and 1956, three different studies were commissioned by the LCC, one

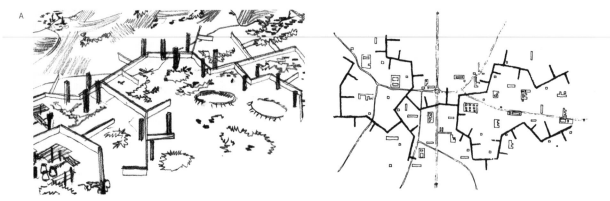

A. Alison and Peter Smithson, Golden Lane Housing Competition, drawings, London, 1952–1953
B. The Lower Precinct, Coventry City Centre, from Tanner Oc and Steve Tiesdell, Safer City Centres: Reviving the Public Realm ©1997 (SAGE Publications Ltd.)

46. Marmaras, *Planning London for the Post-War Era*, 181–183.
47. Exeter-Princesshay new town was designed by Thomas Sharp in 1945, shortly after the publications of Tatton-Brown's *Three-Dimensional Town Planning* and the *MARS Plan* in the *Architectural Review*. Its city center was constructed in 1951 as an elevated system.
48. Sam Jacob and Wouter Vanstiphout, "From Garden City to New Towns: Why Britain Should Be Proud of Its Planners," in *The Guardian*, June 3, 2014.
49. Johnson-Marshall collaborated with Colin Buchanan in 1958 on a two-level proposal for the reconstruction of Berlin, "Plan for a Two-Level City." (See note 52.)
50. Percy Johnson-Marshall, *Rebuilding Cities* (Edinburgh: Edinburgh University Press, 1966), 177–190.

by Martin and the others by Holford.[46] The final master plan for the Barbican was completed in 1954, proposing a program that combined commercial and residential components connected to a system of raised footpaths called the Highwalk.

In the late 1950s, Ling took over the position of city architect in Coventry, leading the implementation of the multilevel pedestrian system began by Percy Johnson-Marshall and Donald Gibson before World War II. Ling would also finally implement multilevel pedestrian systems into many of these new town commercial centers in the early 1960s—including in Stevenage, Harlow, and Bracknell.[47] In the second wave of new towns, Ling designed Runcorn and influenced the ill-fated urban megastructure in Cumbernauld.[48] Johnson-Marshall and Holford were also advisors for the Buchanan Report, "Traffic in Towns" (1963), which advocated elevated pedestrian systems as a standard strategy for cities[49] and is widely credited for the international spread of these multilevel pedestrian techniques in North American and Asia in the late 1960s.

The Pedway, an ambitious elevated walkway project for central London, was planned and partially built by the LCC in collaboration with Holford and Johnson-Marshall in the 1950s and 1960s.[50] By 1965, a confidential LCC document simply titled "Drawing 3400B" defined the London Pedway for the first time as a thirty-mile network from Liverpool Street to the Thames, and from Fleet Street to the Tower of London. Under this scheme, developers had to provide walkways—dedicated public rights of way—as a condition for

– Highwalk system, Barbican area, 2013, Courtesy VJAA Architects, Minneapolis
51. Bob Stanley, "Taking a Walk in the Clouds: A Plan to Build a Pedestrian Way for the City of London Ended Up Going Nowhere," *The Times of London*, August 24, 2004.
52. Tom Avermaete, "Stem and Web: A Different Way of Analysing, Understanding and Conceiving the City in the Work of Candilis-Josic-Woods," in *Sociology, Production and the City* (Delft: TU Delft, 2003), 256–257. [Papers from the conference "Team 10—Between Modernity and the Everyday," organized by the Faculty of Architecture TU Delft, Chair of Architecture and Housing, June 5–6, 2003. This was the second preparatory meeting for the book and exhibition *In Search of a Utopia of the Present*.]
53. William Curtis describes similarly the ongoing work of Lubetkin and Tecton in "Berthold Lubetkin or Socialist Architecture in the Diaspora," in *Architectural Association* (Great Britain)–AAQ, (March 1976): 33–39.

planning consent. Despite this disclosure, the extent of the government's plan for these systems was not publicly known outside of the LCC until the early 1990s.[51] While the elevated pedestrian circulation design for the Barbican was largely successful, employing a podium/bridge strategy to create a large and complex pedestrian zone, the more standardized and ad hoc Highwalk system surrounding the development did not flourish and is currently being slowly dismantled. The multifaceted history of the London Pedway, as a case study, illustrates how the idea of the pedestrian city has spread—sometimes through intimate and interpersonal relationships, sometimes by more circuitous paths, or broadly disseminated through the media.

The Socialist Diaspora

The migration of early avant-gardists to the LCC after World War II influenced more spectacular and experimental urban ideas in the 1950s. Alison and Peter Smithson described this early interwar interval as the heroic period of modern architecture and include a number of architectural works whose trajectory of "invention and social ideals" represent what they were trying to advance. They described with admiration the architects in the LCC while criticizing the paternalistic functionalism into which some projects devolved.

The basic Team 10 understanding of the street as a complex socio-spatial structure can be traced to these LCC connections and influences. An interesting example can be seen in Candilis-Josic-Wood's concept of the "stem and web," which drew from writings on the city by LCC associate Erwin Anton Gutkind, who was an architect, a German émigré, and a member of MARS and Team 10.[52] There were several critical multilevel projects developed by the LCC bureaucracy at this time that can be seen as prototypical projects for the urban application of Pedway systems and influential to the architectural avant garde of the period: the complex of projects at the Southbank Centre (the Royal Festival Hall constructed for the Festival of Britain, the Hayward Gallery and Southbank Centre, the National Theatre); and the Barbican Estate. These projects were all designed by a small group of architects who had been heavily influenced by the poetic strain of Constructivism in the interwar period and the socialist diaspora of MARS, through the Tecton office, the Hampstead Group, *Circle* magazine, and Arthur Korn.[53] This work in turn, influenced more avant-garde practices like those within Team 10 and Archigram.

These urban ideas rapidly spread through various spheres of influence. Whether through professional discourse and dissemination of architectural thinking via groups like CIAM and Team 10, or through colonial and post-colonial influence as ideas passed from London to Hong Kong and Singapore or through publication in international magazines and journals, the concept of the pedestrianized parallel city proliferated worldwide from London in a matter of thirty to forty years. London was central to the dissemination of these ideas

– Candilis-Josic-Woods, Toulouse-Le-Mirail, Toulouse, France, 1963, Courtesy Avery Architectural & Fine Arts Library, Department of Drawings & Archives, and Waltraude Woods

54. Dennis Sharp, ed., *Planning and Architecture: Essays Presented to Arthur Korn* (London: Barrie & Rockliff, 1967). Korn was acknowledged at the end of his career at the AA for the contribution of his early urban proposals for the City of London and the larger region through a series of essays authored by Korn's former colleagues William Holford, Arthur Ling, Patrick Abercrombie, Percy Johnson-Marshall, Ernst May, Erno Goldfinger, and Ludwig Hilberseimer.
55. Jonathan Hughes, "Hospital-City," 266–288.

to North America and Europe through academic and cultural connections. Arthur Korn indirectly promoted multilevel urbanism internationally through his advocacy of key avant-garde practices.[54] This included his introduction of the Smithsons to and as teachers at the Architectural Association (AA), and his advocacy of former students Peter Cook, Elias Zenghelis, Richard Rogers, and Cedric Price, who in turn influenced architects such as Rem Koolhaas and Zaha Hadid.

The other paths of influence followed the professional trajectories of the key promoters within the LCC. Even after the decline of influence of the LCC under later conservative governments, its key leaders and multilevel city advocates shifted their interests to other related areas. Over the years of British colonization, many of the same architects and planners who created the London Pedway vision worked in and influenced development in multiple locations. Architects like Tatton-Brown moved into areas parallel to town planning in government, first working on schools and then as the chief architect of the Ministry of Health (1959–1971); in that position, he redirected similar urban strategies toward large-scale hospital planning. His colleague Johnson-Marshall submitted a "Two-Level City Center" scheme with Colin Buchanan for the Haupstadt Berlin Competition (1957). As an independent consultant, Johnson-Marshall developed multilevel city plans for Halifax, Nova Scotia, and the University of Edinburgh.[55] After guiding the development of multilevel city centers in Coventry, Stevenage, and Cumbernauld, Ling, as president of the Commonwealth Association of Planners, shifted his interest toward planning strategies in UK Commonwealth countries in Africa, Asia, and the Southwest Pacific. After Paternoster Square and his failed proposals for a multilevel development of Picadilly Circus and the thirty-mile Pedway, Holford worked

–   Peter Cook and Gordon
Sainsbury, Picadilly Circus
Competition (highly commended),
model ©1961 Archigram
56.   Iain Gordon Cherry and
L. Penny, *Holford: A Study in
Architecture, Planning and Civic
Design* (London: Routledge, 2005),
250–252.

as a planning consultant in Australia, Hong Kong, Israel, Singapore, Lebanon, Iran, Yugoslavia, and South Africa, and was a juror on the competitions for Brasilia and for the Toronto City Center.[56]

The advocacy for multilevel urbanisms emanating from London had a strong influence in Asia, specifically in Hong Kong and Singapore. The timelines of implementation for all of these systems were roughly concurrent, including the construction of the first elevated systems in Singapore and Hong Kong. The early colonial influence of London has continued in postcolonial Singapore and Hong Kong with the employment of British planners and consultants and through the use of Western-style competitions to design new icons for the cities.

The Multilevel Network

The social processes that fostered and propagated the multilevel urban project internationally cannot be traced in a simple historical chronology, nor can the process be understood solely in terms of individual formal genealogies. The cultural and professional networks though which these ideas were exchanged were surprisingly small and closely knit. The level to which this network of friends and professional rivals was able to maintain its coherence through the

57.   For a developed description,
see the network theories of Bruno
Latour and Manuel Castells.

turbulence of mid-twentieth-century European history is remarkable. The coupling of socialist/communist ideology with the historically magnetic attraction of the multilevel city concept produced a powerful organizing force among the London architectural avant-garde in the interwar and postwar periods.

Simple conceptual but malleable models for social space, in particular the social condenser, were critical to sustaining the multilevel city as a project and maintaining its leverage in the postwar reconstruction process. The engagement of other modernist social and professional networks, like those of CIAM, would serve to extend further the concept while at the same time grafting into the project new actors and forms of individual expression. The social chemistry of these complex interpersonal interactions, the intellectual programming of the movement, and the power of key gatekeepers like Lubetkin and Ling provide an excellent example of actor/network theory in action.[57]

Ultimately it was the success of the multilevel city project that would lead to its ideological collapse. The bureaucratic codification of the elevated city would play a significant role in its failure as projects were completed with diminishing levels of quality and commitment to the originating social principles. In this way, the apparent intellectual failure of the elevated city project in the 1970s and 1980s would mirror the crisis of communism as government-led urban projects were abandoned in favor of a more laissez-faire approach to urban development. However, as systems like the London Pedway stalled and began to be dismantled, they continued to develop in other cities. Where the concepts of multilevel urbanism had been introduced in North American and Asian cities and intermeshed with the interests of capital, they would continue to reproduce and grow. The successful transmutation of the multilevel socialist city concept into an engine of capitalist urban recolonization would extend the project into the next century.

Man walks in a straight line because he has a goal and knows where he is going; he has made up his mind to reach some particular place and he goes straight to it. The pack-donkey meanders along, meditates a little in his scatter-brained and distracted fashion, he zigzags in order to avoid the larger stones, or to ease the climb or to gain a little shade; he takes the line of least resistance. But man governs his feelings by reason; he keeps his feelings and his instincts in check, subordinating them to the aim he has in view.... But the pack-donkey thinks of nothing at all, except what will save himself trouble.... The Pack-Donkey's Way is responsible for the plan of every continental city.

— Le Corbusier, "The Pack-Donkey's Way and Man's Way," 1925

3. DONKEYPATH URBANISM

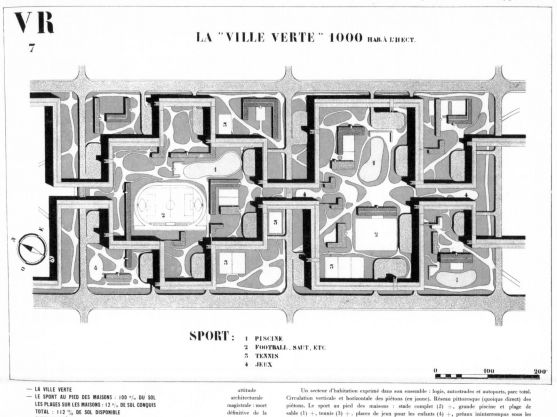

VR 7

LA "VILLE VERTE" 1000 HAB. À L'HECT.

SPORT :
1 PISCINE
2 FOOTBALL, SAUT, ETC.
3 TENNIS
4 JEUX

0   100   200°

— LA VILLE VERTE
— LE SPORT AU PIED DES MAISONS : 100 % DU SOL
LES PLAGES SUR LES MAISONS : 12 % DE SOL CONQUIS
TOTAL : 112 % DE SOL DISPONIBLE
— SUPERDENSITÉ DE 1.000 HAB. A L'HECT.

attitude
architecturale
magistrale : mort
définitive de la
« rue-corridor ».

Un secteur d'habitation exprimé dans son ensemble : logis, autostrades et autoports, parc total. Circulation verticale et horizontale des piétons (en jaune). Réseau pittoresque (quoique direct) des piétons. Le sport au pied des maisons : stade complet (2) +, grande piscine et plage de sable (1) +, tennis (3) +, places de jeux pour les enfants (4) +, préaux ininterrompus sous les pilotis des immeubles, + immense ruban des plages de soleil sur les toits-jardins des immeubles.

– Le Corbusier, "Ville Verte," plan of Radiant City, 1935 ©FLC/ADAGP, Paris/Artists Rights Society (ARS), New York 2016

In studying the plans of elevated pedestrian systems in North America, a fascinating similarity becomes apparent. The branching, informally composed, lattice-like structure of the Minneapolis Skyway System or Calgary's +15 network resemble some of the most provocative urban proposals made by the architectural avant-garde in the 1950s and 1960s. What do these pedestrian systems implemented by municipal bureaucrats in the United States and Canada owe to the European avant-garde? Are these similarities evidence of urban homologies, or are they merely coincidental? Or, are these extant systems the unloved and unclaimed offspring of more experimental and visionary architects like Alison and Peter Smithson, Constant Nieuwenhuys, and Candilis-Josic-Woods, who authored numerous proposals for the multilevel city, but are typically nowhere to be found when this question is asked: Where did these pedestrian systems come from?

The nature of urban modernization and the rationalization of the city, particularly since Baron von Haussmann's Paris, has remained an ideological and aesthetic battleground often fought on multiple levels. From a morphological point of view, the concept of the elevated city spans some of the most contested theoretical terrain in architecture and urban design history. But it is the apparently fungible relationship of aesthetics, function, and rhetoric that remains one of the most perplexing characteristics of utopian urban design thinking, especially with respect to proposals for multilevel cities throughout the nineteenth and twentieth centuries. Le Corbusier's famous attack on picturesque planning, encapsulated succinctly in the epithet "the pack-donkey's way," marked one of the most poignant moments in the vigorous and ongoing debate revolving around the aesthetics and the functional rationalization of the modern city.

1.   Le Corbusier, *Precisions sur un état présent de l'architecture et de l'urvanisme* (*Precisions: On the Present State of Architecture and Planning*), originally published 1930 (Zurich: Park Books, New Edition, 2006), 175.
2.   Catherine Ingraham, "Architecture and the Burdens of Linearity (1998)," in *Architecture Theory Since 1968*, K. Michael Hays, ed. (Cambridge: MIT Press, 2000), 644–650.
3.   Le Corbusier, *Toward an Architecture* (*Vers une Architecture*) (Los Angeles: The Getty Research Institute, 2007), 127.
4.   Tim Benton describes four distinct periods of Le Corbusier's urban thinking: the earliest picturesque, the geometric purity of his work in Paris, the social rethinking in the third phase during La Ville Radieuse and his work in South America, and finally his postwar work of large-scale urban interventions. See Tim Benton, "Le Corbusier," in *Grove History of Art* (Oxford: Oxford University Press, accessed March 5, 2016, http://www.oxfordartonline.com.eep3.116.umn.edu/subscriber/article/grove/art/TO49930.

In La Ville Contemporaine (1922), Le Corbusier's hypothetical city for three million inhabitants, a little more than a decade after first adopting the urban theories of Camillo Sitte and then rejecting them, he would write his famous polemic against both the hapless donkey and the irrationalities of the historical city. Traditional cities, with their irregular street patterns and seemingly chaotic architectural amalgamations, had evolved through intricate, time-dependent processes. These so-called "non-planned settlements" were the target of Le Corbusier's attack from both a functional and aesthetic point of view. With the emergence and continued development of the multilevel city in the twentieth century, these issues remained relevant, and are now critical, to new theories of urban morphogenesis. But as Catherine Ingraham demonstrates in her essay "Architecture and the Burdens of Linearity," it is important when evaluating the ideologies behind visionary proposals for the modern city to make these distinctions if we are to better understand their implications.

For Le Corbusier the metaphorical pack donkey was the true architect of historic cities such as London and Paris, against which he posited the modern city of rational planning and orthogonal aesthetics. Famously criticizing the persistence of traditional street forms in modern cities he summarized his solution to the congested, dark, narrow, and meandering form of the corridor-street with one memorable line, "Kill the street."[1] Orthogonal planning and architecture offered emancipation from the habitus of inherited architectural styles and conventional urban morphologies. For Ingraham this was evidence of Le Corbusier's desire to "violently" remake the historic city in an appropriately rational form: "For cities clogged by these intersection capillaries, Le Corbusier recommends 'surgery': cutting out central corridors (arteries) so that the 'bodily fluids' of the cities can flow."[2]

From his earliest urban vision for a completely elevated city called A Town Built on Piles (1915), with heavy traffic segregated below, to projects like La Ville Contemporaine, Le Corbusier envisioned a modern city of tall office buildings and housing blocks with vehicular traffic flowing freely above and below pedestrian plazas and gardens.[3] It was a city without traditional congested streets. Applying his urban prototype to Paris in Le Plan Voisin (1922–1925), he would extend his orthogonal rationality by proposing an erasure of nearly the entire Right Bank and urban spaces derived, presumably, from irrational forces (e.g., negotiations with nature, terrain, and human behavior).[4]

Le Corbusier's early work drew on the ideas and technical innovations of the previous French planners of multilevel urbanisms: Eugène Hénard, Henri Jules Borie, and Tony Garnier. His urban design proposals would inspire a later generation of modernist architects seeking to reinvent the modern city in a multilevel urban form. But within the extended debate that has surrounded Le Corbusier's radical proposals, a more nuanced and perhaps useful discussion has focused on the nature of urban space—the relationship between the city as a place for work and the city as a place of leisure as well as the role of architecture as a vehicle of cultural expression. The essential question of urban circulation can also be understood as a simultaneous balancing of the need for rational efficiencies and destination-related planning and the desire to see the meandering paths of the city as a place of leisure and connection.

The contextual and incremental adaptation of the city advocated by Sitte was an explicitly aesthetic approach to urban design that could be described as an aesthetics of negotiation, where each urban intervention was made in relation to the spatial opportunities and functional needs of the immediate circumstance. Sitte's incremental and adaptive approach to urban development that attempted to preserve and extend picturesque aspects of the traditional city was anathema to Le Corbusier and viewed as antithetical to rational planning. Woven through this historic debate on urbanism are implications for both the functioning and aesthetics of the modern metropolis and the morphogenesis of the multilevel city. Throughout his career, Le Corbusier's attitude

– Ludwig Hilberseimer, Highrise City (Hochhausstadt): Perspective view, North-South Street, 1924, Gift of George E. Danforth, 1983, The Art Institute of Chicago Photo © The Art Institute of Chicago
5. Richard Anderson, ed., "Ludwig Hilberseimer," in *Metropolisarchitecture* (originally published 1927), 2013, 20–22.

toward the Sitte model evolved. As is described by Jean-Louis Cohen and others, the qualities of the informal, sculptural, and even picturesque, which he first accepted and then later rejected in favor of the grid and geometric abstraction, conceptually reappear in his urban plans for Rio di Janeiro, São Paulo, and Buenos Aires shortly after his visit to Moscow. This work seems to embrace the informality of the forces engendered in the donkey path within a clearer process of planned negotiation.

The City as Infrastructure: Hilberseimer and Garnier

During the interwar period, *Amerikanismus*—a fascination with the technologies and forms of the American capitalist city—was sweeping Germany just as the new socialist democratic Weimar Republic government (1919–1933) was being formed. The period was particularly productive and the beginning of an extended interchange of ideas about how to modernize cities. While appreciating the vitality and urban density of American cities, Ludwig Hilberseimer (1885–1967) became concerned with traffic congestion and how new forms of high-rise building technology could be adapted in an emerging socialist state. Although critical of the chaotic nature of capitalist development in America, with its ad hoc architectural styles and unplanned growth caused by financial speculation, Hilberseimer admired the rationality of the gridiron plan. In particular, his interest lay in its abstraction, reducing architecture and urbanism to circulation and building mass, which he believed were its elemental forms.

Hilberseimer was drawn to La Ville Contemporaine and shortly after a meeting with Corbusier, he proposed the Hochhausstadt (Highrise City, 1924). It was a version of the multilevel city developed from a very different social and political point of view.[5] Highrise City was both a response to and a critique of La Ville Contemporaine and its simplistic planar separation of vehicular traffic below towers, parks, and plazas—a condition that Hilberseimer believed would result in vertical congestion. Highrise City located the pedestrian strata midway between lower-level business with office space and residential and

A. Tony Garnier, La Cité Industrielle, smelting furnaces, 1917, Courtesy Bibliotheque des Arts Decoratifs, Paris, France/Archives Charmet/The Bridgeman Art Library
B. Tony Garnier, La Cité Industrielle, public services detail, 1917, Courtesy Bibliotheque des Arts Decoratifs, Paris, France/Archives Charmet/The Bridgeman Art Library

A

B

commercial space above. The city was portrayed in bird's-eye perspectives as a stark and cellular machine, interconnected with an elevated grid of walkways reminiscent of a diagram of industrial processes—an aestheticized image of the city as pure infrastructure. Hilberseimer was proposing a city that explicitly reflected in its form the principal patterns of movement and building enclosure in both plan and section. Although in principle it was not so different from the sectional zoning of urban programs seen in roughly concurrent proposals by Wiley Corbett, Hilberseimer saw his system of pedestrian walkways and bridges as a means to remove barriers between public and private ownership by redefining the city as infrastructure. Freed of the chaotic development patterns of capitalism, the city could be conceived rationally, thus enabling its rejuvenation.

6.   Richard Anderson, ed.,
Introduction, *Metropolis-Architecture:
Ludwig Hilberseimer* (New York:
Columbia University GSAPP Books,
2013), 30–75. Translation and reprint
of 1927.
7.   In the years immediately
preceding his Hochhausstadt project,
Hilberseimer wrote on the topics of
modern art (abstraction and Dada),
the metropolis, American architecture (1920), and Constructivism
(1922), and began teaching at the
Bauhaus, where he was exposed
to the International Constructivist
movement.
8.   Pier Vittorio Aureli, *The Project
of Autonomy: Politics and Architecture
within and against Capitalism* (New
York: Princeton Architectural Press,
2008), 76–78.
9.   Ludwig Hilberseimer, *Entfaltung
einer Planungsidee* (Berlin: Verlag
Ulistein, 1963), 22.

As opposed to Hilberseimer's view of the city, other early twentieth-cen-tury speculations anticipated less rigid urban forms for a new society. Fifteen years earlier, inspired by the writing of Émile Zola that brought forward and critiqued the Phalanstère, Tony Garnier developed a proposal for a future socialist city with multiple levels. The original 1901 sketch for his ideal city, La Cité Industrielle project (completed in 1904, published in 1917), was based on a reading of Zola's *Travail* (1901).

As Charles Fourier had done for the Phalanstère, Hilberseimer detailed and quantified the life of the community within each block; residential space was proportionally layered above commercial space layered in turn above parking and transit. Elevated streets, balconies, and courtyards connected the living spaces while keeping pedestrians safe from vehicular traffic. For Hilberseimer, this utopian city was both rational and functional; the distribu-tion of volumes—their massing and density—was derived from his quantita-tive analysis. He created an aesthetic image as a total break with history, and its accretional urban form composed of ad hoc styles independent of social purpose. Hilberseimer described this as "an end to the metropolis that is based on speculation and whose very organism cannot free itself from the model of the city of the past, despite all the modifications it has experienced—an end to the metropolis that has yet to discover its own laws."[6] In stripping away the expression of individual agency, principally capitalist in large cities, the Hochhausstadt was a complete rejection of the past through a sublime image of total control.

Hilberseimer's project grew out of his broad interests in experimental art and architecture.[7] In reducing the image of the city to its fundamental func-tional logic, Hilberseimer perhaps inadvertently exposed the contemporary form of the city as a three-dimensional social and economic apparatus and a byproduct of that speculative process. In 2011, Pier Vittorio Aureli described Hilberseimer's radical urbanism through a reading of Manfredo Tafuri as the most honest translation of the economic and productive forces of the metrop-olis, dropping capitalism's architectural mask and thus exposing the hidden mechanisms of its formation.[8]

Ironically, the order and abstraction of the Hochhausstadt proposal was driven by a desire to control the chaos of capitalist development and make the city more humane. But while intended as an analysis of modern urban form, the project also represented the city in a fixed form, a totalizing com-position, sharing with Plan Voisin the authoritarianism of a static image—a process frozen in time. In 1963 Hilberseimer would describe with regret the Hochhausstadt as "more a necropolis than a metropolis…inhuman in every respect."[9] By eliminating evidence of individual and collective agency in the city, the metropolis as a process of cultural expression was rendered inert. The Hochhausstadt project received the most attention and criticism in the USSR, where it was published in 1928, just before the first wave of Soviet urbanization projects.

CIAM's Heart of the City

After World War II, Le Corbusier used the turmoil and urgency of postwar reconstruction to promote the CIAM model for urban modernization. While the multilevel city was initially not one of its agendas, the emergence of a social project for the city was a key factor that would underpin the wide-spread implementation of CIAM's urban models and those of its successor, Team 10. Through a series of events and congresses, CIAM organized a team of international architects around a set of modernist principles promoting architecture as a "social art." Through this exchange, strategies for design and implementation were developed. By CIAM 4 they had expanded their discus-sions to include the transformation of cities, formalizing in the Athens Charter

– Drake & Lasdun, Design for Keeling House, Clarendale Street estate, Bethnal Green, London, section showing residents on the 12th- and 13th-floor balcony areas,1953, Courtesy Lasdun Archive/RIBA Library Drawings Collection

10. Percy Johnson-Marshall, *Rebuilding Cities* (Edinburgh: Edinburgh University Press, 1966), 147.

a set of functionalist principles around rational planning and the separation of functions such as living, recreation, working, and circulation.

Key CIAM members, including Gropius, Cornelis Van Eesteren, and Ernst May, began to develop a technocratic approach toward the implementation of the functionalist principles on a larger scale. In the UK, many of CIAM's strategies and stylistic dictates were adopted by the PTO led by William Holford.[10] Here they were extrapolated into policies and guidelines by the austerity-constrained LCC (1945–1951), with many negative results. The multilevel deck system of William Tatton-Brown (its first promoter in the UK) and the MARS Group had become one of its recurring strategies. While the deck-access concept was widely disseminated in planning reports, publications, and design competition schemes, it was also realized in a number of standardized and poorly built projects for various new towns.

While the multilevel city still held a fascination during postwar reconstruction, the rationalistic formalism of the designs proffered by CIAM and its perfunctory methods of implementation began to be questioned. The banal realities of bureaucratic interpretations of the elevated pedestrian city soon became the focus of criticism by the next generation of modernist architects, who viewed the irregularities of informal historic cities and towns with admiration rather than contempt.

The leading critics of the CIAM model, who would form Team 10, including important voices like Alison and Peter Smithson and Denys Lasdun, were joined by avant-garde architects like Archigram, Archizoom, and Superstudio to challenge CIAM's functionalist planning doctrine and propose elevated urban strategies of their own. Andrea Branzi of Archizoom writes about the

A

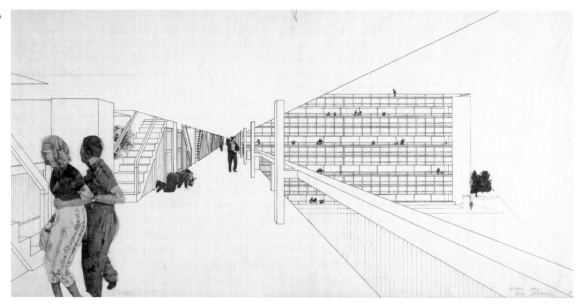

B

C

11.   Andrea Branzi, "Notes on
No-Stop City: Archizoom Associates,
1969–72," in *Exit Utopia: Architectural
Provocations, 1956–76* (New York and
London: Prestel Publishing, 2005),
177–179.
12.   Dennis Sharp, "The New
Architecture in Britain: The
Framework of the Welfare State,"
in *Back from Utopia: The Challenge
of the Modern Movement*, Hilde
Heynen and Hubert Jan Henket, eds.
(Rotterdam: Uitgeverij 010 Publishers,
2002),116–125.

backlash against modernism in the 1950s, and the view "that Modernism as a project (i.e., planning and design) had devolved into a bland social instrument acting in the interests of political authorities." Le Corbusier had even dedicated *Vers Une Architecture* (*Toward an Architecture*) to "the Authorities."[11]

Designing the Donkeypath: Alison and Peter Smithson

The rebellion of the non-plan against the plan initially came from inside CIAM and the MARS Group. Alison and Peter Smithson were first employed within the bureaucracy at the LCC and began their practice after winning its sponsored Hunstanton School competition. Concurrently, they taught at the Architectural Association (AA) with Arthur Korn, and as a result of his advocacy joined the MARS Group and CIAM in 1953. While multilevel pedestrian systems had already been developed within the LCC on work in the Southbank area and for the Barbican area Pedway, the Smithsons coined the expression "streets in the sky" as an alternative to the LCC's more pragmatically named deck-access-system and Le Corbusier's *rue intérieure*.[12] Given that they were

A   Alison and Peter Smithson, Golden Lane Housing Estate Competition, 1951–1952, Courtesy Musée National d'Art Moderne, Centre Georges Pompidou, Paris ©Alison and Peter Smithson ©CNAC/MNAM/Dist. RMN-Grand Palais/Art Resource, NY Photo: Jean-Claude Planchet/G. Meguerditchian

B   Jack Lynn and Ivor Smith, Park Hill, London, 1957–1961, Courtesy Sheffield Newspapers and Sheffield City Council © English Heritage, Aerofilms Collection

C   Erno Goldfinger, Balfron Tower walkways, London, 1967, Courtesy Christopher Hope-Fitch/RIBA Library Photographs Collection

D   Alison and Peter Smithson, Three drawings of Berlin Haupstadt by Peter Sigmonde, 1957–1958, Courtesy the Frances Loeb Library, Harvard Graduate School of Design

D

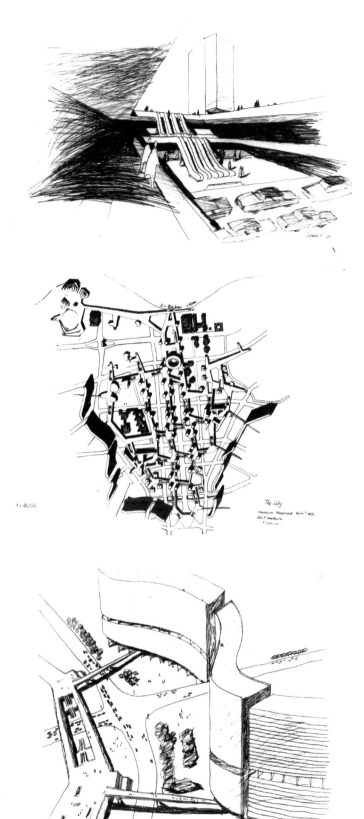

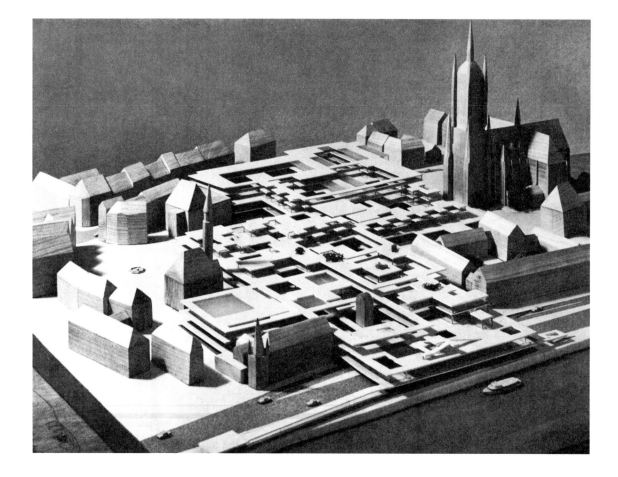

–   Candilis-Josic-Woods, Project
for reconstruction of Frankfurt
Römerberg, Germany, 1963, Courtesy
Waltraude Woods   Photo: Aulnay
Karquel
13.   Steve Parnell, "Reputations:
Alison and Peter Smithson," in
Architectural Review (January 2012),
vol. 232 (1380), 102–103.

nostalgic for the historic city centers destroyed in World War II, their proposals for the Golden Lane Housing (1952) and Robin Hood Gardens (1971) projects were intended to reestablish a sense of community by reintroducing the street as a network of fully connected elevated pedestrian space. By imitating the irregular geometries of informal settlement patterns, the Smithsons were also seeking to re-create the spatial variety and the informal social activities lost in the functionally zoned urban models of CIAM. At CIAM 9 the Smithsons exhibited their new organically composed urban concepts along with their Golden Lane project (1952) and the Urban Re-identification Grid.[13]

In this insurgency led by the Smithsons, Jaap Bakema, Aldo van Eyck, Giancarlo Di Carlo, and Candilis-Josic-Woods, the functionalist modernism of early CIAM was overthrown, initiating a major reconsideration of urban morphologies relative to the social life of cities. The unbuilt Golden Lane Housing project by the Smithsons would prove more influential through its promotion than the competition-winning project that was eventually built. The organic pattern of its elevated walkways overtly referencing informal cities became symbolic of this new kind of urbanism and was adopted by a number of Team 10 members.

In a critical inversion of nearly all previous urban models, Team 10 reversed the figure/ground relationship of building to street—a paradigmatic change that would facilitate a systemic understanding of skyway/subway pedestrian networks as they would soon be developing in North America. This preoccupation with the street had the tendency to objectify its reading, especially when it was elevated or integrated into a superstructure, giving it a figural role in many of their urban proposals. Team 10 also developed the

14.   Jonathan Hughes and Simon Sadler, eds., *Non-Plan: Essays on Freedom, Participation and Change* (London: Routledge, 2000), 99–100.
15.   Simon Sadler, *The Situationist City* (Cambridge: MIT Press, 1998), 47.

concept of the urban "cluster" to support the development of complex spaces of social interaction by replicating and expanding informal spatial patterns.

This approach to urban form was based on observations of human behavior and an analysis of informal settlement patterns. The Smithsons' influence can be seen in the many "cluster" projects that combined diverse programs with multilevel walkways proposed by various architects in the 1950s and 1960s. The pedestrian street became the building in mat-building projects such as the Frankfurt-Romerberg proposal (1963) by Candilis-Josic-Woods and the design for the reconstruction of Berlin (Haupstadt Berlin competition) by Team 10.

Acting against the functionalism of the LCC, the Smithsons and other young architects who had been recruited as the next generation of the MARS Group and CIAM became interested in the idea of *urbanisme*—the interconnection of different programs in the city, the continuity of urban fabric, and the importance of movement patterns in shaping the city.[14] While seemingly catalyzed within the design culture in London, this more organic proposition for streets above streets was also seen extensively in the 1950s in the work of architects and artists such as Yona Friedman, Constant Nieuwenhuys, Candilis-Josic-Woods, and Giancarlo Di Carlo, who emerged as leading advocates of three-dimensional urbanisms through their connections with Team 10. Well-known Japanese architects who formed the Metabolists (e.g., Kenzo Tange, Kikutake Kiyonori, Kisho Kurokawa, and Arata Isozaki) were also affiliated with Team 10 and made a significant and distinct contribution to the conceptual development of the multilevel metropolis.

As opposed to Le Corbusier's rationalistic form of urban renewal, Team 10 advocated a more accretional and respectful redevelopment of the historic city and the replacement of urban systems. In their more comprehensive forms, however, many of these projects suggested a more extreme relationship to existing urban contexts, proposing alternative developments that bypassed or spanned the existing city to create horizontally coexisting, or parallel, cities. This concept of an alternate city freed of contextual obligations and meandering over the outmoded historic city can be seen in the postwar work of Friedman and Constant. These proposals solved the problem of the city by transcending it entirely.

While advocating for freedom and individual control over the environment, it could be argued that Team 10, in reality, tended toward the opposite by proposing excessively deterministic and inflexible circulation strategies. Ironically, the reification of these ideas through rigid designs often precluded the possibility of adaptation and accommodation fundamental to many social and urban processes.

Negotiating the City

Parallel to this interest in organic urban morphologies, there were other more experimental investigations into the informal development of urban space. Among these were the Situationists International, whose key members—Guy Debord, Constant Nieuwenhuys, and Henri Lefebvre—emerged as vocal critics of the sanitized urban spaces of CIAM modernism. Wishing to revive the period of open-ended experimentation in the interwar period, including Futurism, Constructivism, and Surrealism, the Situationists theorized the creative occupation of urban space as a new form of sociality.[15]

Debord's conception of psychogeography and the *dérive* (urban drifting) was an alternative way of understanding urban space against the logic of the capitalist city. It was a creative reoccupation of the existing city. Through the *dérive*, the meandering path of the individual determined the meaning of the city with its atmospheres and terrains or, following Le Corbusier, a "donkey with an agenda." If the functional and rational city represented the life

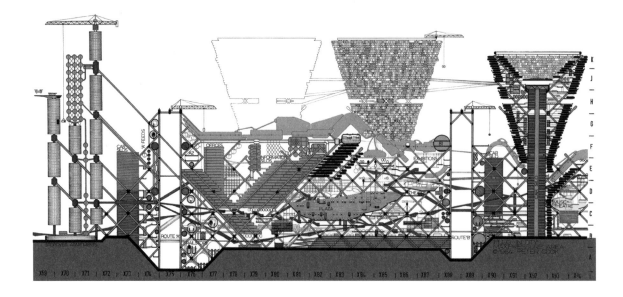

– Peter Cook, Archigram,
Plug-In City section, 1964, Courtesy
Archigram Archives, 2013 ©1964
Archigram

16. Ibid., 33–35.
17. Mark Wigley, "Paper, Scissors,
Blur," in *Drawing Papers* 3, *Another
City for Another Life: Constant's New
Babylon* (New York: The Drawing
Center, 1999), 11–14, 23–27, 30–31.
18. Wigley, *Constant's New Babylon:
The Hyperarchitecture of Desire*
(Rotterdam: 010 Publishers, 1998),
26–30.

and work of modern technocratic society, the world of play was imagined as its opposite. The concept of *homo ludens* (man at play) fueled the creative matrix of Constant's epic artwork *New Babylon* (1959–1974). It also inspired the sociopsychological engagements of the Situationist city and could be seen in the images of children playing in the streets of the Smithsons' postwar cities. If modern conformity was collectively planned, then fostering the creative agency of individuals would require a non-plan.[16]

The concept of the *dérive* was applied at the scale of the megastructure in *New Babylon*. Envisioned as an elevated city made up of transformable structures linked into a meandering urban lattice, it traversed the cities and countryside of Europe. Conceived as a postrevolutionary utopia, it left the existing capitalist cities below, including their bourgeois notions of work, family, and civic responsibility. Instead, *New Babylon* offered its nomadic occupants an endless interior that could be continuously transformed as a space of leisure and play. As Mark Wigley astutely observes, it is in the unresolved techniques of Constant's drawings that he indefinitely postpones the precise representation of the activated interior spaces in order to preserve their potentiality.[17] Apparently, the sequential development of *New Babylon* required no master plan, just the periodic extension of the superstructure's modular components into a rough, ad hoc lattice to be continuously reconfigured and expanded as a field of play on the interior.[18]

Plan versus Non-Plan: City as Process

By the 1960s, state-controlled planning was under heavy criticism from both the political right and left for its paternalistic and overly deterministic protocols that resulted in inflexible and homogeneous urban environments. Out of this critique would emerge some of the most influential proposals for multi-level circulation systems based on the concept of the "non-plan," an approach to urban development that advocated informal strategies that would presumably enable the transformation of the city by its users and its development interests. The emerging concept of "non-plan" was promoted as a means of replacing rationalistic and technocratic methods of organization with process-oriented concepts based on "human association." This moment also represented a shift in formal vocabulary—from rational and gridded to responsive and organic, still led by the model of the Smithsons' Golden Lane Housing.

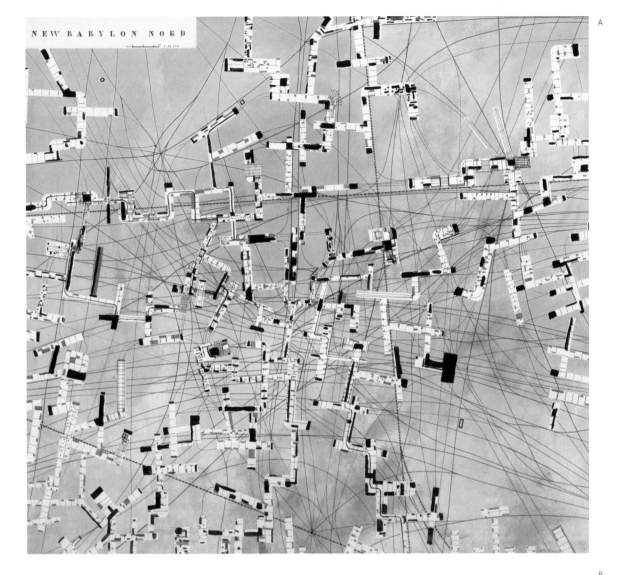

A   Constant Nieuwenhuys, *New
Babylon Nord*, 1958, Collection of the
Gemeentemuseum Den Haag ©2016
Artists Rights Society (ARS), New
York/ c/o Pictoright Amsterdam
B   Guy Debord with Asger
Jorn, The Naked City, 1957,
Courtesy Musée d'Art Moderne
et Contemporain de Strasbourg,
Cabinet d'Art Graphique   Photo:
Musées de Strasbourg, M. Bertola
©BNF, dpt Manuscripts, Fonds Guy
Debord

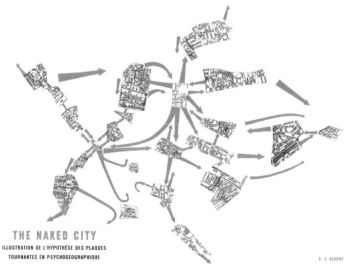

A.   Warren Chalk and Ron Herron, City Interchange, study of a multi-transport mode-node zone, elevation, London, 1963 ©1963 Archigram

B.   Warren Chalk, Peter Cook, Theo Crosby, David Greene, Ron Herron, and Taylor Woodrow, Fulham Study: Redevelopment of Twilight Areas in London, Axonometric showing the corner of a square and the main lift to the access deck, London, 1963 ©1963 Archigram for Taylor Woodrow Construction Ltd.

19.   Simon Sadler, *Architecture without Architecture* (Cambridge: MIT Press, 2005), 30–32.

20.   Ibid., 37–38.

This conceptual shift occurred through the impact of these more experimental practices with global import, centering on the London-based architects—the Smithsons, Cedric Price, and Archigram—who together with a range of international colleagues redefined the multilevel urban project as an organically responsive system. Promoted by international critics such as Reyner Banham, much of this later work was utopian, optimistic, unbuilt, and framed in a dialogue about liberating the city.

These first multilevel projects in the 1960s were planned to grow incrementally and be able to change to accommodate the commercially driven laissez-faire reality of the modern city. Other circulation-centric concepts conceived by Team 10 members, the Metabolists, and Archigram—like the "stem and web" and the "core and stem" were intended to make this urbanism more organic and adaptable to its users. More general concepts such as "streets in the sky" or the "plug-in city" were thus synchronous with the logic of both free-market and consumer culture and what would later be called neoliberal capitalism.

The concept of organic, market-driven urban morphologies seemed capable of reconciling the remaining strains of socialist egalitarianism from the first half of the twentieth century with the individual agency and private ownership ideology of laissez-faire capitalism. This major shift in the political economy of Western states away from strong government had significant impact on the planning profession and architecture alike and was reflected in the emerging models of the modern city.

Archigram members Peter Cook, Warren Chalk, Ron Herron, Michael Webb, Dennis Crompton, and David Greene were influenced by the Smithsons' projects like Sheffield University (1953) and the Berlin Haupstadt (1956), and also the Sheffield Park Hill Project (Womersley, Lynn, and Smith, 1953–1959). Like the Smithsons, they participated as employees and advocates at the LCC in the postwar period and later rejected the larger body of compromised work produced by their former employer. At the same time, Archigram admired the dynamism they saw in the future city visions of Antonio Sant'Elia, Cedric Price, Constant Nieuwenhuys, Yona Friedman, and Buckminster Fuller.

The members of Archigram were proponents of both common multilevel circulation schemes and also their more fantastical forms through the use of machinelike aggregates and megastructures. Through their use of techno-prosthetic architecture, even urban form became an extension of the body. Archigram subverted architecture's traditional role in demarking territories within a relatively fixed field of urban forms. By using infrastructure as scaffolding for docking modules, they allowed every aspect of the city to be seen as an extension of the territorial space of the individual to facilitate spontaneous and temporal urbanisms and, ostensibly, universal connectivity. Many of these speculative projects were promoted through their publication *Archigram*—a compelling Pop art, comiclike digest published in the 1960s.[19]

While known for their futuristic, three-dimensional urban proposals like Plug-In City (1964), Archigram members concurrently produced a number of lesser-known, more cautiously experimental projects, including their work on the Southbank Centre. Members were also concurrently employed with Theo Crosby's firm, Taylor Woodrow Design Group.[20] Of these projects, their Fulham study (an urban renewal shopping mall with elevated pedestrian networks), the multilevel Euston redevelopment scheme (a traffic interchange project), and the urban design for the center of Hereford were more familiar if commonplace forms of contemporary urban pedestrian networks. These were akin to the more standard types of shopping environments constructed in North American cities during the same period and still carried forward as typologies of public space into the twenty-first century.

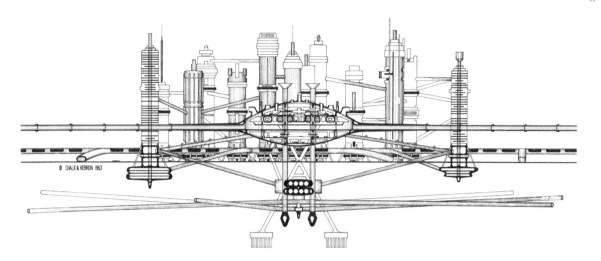

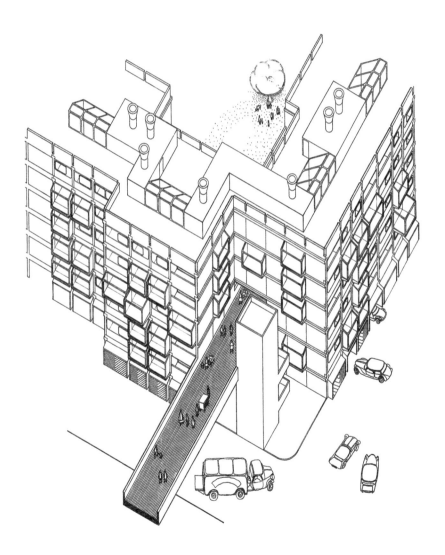

– Cedric Price, Fun Palace, London (helicopter view, circa 1964; interior perspective, between 1961 and 1965), Cedric Price Fonds, Collection Centre Canadien d'Architecture/Canadian Centre for Architecture, Montreal

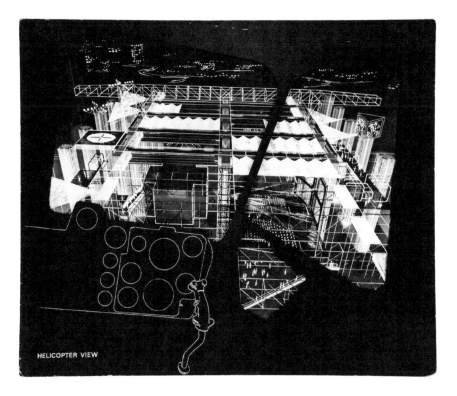

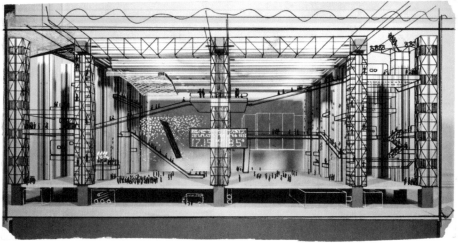

This conceptual shift in proposals for the multilevel city, from the planned and fixed to more organic and responsive systems, resulted from the impact of experimental practices based in London. The new urban project was led by architects like the Smithsons, Cedric Price, and Archigram but expanded outward through a range of international colleagues.

Non-Plan

In reaction to the negative results of rigid postwar modernist planning and processes of the LCC, Cedric Price and the editor of the magazine *New Society*, Paul Barker, coined the term "non-plan" in 1969. The movement

– Rogers Stirk Harbour + Partners, *London As It Could Be*, 1986, Courtesy Rogers Stirk Harbour + Partners

21. Stanley Matthews, *From Agit-Prop to Free Space: The Architecture of Cedric Price* (London: Blackdog Publishing Ltd., 2007), 25–37.

advocated indeterminacy and was influenced by Banham and urban geographer Peter Hall's knowledge of development methods in the United States. Published in *New Society* and intended to provoke controversy, the article was entitled "Non-Plan: An Experiment in Freedom."

A graduate of the AA under Arthur Korn, Price taught alongside Peter Cook (in the mid-1960s through the early 1970s) and had previously worked for MARS Group member Erno Goldfinger. Price had long been inspired by temporary structures, the concept of planned obsolescence, and the work of Buckminster Fuller. He was skeptical of the motivations behind permanent structures and prescriptive regulations, seeing building design and particularly planning as a means to consolidate government control. While modernist planning attempted to determine and permanently fix patterns of urban use, Price believed that the natural form of a city was always in flux, an organic process of self-organization. Instead, in multilevel projects like his Fun Palace (1961), Price argued for a time-based architecture of indeterminacy, giving control to individuals who could reprogram and readapt their environments as their desires changed.[21]

London was home to a number of architects who uniquely influenced more architecture than they actually built through these informal processes. Many of the unbuilt speculative multilevel proposals that appeared in the 1950s and 1960s coalesced around an interest in indeterminacy and non-plan, becoming prototypes and concepts to be applied later by others. Examples include speculative projects such as the MARS Plan, the Fun Palace (which influenced Centre Pompidou and Archigram), and Price's 1984 ferris wheel for London's Southbank (later the London Eye); Archigram's Plug-in City (which influenced Richard Rogers's Lloyds of London building and the work of the Metabolists); and Golden Lane Housing by the Smithsons (which influenced Park Hill and the Barbican).

Centered in the academic culture of the AA under Arthur Korn and Alvin Boyarsky, the ideas of the Smithsons, Archigram, and Cedric Price would heavily influence the later multilevel urbanisms of Rem Koolhaas, Steven Holl,

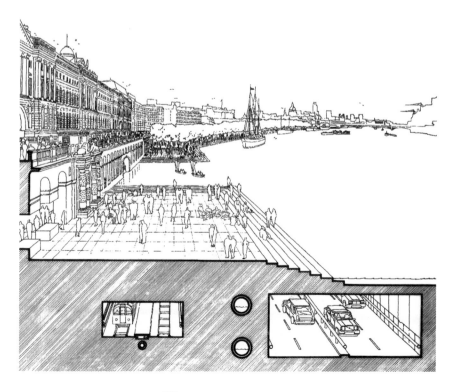

– Rogers Stirk Harbour + Partners, *London As It Could Be*, 1986, Courtesy Rogers Stirk Harbour + Partners

22. Eric Mumford, *Defining Urban Design: CIAM Architects and the Formation of a Discipline, 1937–69* (New Haven: Yale University Press, 2009), 142–148, 166–168, 180.

23. Ibid., 175–479, 185.

Richard Rogers, Norman Foster, and Zaha Hadid. The avant-garde proposals of these architects were also disseminated internationally through exhibitions and publications, their compelling forms easily promoted and widely absorbed in the 1960s and 1970s through advocates such as Banham.

At the AA, planning strategies and urban forms that had evolved through CIAM/Team 10 were initially taught as large-scale urban interventions by Smithson, Price, and Cook, and by Aldo van Eyck and the Dutch Structuralists at schools in Rotterdam and Delft. Other schools led by CIAM and Team 10 members quickly followed, including Harvard and MIT in the United States.[22] Urban design and architecture programs were a critical link in circulating these elevated pedestrian schemes between the avant-garde and the more technocratic mainstream. This eventually led to a standardization of the concept of deck-access schemes for public housing projects and skywalk systems employed in shopping malls, hospitals, and city centers throughout the United States. Concurrent with the attack on planning in general, planning programs by the 1970s were shifted to schools of public policy and administration, leaving the development of multilevel urban systems open to very different agendas.[23] As these typologies developed, a range of new forms evolved within the emergent logic of economic privatization in the non-planned city.

In his research on the impact of non-plan concepts in the 1950s and 1960s, architectural historian Anthony Fontenot describes the movement's development parallel with the writings of neoliberal thinker Friedrich Hayek, a critic who viewed large-scale planning solely as a negative limitation on the freedom of the market economy. The struggle between planning and non-planning in the contemporary metropolis was not only a question of authorship and authority—it had a direct bearing on the definition of public space and individual agency. Framed in simplistic terms as a political choice, planning was an authoritarian technique employed by the socialist state, and

– Yona Friedman, Studies on New York (USA), Drawing of skyway connections over photograph of Manhattan, 1964 ©2016 Artists Rights Society (ARS), New York ADAGP, Paris
24. Anthony Fontenot, "Notes Toward a History of Non-Planning: On Design, the Market, and the State," in *Places* (January 2015): accessed February 10, 2015 www .placesjournal.org/articles/notes -toward-a-history-of-non-planning/.

laissez-faire non-planning was a process of local initiative preferred by advocates of the free market.[24]

Non-plan was equated with economic freedom operating at the scale of the individual transaction—an idea promoted in neoliberal economic theory. This dichotomy of state planning versus individual agency is deceptive. While large-scale planning may be seen as authoritarian, the behaviors of the "atomized agents" of non-plan are subject to programming, and this equally problematic method of control, because it is less visible, could bypass democratic processes. Ironically, as many architects disavowed the processes of top-down formal planning, they gravitated to ad hoc or tactical strategies to incrementally embed "public" social space within privatized urban developments. Additionally, if planning only occurs at smaller circumscribed urban scales, larger urban issues related to infrastructure, particularly systems of movement as public space, become more difficult to sustain. These struggles between ideas of collective coherence and individual agency have remained unresolved in the development of the multilevel city since its emergence.

City as Object vs. City as Process

The critique of CIAM and the city forms that arose out of the Athens Charter centered on its formal planning. Designing a city as if it were a singular object or an aesthetic composition individuated through authorship, rather than an open-ended model of time-dependent processes, leads to the disjunction of form and process. Aside from the critique of Le Corbusier, Hilberseimer, and CIAM planning, this problem can be seen variously in the urban proposals of Team 10 and the Metabolists, and in the work of contemporary architects operating at very different scales. The plans of urban systems produced by these authors are often designed to seem organic—not through the programming

A.   Zaha Hadid Architects, One North Masterplan, Conceptual Lines and Hubs, Drawing Singapore, 2001–2003, Courtesy Zaha Hadid Architects

B.   Zaha Hadid Architects, One North Masterplan, Singapore, 2001–2003, Image courtesy Zaha Hadid Architects; JTC

C.   Zaha Hadid Architects, Galaxy Soho, Beijing, China, 2009–2012 Photo courtesy Iwan Baan

25.   Patrik Schumacher, "Parametricism—A New Global Style for Architecture and Urban Design," in *AD Architectural Design—Digital Cities*, vol. 79, no. 4 (July/August 2009): 87.

26.   Frei Otto, Eda Schaur, *IL 39: Non-Planned Settlements* (Stuttgart: Karl Krämer Verlag, 1992), 8–22.

27.   Frei Otto, *Occupying and Connecting: Thoughts on Territories and Spheres of Influence with Particular Reference to Human Settlement* (Stuttgardt: Edition Axel Menges, 2009), 6, 7, 10–12, 50–65.

of urban processes or performance but through appearance. Conversely, the possibilities of the multilevel city growing and extending indefinitely as an emergent new process of urbanization has been the subject of speculation by experimental urban thinkers such as Yona Friedman and Constant Nieuwenhuys.

In his recent writings on parametric urbanism, Patrik Schumacher, architect and partner in Zaha Hadid Architects (ZHA), has revisited Le Corbusier's hypothetical argument with Camillo Sitte and the debate revolving around the formal plan and the informal development. Prioritizing the direct path over the meandering path, Schumacher describes these techniques simultaneously in rational and aesthetic terms as "a hybrid between minimizing detour networks and a deformed grid" with "a sense of organic cohesion." In this way he reconciles the rational planning objective of efficiency with desirable spatial irregularities.[25]

With an intellectual sleight of hand, Schumacher unites the opposing viewpoints by arguing that new computational design methodologies allow us to understand deeper orders within the pack donkey's way and within informal settlement patterns. He reconciles Sitte's picturesque and localized approach to urban form with the rational ordering principles demanded by Le Corbusier.

In his writings Schumacher draws from the research of Frei Otto on non-plan settlement patterns. He suggests that computational design techniques could finally rationalize the geometries of the informal city—the parametrics of the donkey's path. Using a case study of ZHA's recent master plan for a mixed-use business park, One North in Singapore, Schumacher describes how parametric urbanism enables more malleable and resilient urban morphologies than those composed of platonic orders.

Although parametric urbanism could theoretically enable designers to anticipate and organize the complex variables ordering informal development patterns, this raises an important set of questions. Does the project's totalizing aesthetic allow for this malleability or create new constraints? How are the variables programmed and how are they prioritized? Does an urbanism that depends on the application of an aesthetic style to create cohesion leave room for multiple authors or change over time?

Frei Otto and the Social Parameters of Informal Networks

In 1991 the Institute for Lightweight Structures (IL) in Stuttgart, led by Frei Otto, completed a study of non-planned settlements with Eda Schaur. *IL 39* observed that the growth of the settlements was indeed organized, if not planned, and exhibited many similarities to self-organizing inorganic structures as well as biological and behavioral processes found in the natural world. Rather than an architectural or art-historical analysis of the spatial aesthetics of traditional settlements, the IL study evaluated how informal forms of human settlements optimize their spatial fields based on governing factors related to human behavior, economics, and culture. Through a series of experiments and analysis of human settlements, they attempted to theorize the topographical effects of material surface development and their analogues in human and animal spatial occupations. The IL study demonstrated that, although most traditional human settlements were not planned as complete spatial systems, they nevertheless develop highly articulated structural patterns through a process of self-organization in which individual and collective needs are negotiated over time.[26]

In his more recent work, *Occupying and Connecting*,[27] Otto recapitulated the comprehensive experimental work on human settlement patterns completed between 1972 and 1991. The groundbreaking research established key principles of territorial occupation that explained the negotiated "logic" of so-called non-plan settlements and the morphological properties of city

A

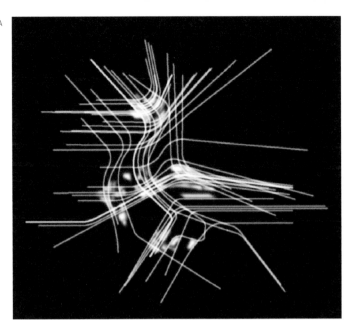

B

C

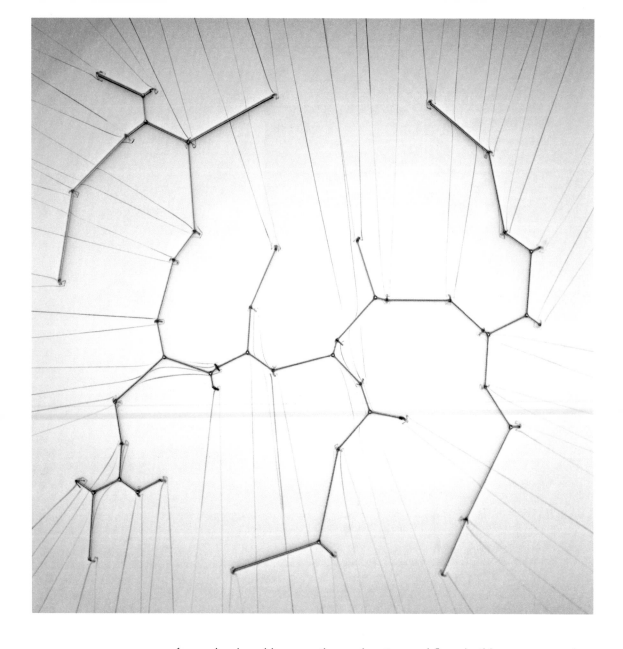

– Frei Otto, Apparatus for computing minimal path systems, 1988, Institute for Lightweight Structures, Stuttgart, Courtesy Institut fuer Leichtbau Entwerfen und Konstruieren, Universitaet Stuttgart, Bildarchiv

forms developed by accretion and patterns of flow. In this sense, non-planning is really planning at a different scale or a form of programming by different agents.

Otto's work investigated the organic processes that form the city from within without superimposing a new order. It also demonstrated that within this informality there is order and a form of public planning in negotiated processes. These patterns suggest a type of intelligence and represent a valid system of form generation that should be acknowledged. Contrary to the more totalizing orders of Le Corbusier and CIAM, the city formations resulting from the pack donkey's way are evidence of intelligent behaviors recorded in the residual layers of the city. The factors affecting urban form include individual human behavior, climate and topography, social territories, and existing contextual conditions, all negotiated over time. Otto also extended his theory of time-dependent spatial development into three dimensions, looking at autocatalytic processes in the formation of cellular solids as well as dynamic behavioral formations such as flocks of birds or schools of fish.

The notion that a city could be conceived in aesthetic terms by an individual architect, or even an organization of architects such as CIAM, assumes that the city can remain frozen in time and not subject to the exigencies of urban development that pass through periods of changing ideologies, shifting needs, stylistic milieus, and technical innovations.

While the examples found in the IL studies are arguably highly successful in aesthetic terms, the small scale of these settlements may not directly translate to issues relevant to the modern metropolis. However, Otto's Analysis does demonstrate that the planning and negotiation that occur simultaneously are two of the most important mechanisms of these emergent forms. It is really a question of agency and control. Rational decision-making, seen at many scales, is also necessarily time-dependent. This understanding, as it applies to contemporary multilevel urban development processes and the challenge of the metropolis, suggests urbanisms that are both planned (prescribed) and negotiated (adapted), directly recognizing the embodied intelligence of human behavior, economics, and culture found in their formation.

As soon as the Socialist government had become the legitimate owner of all the houses in Paris, it handed them over to the architects, with orders to get the best out of them, and especially to establish the gallery-streets indispensable to the new society. The architects carried out the mission entrusted to them as best they could. On the (upper) floor of each house they took over all the rooms overlooking the street and demolished the intermediary partitions; then they opened large bays in the party walls and thus obtained gallery-streets that had the height and width of an ordinary room and occupied the entire length of a block of building…

When all the blocks of houses were thus pierced by galleries occupying the length of their (upper) floor, there was no more to do than connect the separate fragments together and thus form an uninterrupted network embracing the entire extent of the city. This was easily accomplished by establishing covered bridges on each street that had the same height and width as the galleries and were fused with them. Similar bridges, but much longer were even extended over the various boulevards, over the squares and over the bridges, crossing the Seine, so that the gallery-street did not suffer any break in continuity. A pedestrian could thus travel throughout the city without ever being exposed, and, in consequence, was always perfectly sheltered from the rain or sun.

— Dr. Jules-Antoine Moilin, *Paris in the Year 2000*, 1869

4.
SURREPTITIOUS
URBANISMS

– Georgio Vasari, Vasari Corridor, 1565, Florence, Italy Photo: Arnold Paul Sailko/Wikimedia Commons/ GNU Free Documentation License

Jules-Antoine Moilin's socialist utopian proposal to renovate Paris by installing Charles Fourier's elevated "street galleries" throughout the city prefigured the actual development of multilevel pedestrian cities by nearly a century. In his prescient description of a pragmatic implementation strategy, Moilin proposed hollowing out nearly the entire second level of Paris to construct an elaborate pedestrian network of passageways, galleries, and bridges connecting the individual blocks. Had it been constructed, Moilin's pedestrian system would have radically altered the experience of Paris, reducing the existing historic building fabric to little more than an armature for the interiorization of the city.

The parasitism implicit in this approach to the development of multilevel urban space was not new, however, even in Moilin's time. Three centuries earlier, the Vasari Corridor (1565) was designed and built by architect Giorgio Vasari for Francesco I de'Medici to connect his residence in the Palazzo Pitti to the Uffizi and Palazzo Vecchio, the seat of government in Florence. Motivated by a desire to make convenient and secure connections through the city for the Medici family, Vasari introduced into an existing urban fabric one of the earliest examples of an extensive elevated pedestrian way. The path of the corridor was negotiated, and in some cases mandated, resulting in a continuous interior space that extended for nearly a kilometer by penetrating existing structures, winding around others, and bridging the Arno River above the Ponte Vecchio.

The resulting interior space meanders through the city, a hidden passage with voyeuristic glimpses of the city streets through discreetly located windows. The sense of security and exclusivity was enhanced by art-lined corridor walls that periodically gave way to surprising juxtapositions with larger

1. Skyway/Skywalk Cities: Atlanta, Georgia; Calgary, Alberta; Cedar Rapids, Iowa; Cincinnati, Ohio; Dallas, Texas; Des Moines, Iowa; Duluth, Minnesota; Edmonton, Alberta; Houston, Texas; Indianapolis, Indiana; Milwaukee, Wisconsin; Minneapolis, Minnesota; Pittsburgh, Pennsylvania; Rochester, Minnesota; Spokane, Washington; St. Paul, Minnesota; Winnipeg, Ontario.

interior spaces such as the Church of Santa Felicita and the courtyard of the Buontalenti Grotto. Many of the opportunistic and ad hoc strategies used in the construction of the Vasari Corridor, whether from a technical or administrative point of view, were entailed in Moilin's proposal for Paris. Similar techniques would later be applied to the development of grade-separated pedestrian systems transforming cities across North America and Asia.

The grade-separated pedestrian systems that developed in the twentieth century have a variety of names: skyways, skywalks, pedways, footbridges, the +15, and Ville Souteraine. But these have one thing in common—they have radically altered the form and spatial logic of many North American cities. Minneapolis, St. Paul, Des Moines, Dallas, and Calgary all have extensive pedestrian systems that in most cases are still growing. In Asian and Middle-Eastern cities such as Hong Kong, Shenzhen, Singapore, Mumbai, and Riyadh, pedestrian networks continue to crisscross the cities above the original streets. These systems, unlike their predecessors, are generally not promoted by social utopians or the architectural avant-garde, but by more pragmatically inclined advocates and planners ready to embrace both the private sector and municipal authorities in their development. Their principal objectives are to reinforce urban centers by making the cities more convenient, comfortable, and safe for the urban shopper and office worker. Mitigating climatic extremes are also a key factor spurring their development.

Since their beginnings in the 1960s, seventeen significant systems have developed and continue to grow in the United States and Canada with varying degrees of success.[1] The most extensive systems in Minneapolis, St. Paul, Calgary, Atlanta, Des Moines, Cincinnati, and Montreal function as pedestrian networks parallel to the original streets. In Dallas, Winnipeg, and Toronto, tunnel connections and overhead bridges are combined, thus bracketing the original streets. In the United States, the Cincinnati Skywalk is the only significant system that has been terminated and is in the process of being dismantled. More typically, the larger pedestrian systems like those found in Minneapolis and Calgary have grown exponentially over the past fifty years, demonstrating a kind of vitalism that defies conventional modes of urban development.

In the 1960s many North American cities seeking to compete financially with growing suburban developments began to "pedestrianize" their urban centers. Cities responding to the newly minted shopping mall, which offered suburbanites convenient shopping and entertainment in weather-protected interiors with nearby and plentiful parking, looked to connect and consolidate the interior spaces separated in existing individual city blocks. Grade-separated pedestrian systems that both expanded connections to the surrounding city and consolidated pedestrian traffic on a dedicated strata seemed to offer a panacea for cities struggling with economic downturns and suburbanization. In the process of their deployment, the idealistic multilevel urban proposals of early modernist architects and planners rapidly evolved into utilitarian networks built with little concern for their larger impact on urban space and architecture.

What began as a few blocks interconnected with bridges or tunnels became pedestrianized multilevel central business districts (CBD) by the 1970s that may now extend for five to ten miles in many city centers. Although growing rapidly in cities around the world, the component parts are typically viewed as infrastructure and not given serious consideration for the fundamental role they play in the production of urban space.

Economics and Growth
_____

Despite being seen as deviant and untenable urban forms by many designers and urban theorists, these systems are attractive to city planners and businesses because they offer significant urban development opportunities

2.   Trevor Boddy, "Underground
and Overhead: Building the
Analogous City," in Michael Sorkin,
*Variations on a Theme Park: The New
American City and the End of Public
Space* (New York: Hill & Wang,
1992), 123–125, 141–144.

and advantages. The effects of pedestrian systems are often centripetal, enhancing real estate prices and lease values through the concentration of pedestrian traffic and corresponding commercial activity. They also offer easy access to urban amenities, parking, and integrated transit. Once established, grade-separated pedestrian systems typically expand informally based on private and public development interests. The most successful reach an autocatalytic stage, like Minneapolis, where future large-scale developments must be connected to be competitive. Having reached this stage in their development, grade-separated pedestrian networks become durable urban forms and are rarely terminated or dismantled. Although fewer North American downtowns are adopting the skyway model, the existing systems persist and continue to expand into a new urban form. In rapidly growing cities in Asia such as Singapore, Hong Kong, Chongqing, and other new cities in China, the pressure to deploy and extend pedestrian systems grows with increased urban density. Heavily congested cities such as Mumbai are, based on traffic data, tactically introducing new elevated systems to mitigate congestion and enhance pedestrian safety.

Spatial Characteristics

These new urban forms evolved from their earlier precedents to have very particular characteristics. The development of pedestrian systems in North America has typically taken the form of a "thickening" of the street level or a "delamination" of the ground plane into a second-story level above or below grade. This doubling, or sometimes tripling, of the street was described by urban critic Trevor Boddy in the 1980s as an "analogous city."[2] The spatial ambiguity created by the stacked circulation levels—many of which lack sufficient vertical connections—can often render the urban layers as fully independent realms.

A wide range of planning and design strategies has been used in an attempt to mitigate the disjunctive characteristics of multilevel streets. Minneapolis created rules to incrementally regulate the skyway system's overall form through policies that determine the location, orientation, and the basic dimensions of various component links. The city leases air rights over its public streets for bridges roughly centered within each block. Local irregularities are negotiated independently above the gridiron and within each block, producing a regular pattern of bridge connections between labyrinthine block interiors. Design efforts are generally focused on the form of the individual components rather than the overall system, resulting in chaotic paths and loss of orientation. Cities like Des Moines have attempted to improve the relationship between the elevated system and the street by positioning walkways on the perimeter of blocks, parallel to the street. This improves the sense of orientation but significantly reduces the quantity of commercial space fronting the circulation paths. Because they are largely motivated to simply connect into the economically advantageous system where lease value is determined by pedestrian counts, the developers' interest in the characteristics of whole systems tends to be limited.

The Circulation of Ideas

Whether promoted by developers, city planners, or municipal bureaucrats, each city's pedestrian system seems to have its own origin story of a heroic visionary who willed it into existence. However, the individual promoters, including those trained as architects and planners, borrowed their ideas from the mid-twentieth-century European avant-garde. Other popular sources of significance include the 1939 World's Fair in New York and the World Expos of the 1950s and 1960s. The as-built urban systems, however, were rarely

3.   Eric Mumford, *Defining Urban Design: CIAM Architects and the Formation of a Discipline, 1937–69* (New Haven: Yale University Press, 2009), 88, 143.
4.   Arindam Dutta, ed,. *A Second Modernism: MIT, Architecture, and the "Techno-Social" Moment* (Cambridge: MIT Press, 2013), 3–13. Essay in book by Eric Mumford "From Master-Planning to Self-Build: The MIT Harvard Joint Center for Urban Studies, 1959–71," 290–297.
5.   CASE was instigated by Peter Eisenman.
6.   Design à la Carte is derived from a phrase used by Margaret Crawford.

implemented as originally envisioned, but evolved ad hoc as they were spread by a variety of proselytizers.

The main proponents were directly influenced by the work of CIAM and Josep Lluís Sert while he served as dean of Harvard's Graduate School of Design (1953–1969). After relocating to Harvard, Sert continued to advocate many of the ideas of CIAM 8's Heart of the City, particularly the social structure of the urban core and the use of three-dimensional pedestrian network strategies derived from Le Corbusier as well as experimental urban schemes by British architects. Sert promoted the developing discipline of urban design, through which he disseminated three-dimensional design strategies for the revitalization of city centers.

Historian Eric Mumford describes this period and the first Urban Design Conference at Harvard as a merging of the modernism of CIAM with Team 10's critical interest in social practices. Under Sert the two initially adversarial urbanisms became nearly indistinguishable.[3] Among the Harvard Urban Design Conference participants were Victor Gruen and Jane Jacobs. Gruen later published *The Heart of Our Cities: The Urban Crisis: Diagnosis and Treatment* (1964), a clear follow-up to CIAM 8's *The Heart of the City: Toward the Humanization of Urban Life* (1952). Jane Jacobs, an outspoken critic of CIAM zoning, became an advocate of Victor Gruen's pedestrianization strategies, one of many valuable relationships with advocates, clients, and collaborators that Gruen developed through conferences.

At this time, the architectural design and planning faculty at Harvard and MIT coalesced with other familiar figures around a growing interest in grade-separated pedestrian systems. In addition to Sert, this included members of Team 10 like Jerzy Soltan and Metabolists Kenzo Tange and Fumihiko Maki. The Ford Foundation supported the MIT-Harvard Joint Center for Urban Studies (1959–1971), creating a research unit to explore modernist approaches to city planning. This funding was directed toward research-based projects that supported larger domestic and international policy agendas and provided funding for commissions in areas of political interest as test cases. Eric Mumford described the process that refocused architects and planners at MIT in the 1960s culture of postwar federal funding as the "hard sciences" that aimed toward research-driven planning.[4] Architecture and urban design were interconnected with the social sciences, information sciences, and systems theory and integrated with urban research imported by members of CIAM/Team 10 and CASE (the Conference of Architects for the Study of the Environment, 1964–1974).[5] The work of CASE was an ongoing project, creating an American version of European avant-garde process for developing urban proposals. This work ultimately led to the creation of another generation of multilevel experimentation centered at the Institute for Architecture and Urban Studies in New York and an exhibition titled *New City* at the Museum of Modern Art in 1967.

The most significant impact to the development of grade-separated pedestrian systems, however, came not from architects such as Sert, who originally promoted the ideas, but from practitioners and students who would subsequently work directly with developers and city governments. The two most influential figures to set into motion the wide-scale development of multilevel pedestrian systems were Gruen and Vincent Ponte. Both were architects who elaborated on the work of CIAM 8 to invent new urban and architectural typologies that would be applied to a number of urban design proposals for cities such as St. Paul, Minnesota, and Fort Worth and Dallas, Texas.

Victor Gruen: Design à la Carte[6]

The rapid dissemination of these ideas was a direct result of how they were designed and promoted. Architects like Gruen, who first proposed pedestrian

– Norman Bel Geddes and Eero Saarinen's Futurama exhibition for the 1939 World's Fair, Courtesy Harry Ransom Center, University of Texas at Austin, the Edith Lutyens and Norman Bel Geddes Foundation (left); from Bel Geddes' Magic Motorways, 194

7. Victor Gruen, *Centers for the Urban Environment: Survival of the Cities* (New York: Van Nostrand Reinhold, 1973), 192.

systems in a number of cities, understood the complex forces underlying urban development and renewal. While his political background included an unusual combination of socialist idealism and capitalist pragmatism, the practical development of his urban spaces was based on modernist postwar planning principles and incremental methods of implementation.

Prior to his emigration to the United States, Gruen had been educated in Red Vienna, where he had been influenced by the work of Adolf Loos and Erich Mendelsohn. A committed socialist, Gruen connected his political views to his architectural projects, promoting pedestrian separation as a way to create more active and socially oriented urban centers, an interest shared by his mentors. Shortly after arriving in the United States, he began work on Norman Bel Geddes and Eero Saarinen's *Futurama* exhibition for the General Motors Pavilion at the 1939 World's Fair. For Gruen, the project brought together his interest in the design of cities and his early background in retail architecture, an experience that he described rather clinically as "a stimulating task in contemplating and bringing into visual form future ideas for transportation and city planning."[7] Multilevel urbanism centered on retail environments would become one of his passions, and fifteen years later Gruen proposed his first downtown skyway linkages as part of his plan to create a pedestrian center in Fort Worth, Texas.

In 1956, the same year as his proposals separating traffic for Forth Worth were published, he opened Southdale Center, the first interior shopping mall in the United States in the Minneapolis suburb of Edina. The project had strong social ambitions and attempted to create the type of complex, socially conducive civic space that might be found in a traditional European town square. The mall would be a center for local art and culture as well as provide for the necessities of everyday life. While initially implemented, Southdale's cultural program evolved over time into something completely different—a more typical shopping center with renovations to accommodate ever-shifting national brands and chain stores.

In his urban proposals, through a comprehensive master plan, Gruen introduced something that in contemporary terms could be described as a form of tactical urbanism: a recognizable vocabulary of adaptable components

– Victor Gruen, Street-level renderings, Plan for Fort Worth, 1956, Courtesy Gruen Associates

8. Jane Jacobs, "Downtown Is for People," in *Fortune* (April 1958): accessed July 14, 2016. www.fortune.com/2011/09/18/downtown-is-for-people-fortune-classic-1958/.

such as pedestrian bridges, plazas, and arcades that could be deployed selectively. Due to this adaptability, the construction of the system could proceed incrementally, radically changing a city over time. Gruen's plan for Fort Worth proposed a reordering of the city around a central pedestrian plaza with shopping. Vehicular traffic would be located on the periphery along with access to surrounding freeways. Elevated pedestrian bridges would connect the peripheral parking ramps to the pedestrian core. While framed within a compelling narrative referring to experiences of everyday life and historic European cities, Gruen's alternative was distinctly modernist.

Jane Jacobs advocated Gruen's approach in the Fort Worth plan in her famous essay, "Downtown Is for People."[8] In contrast to the early modernism of CIAM or Robert Moses's version of urban renewal, she argued that the

– Athelstan Spilhaus, *Our New Age: Experimental City*, March 5, 1966, Courtesy Athelstan Spilhaus Papers, Dolph Briscoe Center for American History, University of Texas at Austin

9. The Institute of Technology at the University of Minnesota was led by Dean Athelstan Spilhaus, instigator of the MXC. Faculty and students were involved in the federally supported project. Spilhaus also hired Architecture School head Ralph Rapson, who studied under Eero Saarinen at Cranbrook (1939) and worked in his office (1940–1942) during the period of the Futurama project.

success of Gruen's plans would be found in the variety and detail of activities proposed at the street level. While broadly endorsing his social programming, she warned that his clients or those who enacted his plans would overlook this critical point, focusing instead on his strategies for traffic management. As Jacobs had predicted, Gruen's model for development was tenuous. City governments allowed their plans to evolve with little guidance, selecting various components desirable to particular political constituencies and independently acting entities of government. The urbanistic goals that were crucial to Gruen's vision, such as vehicle-free centers that required an integrative and comprehensive approach, were often not maintained as the cities evolved.

A Dialogue of Two Cities

In the Twin Cities of Minneapolis and St. Paul, the multilevel city has been an ongoing fascination since the 1950s. In Minneapolis, civic-minded businessmen drove the development of the Skyway System along with figures such as Victor Gruen, inventor Athelstan Spilhaus, and engineer R. Buckminster Fuller.[9]

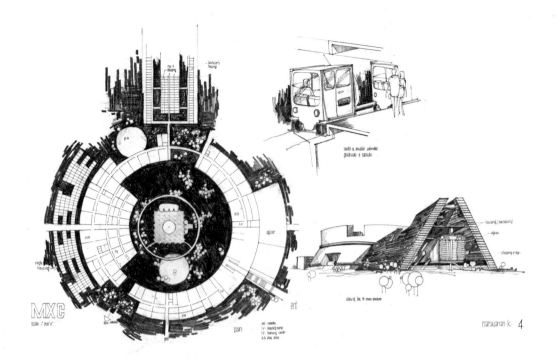

– Athelstan Spilhaus and R. Buckminster Fuller, Minnesota Experimental City (MXC), 1969–1973, drawing by Krishnan Narayanan, 1971 master of architecture, Courtesy Northwest Architectural Archives, University of Minnesota Libraries

Gruen initially worked with both St. Paul (1957–1961) and Minneapolis (1952) to transform their downtowns. As soon as Southdale Center opened in 1956, the downtown businesses of Minneapolis and St. Paul were overwhelmed by its success. Civic leaders in both cities first looked to Gruen for concepts to reactivate their commercial cores. He was initially hired to look at the early development of the IDS office and retail complex in downtown Minneapolis in 1952 (which became a central hub of the Minneapolis Skyway System in 1971) and for downtown St. Paul in 1957 as part of the Capital Centre project, a centralized pedestrian mall in the form of a twelve-block urban renewal zone intended to compete with Southdale. Although Gruen is simply credited with building a department store and parking ramp, his larger urban scheme evolved into the first comprehensive proposal for a skyway system that was later used by the city of St. Paul to acquire federal funding for urban renewal and an initial nine-block network of walkways. His proposals for St. Paul were also instrumental in the development of the Minneapolis system.

Gruen was later contacted about the multilevel Minnesota Experimental City (MXC) project, the brainchild of Spilhaus, perhaps best known for *Our New Age*, his syndicated science-based comic. MXC was to be a self-sufficient new town proposed as a compact multilevel city, with pedestrians elevated above vehicular traffic and utilities. The city, first contained under a dome proposed by Fuller, was later reimagined in its last iteration as a floating island before it was abandoned as federal funding for its implementation was withdrawn. Gruen's influence can be found in many other cities, most significantly Cincinnati's downtown skywalk system, which was first proposed by him but implemented and expanded by others.

The "First" System

In cities like Minneapolis and St. Paul, master plans were produced for independent, nongovernmental entities (e.g., downtown business councils, chambers

– Grover W. Dimond Associates, Capital Centre project, St. Paul, Minnesota, 1962–1970, Courtesy Grover W. Dimond Associates papers (N32), Northwest Architectural Archives, University of Minnesota Libraries, Minneapolis

10. Grover Dimond completed the first skyway and several buildings in the district and was the local architect for Gruen on the Dayton's department store.

of commerce, etc.) sharing an interest in the success of their city centers. Government agencies such as the highway department enacted parallel and selected components of the plans as they fit within their agendas.

In 1956, based on Gruen's Fort Worth plan and the success of Southdale Center, a group of local young architects proposed an automobile-free zone with skyway connections for downtown St. Paul. A similar group at the University of Minnesota (under Walter Vivrett, a graduate of MIT and an MXC project leader) presented one such plan for downtown Minneapolis in 1957. All of these young architects were aware of the ongoing and international interest in the multilevel city, largely promoted through Team 10.

In response, Gruen was hired in 1957 by a private entity, the Greater St. Paul Development Inc., to work on the twelve-block Capital Centre plan, applying the principles of his Greater Fort Worth plan to St. Paul. The original three architects (Louis Lundgren, Grover Dimond, and Brooks Gavin) who had proposed the system took over the project in 1961 as the architects for a new

– Minneapolis Skyway system
phased growth (clockwise from
upper left): 1970s, 1980s, 1990s, 2016,
drawings by VJAA, 2016
11.   Jeffrey A. Hess and Paul Clifford
Larson, *St. Paul's Architecture:
A History* (Minneapolis: University of
Minnesota Press, 2006), 202–212.

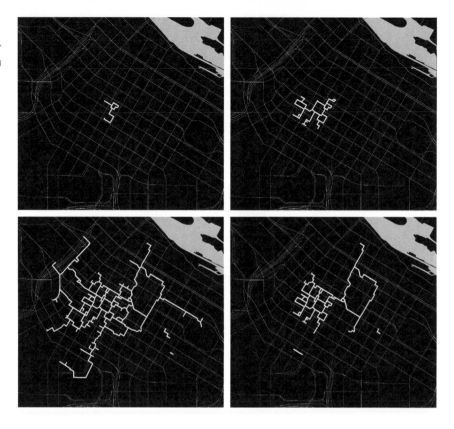

urban renewal district.[10] In St. Paul, the local Department of Transportation had the most political power because it directed the majority of federal funding, while the city planning group had less financial clout and relied on regulations and incentives to support urban renewal efforts when implementing projects at a large scale.

As a result of this earlier work, the city of St. Paul proposed a skyway system to be funded by federal money; it was redesigned by 1962 to cover nine blocks.[11] Gruen completed Dayton's department store in 1963 as the core of the network and the district followed select strategies derived from his work. Meanwhile, neighboring Minneapolis, also concerned about the competition posed by new suburban malls such as Southdale, used planning strategies similar to those being promoted in St. Paul. But Minneapolis bypassed the federal funding, which allowed it to implement its system first. The first skyway bridges were completed in 1962 and 1963 as part of a private development. The first transit-oriented pedestrian mall (Lawrence Halprin's Nicollet Mall) was completed in 1968. The skyway as a system was defined with the construction of its hub, the IDS Center (1972), by Philip Johnson.

St. Paul finally began construction of its downtown skyway system in 1967. Like Minneapolis's eight-mile network, the St. Paul skyway is fully enclosed and now extends for more than six miles. But unlike Minneapolis, the St. Paul system was created as a publicly owned network by using easements to include interior horizontal and vertical circulation for public access and control. The placement of the bridges in this unified system was determined by the Department of City Planning, and the designs were based on a single prototype. Construction was regulated by the Minnesota Department of Transportation. Federal money received through the US Department of Transportation made possible the full development and implementation of the system. This was in contrast to Minneapolis' private system, in which

12.   William H. Whyte, *City: Rediscovering the Center* (Philadelphia: University of Pennsylvania Press, 2009), 228
13.   Vincent Ponte, "The Multilevel City," in *The City as a System; Proceedings, Boston Architectural Center Workshop Series on Environmental Design for Decision-Makers in Government, 1967–68, Boston, Massachusetts* (Boston: Boston Architectural Center, 1968), 19–65.

building owners negotiated with the city for air rights over the street; in St. Paul, public right of way was taken through private property by local government. Because St. Paul has more historic buildings than Minneapolis and an irregular sloping topography, bridges were designed to adapt to highly complex existing conditions, creating a very circuitous network. Urbanist William H. Whyte criticized the system, calling St. Paul the "blank wall capital of the United States," a reference to the system's disorienting interior spaces and walkways that passed by the windowless side walls of buildings.[12]

Working at the height of suburbanization in America with its dependence on the automobile meant that Gruen's plans for car-free downtowns in cities like St. Paul were rarely implemented. Instead, to provide a similar level of convenience and shopping opportunity, city planners and developers spanned streets with footbridges, or tunneled under to create a more unified and interconnected urban retail experience. Pedestrian safety in the city was also a major concern in a period of suburban flight. Gruen's imagined journey for a Fort Worth suburban resident consisted of getting into a car, driving into downtown, and parking in a ramp with an elevated bridge connected to a continuous interior space, which meant that actual street life could be kept at a safe distance. From his work on the enclosed shopping mall in Minnesota, Gruen also realized that in many cities climate was also a key factor—whether rain, winter cold, or summer heat. Cities retroactively embraced these systems for the comfort and convenience of urban residents and visitors. The financial competition between cities and suburbs led to the "mallification" of many downtowns, a phenomenon augmented by the implementation of convenient and secure pedestrian pathways over and under existing city streets.

The Multilevel Man

Vincent Ponte was a very different kind of protagonist. Described in a 1970 *Time* magazine article as the "Multilevel Man," he developed incremental mixed-use superblock plans in the 1950s and 1960s for numerous cities, including Montreal and Winnipeg in Canada and proposals for Miami, Columbus, and Dallas in the United States. At Sert's 1956 conference at Harvard, which continued the ideas and influence of CIAM 8, Ponte was a key speaker and participant. As planner for Montreal's La Ville Souteraine (The Underground City, 1962), he promoted the rights of the pedestrian and the separation of automobile traffic as advocated at CIAM 8. Montreal was the first example of a comprehensive below-grade pedestrian system implemented at an urban scale.

Although attributing urban decay to suburban sprawl, Ponte was more economically driven than socially or environmentally motivated. Working with Montreal City Transit and Eatons Department Stores, he catered to the interests of downtown business communities and local politicians, and was particularly skillful with the media. While participating in numerous conferences, such as the City as a System that took place in Boston in 1967 and 1968,[13] Ponte suggested that his visions of multilevel interconnected cities were inspired by Leonardo da Vinci's ideal cities and Antonio Sant'Elia's plans for Rome, eschewing the ideas of Le Corbusier, Sert, and CIAM 8's Heart of the City group. His work, like Gruen's, was implemented by others—while framed in terms of a "plan," he introduced skyways as a malleable urban tool and left it to others to develop them.

Most skyway cities are clearly hybrids that combine characteristics of both planned and self-organizing systems. Montreal is an excellent example of the same process in a subterranean pedestrian system. Emulating Rockefeller Center, La Ville Souteraine was conceived by I. M. Pei and Henry Cobb in the 1960s as a self-contained, fully complete underground pedestrian zone. It was subsequently expanded by Ponte, and ultimately evolved into a loose network moving beyond its original boundaries and displaying

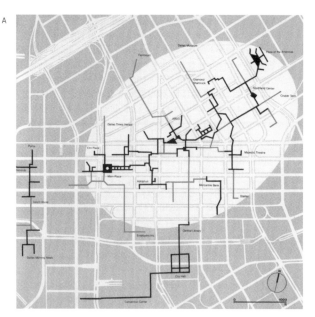

A.   Vincent Ponte, Plan for Dallas
(1979)
B.   Vincent Ponte, Place Ville Marie,
1962, Montreal, Canada ©Mark
Pimlott
C.   Vincent Ponte, Plan from "A
Report on a Sheltered Pedestrian
System in the Business Center,"
prepared for the City of Dallas
and the Central Business District
Association, 1979, Courtesy City of
Dallas and Downtown Dalls, Inc., and
the Frances Loeb Library, Harvard
Graduate School of Design
14.   David Dillon, "How Best-Laid
Plans of the '60s Helped Create
Urban Division," *Dallas Morning News*,
December 8, 1991.

self-organizing characteristics similar to many other ad hoc systems in the United States and Canada.

Similar to his superblock proposals in Montreal with their integration of shopping malls and transit, Ponte's concepts for the Dallas Pedestrian Network encompassed the entire downtown. His clients were the downtown corporations that occupied the majority of the office space, including powerful oil and tech companies. The three-mile system comprised a mile of overhead walkways and two miles of underground tunnel links connecting a total of thirty-six blocks. While the system was the outcome of a comprehensive master plan, it too evolved into a more informal configuration and the combination of above- and below-grade connections only served to increase the discontinuities of the network. In the car-centric culture of Dallas, parking ramp connections and vertical links to surface parking lots were given priority, supporting the interests and desires of white-collar office workers. Critic David Dillon described the city's fragmentary interiorization as the outcome of individualized agendas of the developers of downtown office buildings. For Dillon this amounted to taking a progressive idea and making it regressive, where "downtown streets belong to the poor, the homeless, and the politically disenfranchised" and the air-conditioned upper level belonged to a homogenous population of office workers.[14]

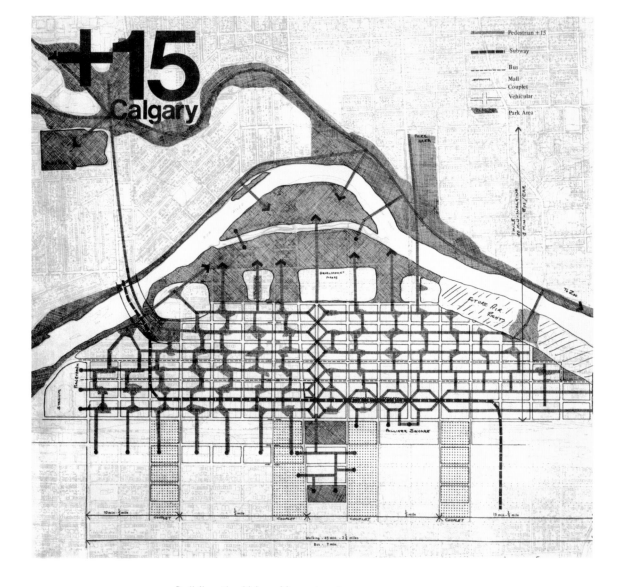

Legend (top right of figure):

- Pedestrian +15
- Subway
- Bus
- Mall
- Couplet
- Vehicular
- Park Area

–   Harold Hanen, +15 Plan,
Calgary, Canada, from "A
Development Plan for Downtown,"
Architecture Canada (November/
December 1966), Courtesy Royal
Architectural Institute of Canada
(RAIC) Image courtesy University of
Minnesota Libraries

Building the Urban Megastructure

It is interesting to trace the spatial characteristics and typological evolution
of these systems through the 1960s and early 1970s. In their initial incarnation
in the early 1960s, these projects followed the trends promoted by CIAM and
Team 10. First appearing in England as buildings interconnected with open-air
bridges, they quickly evolved into more spatially complex mat buildings, megastructures, and fully interiorized urban networks. Some of the most interesting
aspects of skyway/subway cities in North America are the striking similarities
in scale and patterns of growth. Unlike rationally planned gridiron cities, they
exhibit similar self-regulating behaviors in their organic development. Their
incremental and almost unrecognizable growth is synthetic and evolutionary.
Depending on large-scale economic development forces, political and bureaucratic agendas, the systems are regulated and modified by the immediate scale
of existing city blocks and architectural conditions, building codes, and the
particular economic and security interests of each property owner.

While many of these systems began with master plans that were rarely
followed, Calgary, Alberta is the one of the few cities that was conceived as

— Allied Works, National Music Centre of Canada, Calgary, 2016, Courtesy Allied Works

15. Harold Hanen, et al., "Places of Interchange in the Northeast Corridor Transportation System" (master's thesis, MIT, June 28, 1965).
16. +15 Coordinator Ron Ference, interview with the authors, 2002.

a complete urban system and strategically implemented over time. Chief city planner Harold Hanen acted as both a social justice advocate and an environmentalist when he began to develop his plan for Calgary's +15, the elevated pedestrian system so named because footbridges are fifteen feet above street level. A recent graduate of MIT, Hanen had Team 10 member Jerzy Soltan as an advisor and was immersed in the work of Team 10 and Le Corbusier as well as the Metabolists. His final thesis (a group project primarily crediting Soltan) was a multilevel city with a fully integrated public transit system.[15] Hired immediately after graduation in 1966, Hanen proposed a similar comprehensive system for Calgary within his first six months, including mass-transit and the bonus-density incentive system that would accelerate the development of the network throughout the city.

Although his position as chief planner did not last, his plan did, and the desire to realize the full scheme still guides planning decisions.[16] Implementation strategies such as city acquisition of public right of way through private buildings and the bonus-density system were employed to facilitate the creation of urban amenities like the Devonian Gardens, an elevated, interiorized public park described as an urban oasis. The only public gardens on the system, they generate revenue for the city as the site for weddings, parties, and corporate events. Recent projects like the National Music Centre of Canada (2016) by Allied Works Architecture leverage the city's bonus-density logic further—extending large volumes of space over the street and making interior connections that tie into the city's emerging +30 and +45 levels.

What gave all of these actors the ability to realize these systems where their predecessors had failed was their mastery of the public policy tools available for implementation, and their personal charisma and passion for the

17. Regional Plan Association, Urban Design Manhattan (New York: Viking Press, 1969), 5–7.

multilevel city. While they were less driven by the need to design the physical form or architectural experience of the city beyond the efficiencies of the system itself, they were well-schooled in the economics of city governments and the political power of tax incentives. As a result of their promotional skills and acumen in planning and public policy, a few men almost single-handedly transformed more than a dozen cities in North America, some of them without the typical tools of the profession such as drawings, designs, or detailed plans. Instead, they devised policy-based strategies including regulatory codes and tax incentives that could be described as programmatic strategies rather than master planning. Even the systems that were planned at their inception tended to be developed more informally as the rules governing their implementation evolved over time, demonstrating the resiliency of the programming script.

The most extensive systems have been built incrementally over time under the jurisdiction of municipal bureaucracies. The complex incentives offered to developers often redefine property rights and blur the distinction between public and private space. To achieve more continuous and interconnected tenant spaces, cities may lease airspace over streets to developers and property owners, who trade right of way through their buildings for additional, buildable, gross floor area ratios (FAR). Driven by short-term commercial interests, these multilevel systems are often the result of negotiation. Connecting to, be or "plugging-in," is typically viewed as beneficial, if not indispensable, by developers as access becomes more fluid and convenient. This in turn encourages densification. Under the prevailing logic of the systems, every major new commercial development must be connected to succeed economically. Once established with a certain critical mass, these public/private systems establish a permanent network parallel to the original street.

Manhattan: Access Trees and Hubs

One of the more radical proposals for the multilevel city was developed by the Regional Plan Association in the late 1960s, and published later as *Urban Design Manhattan*. Referring to the early multilevel proposals of the first Regional Plan for New York and Harvey Wiley Corbett's multilevel scheme, this publication was one of a series of reports leading to the Second Regional Plan for the New York Metropolitan Region. From 1960 to 1968, the study was led by planner Stanley Tankel, a proponent of garden cities who had studied under Walter Gropius at Harvard and worked for the London County Council on the city's post-Blitz multilevel reconstruction. After returning to New York City in the early 1950s, Tankel, along with other professionals in Greenwich Village, including Jane Jacobs, created the Village Study in 1956 to examine pedestrian and vehicular traffic segregation. Tankel hired planning consultants Rai Y. Okamoto and Frank E. Williams to develop the proposals in "Urban Design Manhattan."[17]

In the report, Grand Central Station and Rockefeller Center were described as prototypical multilevel "access trees," and it promoted the intersections of multimodal transit systems with mixing chambers, or social hubs. The proposal identified specific multilevel districts to concentrate multiuse public spaces and identified diagonal connectors to link the different zones against the generally orthogonal matrix. This included Midtown Manhattan, connecting sites like Grand Central Station, Times Square, Columbus Circle, and Rockefeller Center. This work culminated with the Greenwich Street Special District, approved in 1971, which attempted to zone a complex multilevel urban design solution into an area around the World Trade Center (WTC) in lower Manhattan.

The history of the WTC district, beginning in the 1970s until the World Trade Center Design Competition after 9/11, represents in many ways the end of one kind of three-dimensional urbanism oriented toward the street,

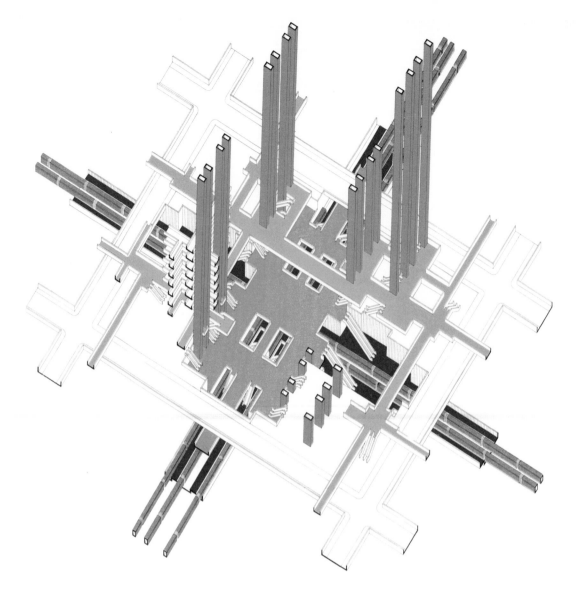

– Regional Plan Association, The
Access Tree Diagram, *Urban Design
Manhattan*, 1969, Courtesy Regional
Plan Association

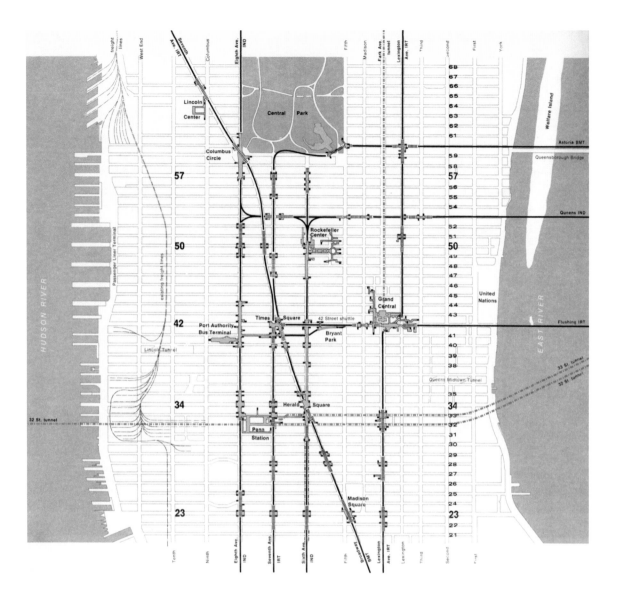

–   Regional Plan Association,
Existing Movement and the First
Mezzanine Level, *Urban Design
Manhattan*, 1969, Courtesy Regional
Plan Association

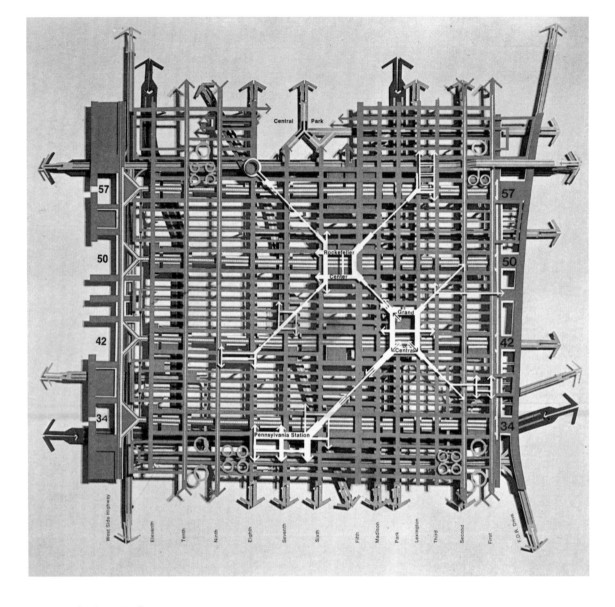

– Regional Plan Association, The
Access Tree Diagram, *Urban Design
Manhattan*, 1969, Courtesy Regional
Plan Association

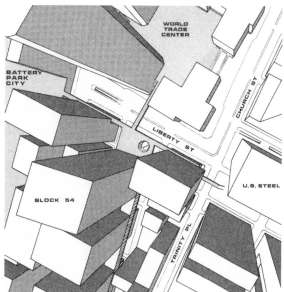

A. World Trade Center site, special Greenwich Street development district (New York: Office of Lower Manhattan Development, Office of the Mayor, 1969), Courtesy New York City Municipal Archives, Department of Records, Regional Plan Association Image courtesy Canadian Centre for Architecture, Montreal
B. Regional Plan Association, A New Office Cluster, *Urban Design Manhattan*, 1971, Courtesy Regional Plan Association
18. Office of Lower Manhattan Development, *Special Greenwich Street development district* (New York: Office of Lower Manhattan Development, Office of the Mayor, 1971), 20-55.
19. Jerold S. Kayden, *Privately Owned Public Space: The New York City Experience* (New York: Wiley, 2000), 14–17, 24–28.

and the transition to another future city form based on the elevated enclave. Beginning in the 1970s, the Special Greenwich Street Development District was created to promote the orderly and vertical expansion of commercial development to accommodate multilevel public spaces in Lower Manhattan in the area adjacent to Battery Park City and the World Trade Center. The district was targeted for grade-separated pedestrian circulation improvements with strong connections to street-level retail and transportation hubs. It used familiar incentives like floor area bonuses, but created a diverse set of design prototypes to achieve specific planning objectives defining the parameters of the system through a set of spatial typologies. The prototypical components were to be implemented by private entities through a range of strategies that were either mandatory or elective depending on the specific case.[18]

Focused on interconnecting the first two levels of the city, this expansion of street-level programs was enabled by more spatially complex versions of bridges and vertical circulation. Although intended to conjoin buildings into megastructures, in reality its impact on the proposed system was less visible or significant. The first project built using this system was the multilevel Deutsche Bank Building complex designed by the architectural firm Shreve, Lamb & Harmon at what was formerly the Bankers Trust Plaza (1971–1973). The first elevated bridge and tower plaza was designed by M. Paul Friedberg in 1974. It was later damaged on 9/11 and demolished along with three pedestrian bridges at Liberty, Vesey, and Chambers streets. Public reaction forced their replacement with new bridges designed by SHoP Architects (2002, 2003) at Rector Street. Formal regulations for elevated pedestrianization in the district ended in 1998.[19]

The sectional logic of the city has been a central concern from the first proposals in the "Regional Plan of New York and Its Environs" of 1929 that were driven by a desire to accommodate ever-increasing urban densities through the layering of the city's transportation systems and the regulation of building mass to permit light and air onto the street. The "Second Regional Plan for Manhattan" was based on the systems thinking in the 1960s and proposed the rationalization of the Manhattan gridiron as a three-dimensional infrastructural problem driven primarily by the efficiency of movement between commuter hubs and workplace destinations, thereby facilitating maximum connectivity. Concurrent with these proposals for comprehensive networks, other forms of

– SOM, Grand Central Station
Next 100 Years, 2012 ©SOM/Crystal
CG

three-dimensional urbanism would continue to develop in Manhattan as super-blocks, megastructures, and other kinds of clustered developments. By the beginning of the twenty-first century, it would be clear that the urban enclave as a model of three-dimensional urban development had replaced the preoccupation with urban networks in the design profession.

Architects wishing to create interconnected public or quasi-public space within consolidated architectural projects gravitated toward ideas that corresponded more naturally with the concentrated capital investments of public/private developments. Among the design submissions for the reconstruction of the World Trade Center site, eight out of nine of the schemes proposed elevated bridges or tangential intersections connecting building clusters high above the streets of Manhattan. The international attention focused on the competition further legitimized the three-dimensional urban enclave as the quintessential form of interiorized neoliberal urbanism. Networks that were primarily driven by public investment, outside the boundaries of individual projects, seemed to be a thing of the past.

A more recent proposal by SOM for Grand Central Station in 2012 suggests that a synthesis of all of New York's previous forms of multilevel urbanism is indeed possible if not inevitable as the city continues to grow. The new proposal for a high-density cluster of towers surrounds the station with densely layered transportation systems, including pedestrian walkways and concourses, mass-transportation, shopping malls, rooftop gardens, and a circular observation deck that rises to the top of the towers to hover over Grand Central Station like a halo. In this way the project combines the cosmopolitanism of Corbett and the "mat building" logic of the "access tree" from the Second Regional Plan with the multilevel enclave and branded urban spectacle of contemporary neoliberal developments.

A.   Central Escalator, Hong Kong,
Courtesy WingLuk/Wikimedia
Commons/GNU Free Documentation
License
B.   Hong Kong, podium level,
Courtesy Fomukimai/Wikimedia
Commons
20.   Keller Easterling, *Extrastatecraft:
The Power of Infrastructure Space*
(New York: Verso, 2014), 28–29,
48–49.

Hong Kong: City as Process

> Space, it is said, is both socially produced and produces the social;
> but to this we will have to add that it has become so complex
> and enigmatic that it cannot be directly described. Urban spaces in
> particular are like black holes: we perceive them only in the effects
> they produce.
>
> — Ackbar Abbas, "Between the Visible and Intelligible in
>   Asian Cinema," 2010

The multilevel pedestrian system in Hong Kong is the most extensive in the world. Its form has evolved organically from a need to reconcile the city's complex street system with the steep hillside terrain. Although not intentionally influenced by the Metabolists, the growth of the city's seven hundred footbridges may be one of the best contemporary examples of the Metabolist concept of the "city as process." Cities like Hong Kong have followed a distinct trajectory since the 1960s, using multilevel urbanisms reactively to accommodate increased density and reduce congestion, pollution, and crime while promoting economic development.

The growth of the pedestrian system in Hong Kong has always been driven by an underlying economic motivation to promote commercial investment. British free ports were established as Free Trade Zones in Singapore (1919) and Hong Kong (1849) under the planning purview of the British government. While all land in Hong Kong was technically owned by the crown during the period of British colonial governance, regulations and infrastructure were designed and constructed around the interests of foreign corporations based in the city and the local workforce.[20]

This economic and political system of governance underlaid colonial planning studies produced in the UK for Hong Kong at the time. The studies included the Hong Kong Preliminary Planning Report of 1949 authored by Patrick Abercrombie and his collaborators shortly after their successful work on the Greater London Plan of 1944. Despite the differences in contexts and cultures, the framework and planning principles they advocated were similar. While Abercrombie advised on the sectional improvements in Hong Kong

– Hong Kong skyway system phased growth (clockwise from upper left): 1963–1975, 1975–1988, 1988–1995, 1995–2010, drawings by VJAA, 2016

21. Zheng Tan and Charlie Q. L. Xue, "Walking as a Planned Activity: Elevated Pedestrian Network and Urban Design Regulation in Hong Kong," in *Journal of Urban Design* (London: Routledge, 2014), 723–727.

22. Transport Department senior engineer Wai Chung Chan, interview with the authors, 2010.

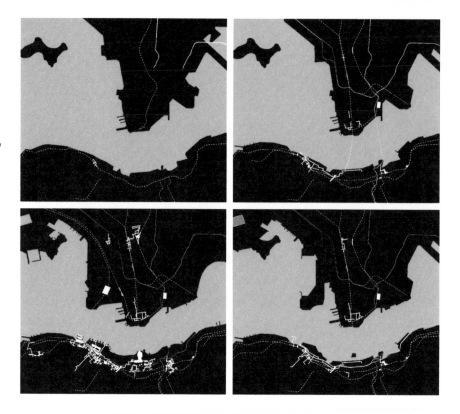

(1948) and the need for traffic separation at its center, it wasn't until 1961 that the Central Area Redevelopment Plan proposed an elevated pedestrian network connecting the Central and Admiralty districts. This plan was influenced by Colin Buchanan's Traffic in Towns research but also by the recent construction of megastructures in new towns like Cumbernauld. Hong Kong's Colony Outline Plan document of 1969 described a more complete vision; a multilevel city with elevated public spaces connecting housing, businesses, offices, and parking in a single megastructure elevated above a mass transit line.[21]

After the first elevated footbridges were constructed in 1963, a more continuous and interconnected system began to take form beginning with the creation of Connaught Place in the Central District in 1970. Additional "flyover" connections across congested streets and roadways enabled greater commercial development in the Central District as well. Due to government ownership of all lands and Hong Kong's lack of a significant historic conservation agenda, the implementation of this system would be far more successful than it had been in London.

Elevated walkway systems now span the majority of the Sheung Wan, Central, Admiralty, and Wan Chai districts. Under the current political system, land ownership is still held by the government, which then leases land to developers, creating a system that is inherently more temporal and adaptable. Hong Kong's planning department employs various multilevel circulation strategies through what is called "on-demand planning" and the use of data-mapping techniques.[22]

The Hong Kong pedestrian network is composed of a range of connector prototypes, including deck-access plazas and podiums, flyover bridges, open-air footbridges, and high-bridge networks (exterior pedestrian bridges over streets), interiorized walkways, elevated parks, and exterior escalators that scale the steep hillsides. The most significant of these is the Central Escalator,

23. Ibid.

a two-thousand-six-foot-long series of moving, covered walkways connecting Hong Kong's central business district to the Mid-Levels residential district. This seeming patchwork of strategies uses on-demand planning techniques to develop and refine the system and respond to changing circumstances. Planners focus on specific districts and neighborhoods rather than trying to achieve a continuous urban network.[23]

The process for each new development in contemporary Hong Kong is not simply about negotiating a building on a site, but integrating each new component as part of a larger interconnected urban condition. The use of on-demand planning development is accretional and adaptive, supposedly allowing the conditions to generate the form. While this system is enacted on behalf of the public, there are inevitably political and economic agendas underlying decisions made about control and access.

As Hong Kong and its surrounding districts grow in population, the city continues to evolve into greater three-dimensional complexity. Since the initial land reclamation projects of the 1890s, the process has accelerated to create more than six thousand hectares of new land concentrated along the waterfront at the beginning of the twenty-first century. This expansion along the sea frontage has been accompanied by massive multilevel infrastructural improvements and building development. What began in the 1960s under British and Hong Kong planners as measures to ameliorate conflicts between congested city streets and the steep natural topography has now escalated into complex interconnections within the new artificial topography of the autonomous urban city form. Emerging from underground transit hubs, networks of walkways connect exterior terraces and podia with interior atria, shopping mall spaces, and the extended urban realm. Analogous to the ossification and resorption of growing bone tissue, the transformations of Hong Kong reveal the metabolism of the modern metropolis.

Centripetal and Centrifugal Flows in the Three-Dimensional City
---

It is interesting to compare contemporary pedestrian systems with their historic antecedents. In some ways Moilin's Paris of 2000 is actually Minneapolis or Calgary in the twenty-first century, if not in their forms or intent, then in their procedural methods of development. Paris of 2000 was a speculative plan to transform the city in fifteen years through an initiative sponsored by a strong central government with the resources to intervene on a massive scale, much like Haussmann's plan for the city. Had Moilin's plan for Paris been undertaken, it is hard to imagine how far the historic city would have been transformed. The implementation strategy he proposed has been proven viable, even resilient, in North American cities in the mid-twentieth century. Once initiated, the systems may develop rapidly as they reach a self-generating or autocatalytic stage. In other cases such as London or New York, where the historic character is more deeply rooted in the city's cultural identity, fear of the invasive nature of the systems has been sufficient to forestall the development of large-scale networks. Although the London Pedway had taken a similar approach to incremental development, it was ultimately blocked, due in no small measure to the efforts of historic preservationists. In North America they would take root where there was less resistance to the radical changes entailed in their urban and architectural forms.

While seemingly lacking in invention, many of these cities implemented very ambitious proposals through creative methods that were conceived in bureaucratic, legal, and economic terms. While the most provocative and imaginative forms of multilevel urbanism are currently found in discrete architectural projects, the pragmatically driven and rapidly growing informal systems are much more radical forms of urbanism. For this reason, they should not be ignored. Critically considered in both sociological and experiential

24. Albert Pope, *Ladders* (New York: Princeton Architectural Press, 1996), 61–64, 153–156.
25. Sarah Whiting, "Superblockism: Chicago's Elastic Grid," in Rudolph El-Khoury and Edward Robbins, *Shaping the City: Studies in History, Theory, and Urban Design* (London and New York: Routledge, 2004), 74.

terms, they may be viewed as "demonstration projects" suggesting the positive and negative potential of these new urbanisms. Critics of grade-separated pedestrian systems warn of the possible negative social effects of multiplying the levels of the street or short-circuiting the gridiron matrix.

The inherent openness and centrifugal effects of gridiron cities or other latticelike geometric planning systems has been contrasted with the centripetal effects of the cul-de-sac, or branching geometries. In his book *Ladders*, Albert Pope argues that more open and interconnected planning geometries facilitate extension and interconnectivity and are inherently more public. This is what we might call, in more general terms, their cosmopolitan tendency. Conversely, he proposes that a centrifugal system is by nature closed and insular, and more easily privatized or controlled by financial interests.[24] While this distinction is important, Sarah Whiting argues against this binary framework in her analysis of the superblock in Chicago, describing the elasticity of a "closed system" in social terms. Her subtle distinction of "superminiurbanisms" alludes to the innate and simultaneous development of bounded and articulated social space and its complementary relationship with the open and interconnected characteristics of a centrifugal city.[25] We use the term "communitarian" to describe this tendency in positive terms. In fact, in the three-dimensional city, the concepts of open and closed, public and private, or inclusive versus exclusive always occur simultaneously and relatively, in ways that may be positive or negative depending on circumstance.

I can go from my office and all the way to Frankfurt, Germany and not put on a coat. I won't get wet. I get out and take a train into downtown. What the hell is wrong with that?

— John Portman, March 2013

We do not yet possess the perceptual equipment to match this new hyperspace, as I will call it, in part because our perceptual habits were formed in that older kind of space I have called the space of high modernism. The newer architecture therefore—like many of the other cultural products I have evoked in the preceding remarks—stands as something like an imperative to grow new organs, to expand our sensorium and our body to some new, yet unimaginable, perhaps ultimately impossible, dimensions.

— Fredric Jameson, *The Cultural Logic of Late Capitalism*, 1991

5. THE CONTINUOUS INTERIOR

5. THE CONTINUOUS INTERIOR

1.   Manfredo Tafuri, *The Sphere and the Labyrinth: Avant-Gardes and Architecture from Piranesi to the 1970s* (Cambridge: MIT Press, 1987), 28–54.

The Charismatic Interior

While convenience and comfort are two of the principle objectives of the enclosed and connected grade-separated pedestrian city, the spectacle of the grand interior remains an equally important, if complementary, reason for the resiliency of the concept of the interiorized city. In Atlanta, Georgia, the Peachtree Center, designed by architect-developer John Portman from 1965 to 1992, is a city-scaled urban development made up of offices and residential towers, convention hotels, the Americas Mart trade center, shopping arcades, parking ramps, and mass transit. A network of corridors, bridges, and tunnels connects twelve blocks, forming a largely interiorized urban enclave in downtown Atlanta. The four block-size buildings of the merchandise mart are grafted together with multiple bridge connections to form a superblock.

But Portman's signature architectural device—the atrium, which is used repeatedly throughout the Peachtree Center—gives the entire complex its notoriety. The vast scale of the atria in the Marriott Marquis, the Hyatt Regency Hotel, and the Americas Mart brings to mind Fredric Jameson's description of Portman's Bonaventure Hotel in Los Angeles as a "hyperspace"—the new and as yet untheorized form of the city of "late capitalism." The alienation, likely coupled with awe, that Jameson experiences in the hotel is echoed by geographer Ed Soja, who described the Bonaventure's inversion of inside and outside as the very metaphor for the postmodern city itself.

The fact that many of these new spaces are not exterior but interior is crucial. From a psychological point of view, the success of Portman's formula seems to fundamentally depend on the apprehension of incomprehensible scale and precision as one enters from the street or other areas of a more familiar scale. The grand atria are remarkable for their geometric clarity and the seemingly effortless pulsing of their glass elevators. These charismatic interiors, like those of Fourier and Considerant, are amplified to the level of the sublime. The vast emptiness, as Jameson notes, is simultaneously vacant and populated—a panopticon of pleasure providing maximum visibility across the central atria to blank walls with doors that periodically open to discharge residents laterally along the layered balconies.

The Absent Proprietor

The concept of the continuous interior has taken on various guises over time, alternating between utopian and dystopian images of the city. In a near perfect inversion of Portman's paternalistic spaces, Giovanni Battista Piranesi's etchings, *Carceri d'invenzione* (*Imaginary Prisons*, 1761), provide an alternative and nightmarish image of three-dimensional urban interiors made up of catwalks, stairways, and ambiguously layered architectural space. In the *Carceri* the halls seem to be abandoned. There is no proprietor and no authority, only the residue of past occupations. Manfredo Tafuri described the *Carceri* as a heterotopic space, defined by characteristics that are both real and imagined—an image resembling a centered and figural space where none really exists. Through Piranesi's perspectival manipulations, the *Carceri* etchings represent what appears to be a single cavernous space that is immediately undermined by a series of individually deployed spatial events that are "off-center to one another and dislocated onto independent rings" as a "systematic criticism of the concept of 'center.'" Intentionally avoiding any comprehensive understanding of the whole, there is not an absence of space, but instead the creation of a sense of infinite expandability through a "chain of associations."[1]

Although proffered by Tafuri as a "negative utopia" that warns of the city's future, Piranesi's etchings clearly exploit the sublime spectacle of the continuous interior for dramatic effect. Tafuri also connected Piranesi's project to the Russian Constructivists and Soviet filmmaker Sergei Eisenstein's

– John Portman, Peachtree Center, Atlanta, 1961, Courtesy the authors

– Giovanni Battista Piranesi, The Drawbridge, Plate VII from the series *Carceri d'Invenzione*, 1745 Photo: Cooper-Hewitt, National Design Museum, Smithsonian Institution/Art Resource, New York

2.   Ibid., 55–60.
3.   Anthony Vidler, "Phobic City" Psychopathologies of Modern Space," lecture at the Architectural Association, June 22, 1994, accessed January 15, 2016.

interest in the *Carceri* between the two Soviet Five Year Plans of reconstruction. Through a reading of Eisenstein's film techniques, Tafuri identified a duality in the imagery containing the abstract promise of an avant-garde vision that is simultaneously suggestive of a loss of vision experienced through its realization.[2] This duality—a project conceived in utopian terms, while inevitably containing its negative real-world realities—can be found in many elevated interior projects since the 1960s.

In Eisenstein's cinematic montage technique captured the constant motion and fragmentary experiences of modernity in the early twentieth century, the Dadaist paintings of George Grosz represented the anxiety and dread of urban life that accompanied the development of the modern metropolis. The multifarious psychological effects of dense urban space have been a key motivator in the development of multilevel urbanisms.[3]

In his book *Warped Space*, Anthony Vidler explores the fears and phobias underlying the social transitions from the physically impacted urban conditions of nineteenth-century Europe through the emerging modern spaces of

A.   Constant Nieuwenhuys,
*Symbolische voorstelling van
New Babylon*, 1969, Collection
Gemeentemuseum Den Haag
©2016 Artists Rights Society (ARS),
New York / c/o Pictoright Amsterdam
B.   Constant Nieuwenhuys,
*Gezicht op eukele New-Babylonische
sectoren*, 1971, Collection Gemeen-
temuseum Den Haag ©2016 Artists
Rights Society (ARS), New York / c/o
Pictoright Amsterdam
4.   Anthony Vidler, *Warped Space:
Art, Architecture, and Anxiety in
Modern Culture* (Cambridge: MIT
Press, 2001), 26–46.
5.   Mark Wrigley, *Constant's New
Babylon: The Hyper-architecture of
Desire* (Rotterdam, 010 Uitgeverij,
1999), 160.
6.   Constant Nieuwenhuys, "Une
autre ville pour une autre vie"
("Another City for Another Life"), in
Internationale Situationniste, no. 3
(December 1959): 37–41.

Baron von Haussmann's Paris and Vienna's Ringstrasse to the sublime and "ineffable" space of Le Corbusier's modernism. Vidler parallels the development of early modern psychiatric theories with the emergence of radically different theories of architectural and urban space. If the fear of going outside, of being exposed in the vast spaces of the city was associated with the newly diagnosed psychological disorder of agoraphobia, then claustrophobia—the fear being trapped, of proximity and intimacy—was its opposite. That these two characterize as psychopathologies the binary relationship of the interior and the exterior suggests the importance of this dichotomy in the theorization of the multilevel city and the interiorization of urban space.[4]

The Continuous Interior

Artist Constant Nieuwenhuys began to develop his plan for an elevated city called *New Babylon* in 1956. Named after Grigori Kozintsev and Leonid Trauberg's 1929 Russian Constructivist film about the Paris Commune, the indefinitely extending megastructure would consume Constant's efforts as an urbanist for the next eighteen years. *New Babylon* was a radical new city conceived as a continuous interior space—a social place of creative free play in an endless chain of varying atmospheric environments. Borrowing the term *homo ludens* (man at play) from cultural historian Johann Huizinga, Constant imagined that the postrevolutionary citizen "will respond to his need for playing, for adventure, for mobility, as well as all the conditions that facilitate the free creation of his own life." Growing out of the Situationist interest in

A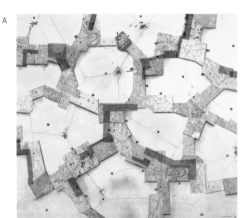

 B

both Surrealism and Fourierism, Constant's *Une autre ville pour une autre vie* (*Another City for Another Life*) (1959) framed *New Babylon* within the context of the postwar critique of the functionalist city.[5] *New Babylon* was for him a critical tool directed at the "concrete cemeteries" of CIAM where "the masses are condemned to die of boredom" and where the over-scaled open spaces limit "people's direct relations and collective activities." Constant promoted the use of new technology for the purposes of "leisure" but questioned its value when employed without imagination. Instead, a "happier life" could be achieved through an alternative "unitary urbanism" that would create new situations, adventures, and changing experiences through "atmospheres" combined with mobility to create "an urbanism designed for pleasure." This new communal environment devoted to leisure, "collective creativity," and social intercourse is achieved through "the urban network" and "a social conception of urbanism."[6]

In his detailed description of *New Babylon*, Constant made clear the significance of the meandering path, or *dérive* (drift). In the "covered cities in which the layout of roads and separate buildings will be replaced by a

– R. Buckminster Fuller, Model of Triton City, 1967 Photo ©Bob Daemmrich

7. Ibid., 37–41.

continuous spatial construction elevated above the ground, including clusters of dwellings as well as public spaces (permitting changes in use according to the needs of the moment).... The multitude of different traversable spaces of which the city is composed will form a complex and vast social space." The new city of leisure could only be achieved by overriding the historic city below. "The city of the future must be conceived as a continuous construction on pillars ... leaving the ground level free for traffic circulation and public meetings.... In this way it will be possible to create a multilayered city: underground, ground level, upper stories and terraces, with areas ranging from that of a present-day neighborhood to that of a metropolis."[7]

The optimism of this utopian proposal to house human society in a vast, vaguely defined interior is as seductive in its allusions to creative communal life as it is naïve in its proposed implementation, not to mention its implications for human sociality or governance. As Constant's work progressed, the project began to display signs of its dystopian opposite. Rather than a field of continuous play, *New Babylon* in later paintings became increasingly reminiscent of Piranesi's infinitely extended interior spaces. The vaguely threatening imagery, including evidence of recent violent incidents or crisis, brings to mind key characteristics of the *Carceri* and the implied dangers of nebulous and unsecured interior urban space. Interestingly, some of the exterior collaged images of *New Babylon* also suggest the ad hoc expediencies of non-planned development raising more questions about the economic and political systems underpinning this new society. The images bear a striking resemblance to the actual forms of many contemporary skyway cities driven by capitalist development.

– Superstudio, Monumento
Continuo (The Continuous
Monument), circa 1969, Musée
National d'Art Moderne, Centre
Georges Pompidou, Paris © Gian
Piero Frassinelli Photo: Georges
Meguerditchian ©CNAC/MNAM/
Dist. RMN-Grand Palais / Art
Resource, NY
8. Andrea Branzi, Notes on
No-Stop City by Archizoom, in *Exit
Utopia: Architectural Provocations,
1956-76* (London: Prestel Publishing,
2005), 6–7.
9. Peggy Deamer, *Architecture
and Capitalism: 1845 to the Present*
(London: Routledge, 2013), 138–140.

The Interiorization of Capital

If Constant's epic project evolved from utopic to dystopian, Archizoom Associati's No-Stop City (1969) offers an ironic vision of the continuous interior influenced by Ludwig Hilberseimer, where the future is imagined as an endless, artificial interior built on mass consumption. According to Archizoom member Andrea Branzi, the next generation of architects were interested in architecture not as a tool for benign mediation, or creating an alternative city, but representing and reframing the "mechanisms of power." The true political project of No-Stop City became not "how to improve the functioning of the city, but instead, how to disrupt it." For Branzi, the social uprisings of 1968 were in many ways similar to the French Revolution that had influenced the socialist utopians. The social transformations that had already taken place were made manifest to conservative political powers slow to recognize the new order.[8]

Manfredo Tafuri observed in the late 1960s that only two utopian architectural projects understood the impact of capitalism on the city, whether they intended it or not: Hilberseimer's Highrise City (1924) project and Le Corbusier's two-level city, Plan Obus, Algiers (1932). Drawing from Taylorism and industrial modes of production, both projects absorbed the buildings as objects, instead organizing the elevated traffic of the city around the "processes of production." Archizoom and Superstudio adopted these images of rationally ordered and stratified urban space as a vehicle for theorizing the continuous interior in political terms. Criticizing the condition of the capitalist welfare state as fundamentally authoritarian, Archizoom created a new urban form as a provocation, using the concept of an endless commercial interior to expose how modern capitalism links production with consumption for economic and political ends.[9]

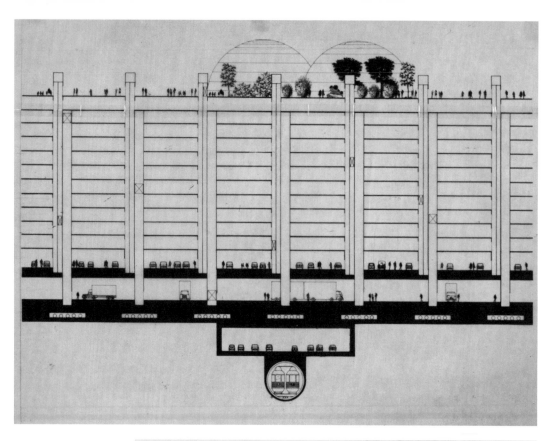

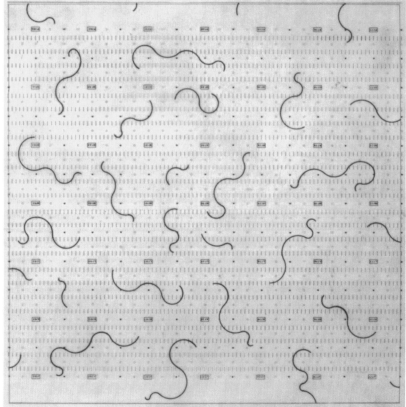

– Archizoom Associati, No-Stop
City, 1970, Courtesy Centro Studi
e Archivio della Communicazione
(CSAC)–Università di Parma

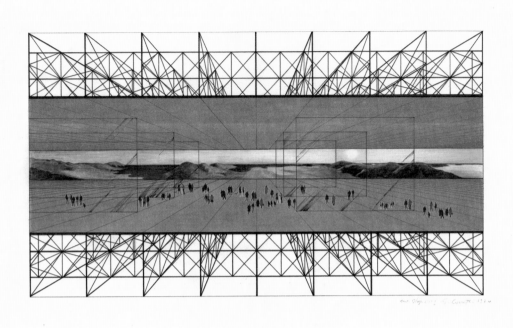

– Gilberto Corretti (Archizoom Associati), No-Stop City, 1970, Museo Novecento Firenze, Courtesy Archivio Gilberto Corretti

10. Reyner Banham, *Megastructure: Urban Futures of the Recent Past* (London: Thames & Hudson, 1976), 45.

11. Zhongjie Lin, *Kenzo Tange and the Metabolist Movement: Urban Utopias of Modern Japan* (London: Routledge, 2010), 71–72.

Inside the Metabolic City

Immersed in the context of the cultural and political climate of the 1960s, the Metabolists in Japan also viewed their work through the lens of social change. The classic notion of the megastructure and its interiorization of the city can be gleaned from the work of R. Buckminster Fuller of the late 1960s and early 1970s, where it is based on singular concepts and technical invention: multi-level cities interiorized under bubbles (Dome Over Manhattan, 1960); elevated cities that float (Triton City, 1967); and others derived from their internal structural logics (Hyperboloid Housing Towers, 1964). By contrast, the Japanese Metabolists conceived of megastructure (and the term Metabolism itself) as part of society's inherent processes of urbanization.[10] Kenzo Tange introduced the Metabolist concept of the "city as process"—the belief that the metropolis was no longer a fixed, stable entity with a separation of buildings and infrastructure in exterior space, but was synthesized into a dynamic, organic interiorizing whole.

Flexibly inhabited and flowing over existing cities and streets, the Metabolists' large superstructure networks projected a very different form of urbanism. In Tange's iconic Plan for Tokyo (1960), he used the pilotis and core method of separating traffic from pedestrians, creating continuous urban space. Exhibited at CIAM XI in 1959, projects such as Kikutake Kiyonori's Sky House and Marine City (both 1958) reflected the Japanese interest in the floating city as a reaction to the problem of a densely populated island country. Architects such as Arata Isozaki saw his City in the Air, Proposal for Tokyo (1961) as a way to move past the architectural limitations of the historic city; "Tokyo is hopeless. I am no longer going to consider architecture below thirty meters in height. I am leaving everything below thirty meters to others."[11]

– Kenzo Tange, Plan for Tokyo
Bay, 1960 Photo: Akio Kawasumi and
Osamu Murai

A.   Kenzo Tange, Fuji Television building, Tokyo, 1996 Photo: Liao Yusheng
B.   Arata Isozaki, Joint Core System, Shinjuku, Tokyo, 1960
©Arata Isozaki digital image ©The Museum of Modern Art/Licensed by SCALA/ Art Resource, New York
12.   Ibid., 58–72.
13.   Ibid., 81.

A

B

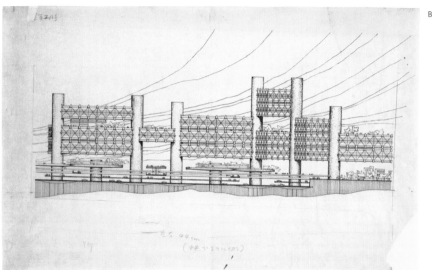

The principles of Metabolism also suggested an idealized pattern of growth with a biological imperative. It advanced a balance and symmetry of parts, including the conditions of heterogeneity and the equilibrium of diverse factors that the real political and economic forces of urbanism lacked. Fumihiko Maki's concept of Group Form reduced to a formula the accretional growth of these systems, conceived of as an aggregate of components around an armature. Projects like Kisho Kurokawa's Agricultural City (1960) and Helix City (1961) and Kikutake Kiyonori's Ocean City were derived from earlier socialist mass housing projects.[12] Composed of multilevel components connected by elevated walkways, the large infrastructural elements were dubbed "urban connectors," a term created by Marxist scholar Noriake Kurokawa and loosely based on the Soviet social condenser. The urban connector mediated between the scale of the city and the scale of the individual, and between the individual and the collective, as is also seen in Kisho Kurokawa's Nakagin Capsule Tower (1972) or in Kenzo Tange's Riojo Housing complex (1969) in Buenos Aires.[13]

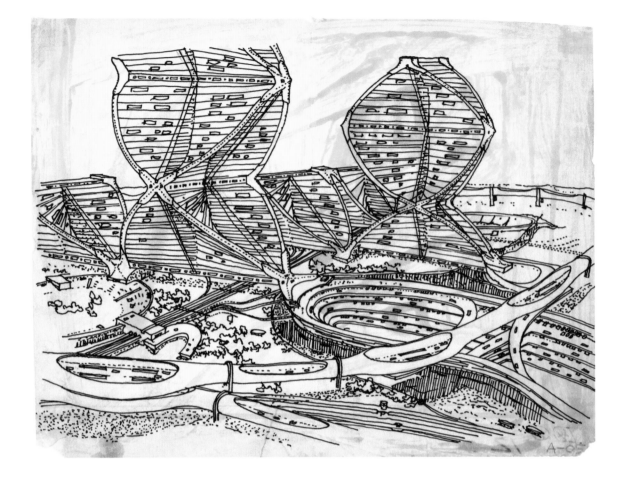

– Kisho Kurokawa, Helix City, 1962 ©Kisho Kurokawa Architect & Associates   Photo ©Centre Pompidou, MNAM-CCI/Georges Meguerditchian/Dist. RMN-GP

14.   The Planning Techniques Office (PTO) can be seen as a precursor of the computational strategies currently being employed with parametrics. What is interesting about this data-driven model of design and its ties to the early beginnings of these movements is its development of methods of geometric design through the selection of data sets. In the case of the PTO, the architects adapted land-use and density strategies of the Garden City, the programmatic zoning of early functionalist CIAM, health and economic factors of the Existenzminimum, and massing studies that emphasized access to daylighting as an isolated condition to generate form. Many of these techniques created urban conditions that were simply topographic maps of data, abstracting the original social agenda underlying the PTO's purpose. Martin's research into the science of form generation took a more academic trajectory: when he applied these methods to typological analysis, he used density, performance, and environmental factors.

The Megastructure in Britain: The Interiorization of Geometric Space

Concurrent with the Metabolist's project, an alternative concept of urbanization began to develop in the United Kingdom driven by the forced fusion of technology and social form. The megastructure, initially the preoccupation of academic architects in the 1960s and 1970s, was defined by Reyner Banham as an urban armature, layered up from the ground plane with a more fine-grain build-out to suit the temporal needs of occupants. Typically driven by the logic of a definitive section, the megastructure was an extensive form capable of growing to unlimited lengths. According to Banham, Cedric Price most succinctly described the megastructure as "any building with more than four expansion joints." An emerging interest in multilevel megastructural forms can be seem in early British projects like the Brunswick Centre by Leslie Martin and Patrick Hodgkinson (1967). After completing early studies for the project in the late 1950s and after completing the Royal Festival Hall, Martin left the LCC for a position at Cambridge University, where he carried forward his work with the research-based PTO and his multidisciplinary collaborations in the early Hampstead Group. He subsequently founded the research group Land Use Built Form Studies (LUBFS) at Cambridge with Lionel March. LUBFS used scientific and mathematical models to develop an intellectual basis of form, leading to the beginnings of integrated data and computation in architectural design.[14]

Expanding on an interest in organic patterns of urban growth combined with a critique of both Sitte's picturesque model of urban design and CIAM's

– Leslie Martin, Whitehall proposal, London, 1965, from L. Martin and C. D. Buchanan, "Whitehall: A Plan for the National and Government Centre London": HMSO, 1965

15. Leslie Martin, "The Grid as Generator," in Leslie Martin and Lionel March, *Urban Space and Structures* (Cambridge: Cambridge University Press, 1972), 6–27.

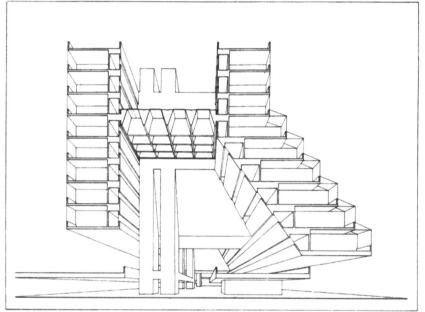

prescriptive functionalism in planning, Martin wrote the essay "The Grid as Generator." Influential on early computational strategies in design, it was first presented as a lecture at Harvard in 1966. Martin proposed a new approach based on historically organic developments within artificial patterns (the grid). He concluded with the work of Colin Buchanan and the creation of an elevated pedestrian "net" (deck-system) to allow for continuous movement unobstructed by traffic.[15] This academic research was based on a series of projects developed with LUBFS at Cambridge that used serialized geometric diagrams to test perimeter block strategies on a site. This work culminated in Martin's radical megastructural proposal for Whitehall (1963–1965), achieved in collaboration with Buchanan, a skywalk advocate. Proposing an overlaid grid of low-rise perimeter blocks with mathematically and spatially complex geometric patterns of elevated walkways and courtyards, the LUBFS group identified generative conditions to manipulate the overall grid and optimize

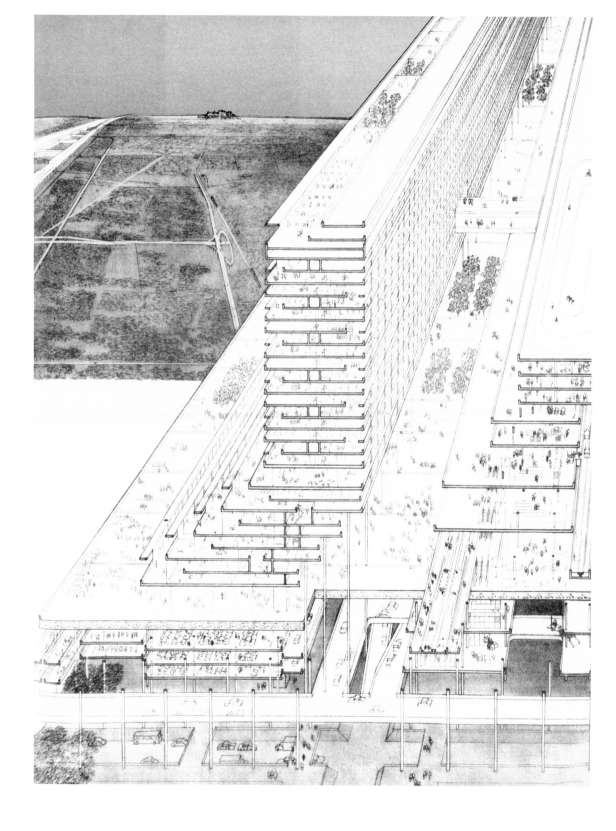

–   Peter Eisenman and Michael Graves, Views of Linear City/Jersey Corridor Project, 1965, Courtesy Michael Graves Architecture & Design and Eisenman Architects
16.   Adam Sharr and Stephen Thornton, *Demolishing Whitehall: Leslie Martin, Harold Wilson, and the Architecture of White Heat* (London: Ashgate, 2013), 95–103.
17.   Altino João Serra de Magalhães Rocha, *Architecture Theory 1960–1980: Emergence of a Computational Perspective* (PhD diss., Cambridge: Massachusetts Institute of Technology, 2004).
18.   Arie Graafland, Review of Peter Eisenman: "The Formal Basis of Modern Architecture" (PhD diss., Cambridge University, 1963) in *Footprints, Issue 1: Trans-Disciplinary*, (Delft: TU Delft Publishing, 2007): 93–96.
19.   Suzanne Frank, *IAUS, the Institute for Architecture and Urban Studies: An Insider's Memoir* (Self-published, Authorhouse, 2010), 18–22.
20.   Howard Mansfield, *Cosmopolis: Yesterday's Cities of the Future* (Piscataway, New Jersey: Transaction Publishers, 1990), 110.
21.   Reyner Banham, *Megastructure: Urban Futures of the Recent Past* (London: Thames & Hudson, 1976), 11.

density, including movement patterns, open space, and building height. Adapting the stepped section of elevated walkways and linear gallery space of earlier projects, the final scheme created legible hierarchies, particularly circulation patterns, within the more familiar megastructural form. Roads pass below the linear gallery spine and pedestrian bridges crossed overhead.[16]

Architect Peter Eisenman, who studied under Martin at Cambridge (1960–1963), also used these early computational strategies to develop methods of form generation in architecture. Eisenman's thesis at Cambridge, with Martin as an adviser,[17] entitled "The Formal Basis of Modern Architecture," used similar methods of diagrammatic analysis to shift the concepts of modern architecture away from the subject and toward the object, with the form of volumetric solids established through a language of structure and techniques.[18] After leaving Cambridge, Eisenman created linear urban proposals similar to the interiorized megastructural forms of the LUBFS in projects like the Jersey Corridor (1965) and in the exhibition *The New City* focusing on Harlem while teaching at Princeton.[19] Eisenman and collaborator Michael Graves describe the Jersey Corridor project as a prototype for a new city as a framework for a better way of life: "Our society can send a rocket safely to the moon. Our society now will have a city that will send a person in dignity to the opera. A glorification of our society. Not for posterity ... but for now."[20] This work influenced a number of significant multilevel megastructural projects proposed in the United States in the late 1960s through the early 1970s, including Paul Rudolph's Lower Manhattan Expressway Project (1971).

While advocating the megastructural form during the height of its popularity, critic Reyner Banham in hindsight faulted its unlikely occurrence within the logic of urban speculative development. At the time, he cautioned that the formation of megastructures had limited economic value, asserting that they could be built only through the centralized authority of municipal governments, expositions, and universities.[21] But in the 1970s Banham didn't predict the consolidation of capital that would result in their use for massive infrastructurally scaled architectural developments like megamalls, or in the CBDs of global cities or in shopping complexes such as megamalls. He also didn't fully appreciate the incremental but massive redevelopment of urban centers where entire cities would gradually morph into multilevel cities with pedestrian systems built incrementally through a range of public-private partnerships. Critiquing the megastructure and expansive urban forms like the Phalanstère

– World Trade Center Memorial Competition, Scheme 1, 2002, New York, Courtesy Steven Holl Architects

22. Reyner Banham, "Megastructures 1," October 15, 1974, lecture at the Architectural Association, accessed December 10, 2015, http://www.aaschool.ac.uk//video/lecture.php?ID=2774.

23. Kenneth Frampton, *Megaform as Urban Landscape* (University of Illinois at Urbana Champaign School of Architecture, 2010), 34–35.

as fundamentally utopian, Banham concluded that "the megastructure is an ideal city containing someone else's utopia."[22]

Exteriorizing the Interior

In Kenneth Frampton's survey on megastructural form, he offers the megastructure as an antidote to the ubiquitous "sub-urbanized" conditions that surround and isolate the contemporary city. Suggesting a new terminology of "megaform" to reposition the megastructure as a topographic feature and recognize its exteriority, Frampton identifies a series of projects that combine massive large-scale interiorized conditions with exterior landscapes developed as an integral part of their forms.

While beginning with elevated urban projects of the past, such as Le Corbusier's Plan Obus, Algiers and his project for Rio de Janeiro that conjoin landscape and infrastructure in quasi-urbanized architectures, Frampton also includes two of Steven Holl's recent elevated urban megaforms: the Linked Hybrid, Beijing (2009) and the Vanke Center, Shenzhen (2009).[23] For

A. Steven Holl, Linked Hybrid, Beijing-Diagram of Beijing Section-phases of growth of system ©Steven Holl Architects
B. Steven Holl, Linked Hybrid, Beijing—Diagram of circulation loops—axonometric (three public circulation loops: at ground level, on top of the lower buildings, and the loop of skybridges) ©Steven Holl Architects
C. Steven Holl, Linked Hybrid, Beijing, China, 2008 Photo ©Iwan Baan

A

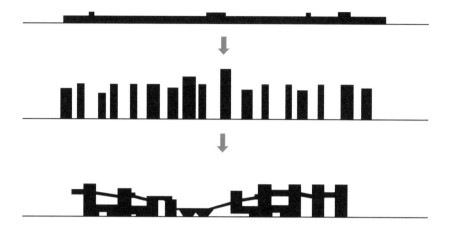

B

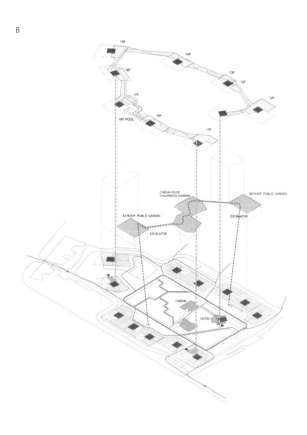

C

133

A.   Steven Holl, Vanke Center,
Shenzhen, China, 2006–2009,
Courtesy Steven Holl Architects
B.   Steven Holl, Vanke Center,
Shenzhen, China, 2006–2009,
Courtesy Steven Holl Architects
Photo courtesy the authors
24.   Kenneth Frampton, "The Mega-
form and the Helix," in Steven Holl,
Urbanisms: Working with Doubt (New
York: Princeton Architectural Press,
2009), 272–274.

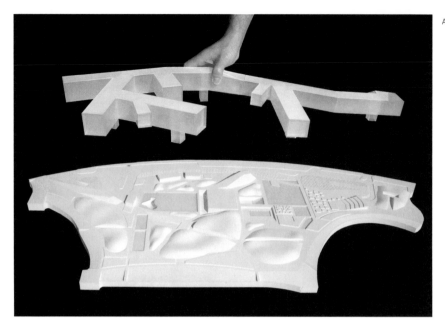

A

B

Frampton, "megaform" is also informed by a second tendency in Holl's work, which had been present since the late 1980s: the concept of "intertwining." This use of interwoven circulation strategies is often inspired by infinite forms like the double helix that expand the possible points of intersection and exchange in social space.[24] The idea of the "lyrical path" had previously appeared in Le Corbusier's post-Moscow work where, in a similar way, he identified moments of social catalysis in which movement, diverse programs, and open space intersect.

Holl also appropriated the Soviet idea of the social condenser, renaming it initially the "social bracket." According to an early press release on the Linked Hybrid project, the social bracket is a network of "double height and triple height social spaces—as an urban interface." Shown in early sketches as

134

25. Holl, *Urbanisms*, 137–138.
26. Ibid., 169.
27. Henri Lefebvre, *The Production of Space* (Oxford: Blackwell Publishing, 1992), 59.

a series of elevated loops of circulation, the loop on the ground level interconnects with exterior civic spaces and an interior garden level that is open to the public and includes schools, a cinema, restaurants, and recreational space. On the higher levels there are bridging and ramping elements called "social condensers"[25] that connect cafes, exterior gardens, and fitness centers with a hotel and residential amenities. The looped circulation enables continuous patterns of movement through a series of differentiated landscape "atmospheres" defining a series of age-specific recreational mounds designed for play, speed, socialization, relaxation, and meditation. Holl also speculates on the possible expansion of the project on an urban scale in a series of sectional drawings that show the evolution of Beijing from a low-density city to a city of towers to a multilevel city of linked hybrid urbanism. The sections demonstrate how breaks in the three-dimensional lattice system allow for connections to the ground plane and across various levels.

Holl's Vanke Center revisits El Lissitzky and Mart Stam's horizontal skyscraper concept as an extended urban form. Although physically bounded, Vanke Center creates continuous interior urban space on multiple levels. The hybridized mix of building programs blends together public and private functions while maintaining visual connections to the surrounding mountains and sea. The horizontal forms layer offices, a conference center, a hotel, and residential spaces. Large community rooms are raised above the ground plane and located at the points of intersection between vertical and horizontal circulation, while the space below is left open and unbounded as a public park connecting to the surrounding urban context. For Holl, the underside of the building is the "sixth-elevation" for the public open space.[26]

Both of these projects create innovative forms that extend the social project of the city, combining closed and open systems with vertical connections to allow for a range of atmospheres and spatial interactions interweaving both public and private realms. While experientially choreographed, the aesthetic of Holl's work and its ad hoc qualities of massing and composition allow for adaptability in an expanded field of development. He uses the concepts of hybridization, grafting, intertwining, and other metaphors to generate new urban morphologies as architecture, landscape, and infrastructure are composed as a totality. The model suggests a possible solution to the dilemma of planning versus negotiation and inevitable exigencies of time-dependent urban growth. As Frampton points out, in terms of the coherent conceptualization of urban form, the scale of each development matters. On the other hand, so does the model of programming and spatial composition. It could be argued that the ability for urban development to carry on coherently in the hands of others is just as important. Holl's hybridized work offers a possible model for its theorization.

Henri LeFebvre criticized the Constructivists for failing to design new forms of space to support the relations they desired in society, instead choosing to apply modernist forms and symbols of social connectivity to traditional models of spatial organization. The functionalist city of the Stalinists and of modernism failed by focusing only on its needs through austerity and not on the other aspects of human socio-spatial life, including pleasure. The capitalist city failed by interiorizing the city and filling it with products or spectacle, substituting consumption for experience. In Lefebvre's words: "Change life! Change society! These ideas completely lose their meaning without producing an appropriate space. A lesson to be learned from Soviet Constructivists from the 1920s and 1930s, and of their failure, is that new social relations demand a new space, and vice-versa."[27] While there is much truth in this criticism, it becomes more complex as you evaluate the Constructivist project of the city in terms of its impact over time. The product of its experimentation can be seen as the catalyst for a continuing social project carried forward by other projects in other locations and

28. Fourier's project was differentiated from the modernist socialist project based on its acceptance of human behavior and creating an urbanism that relied on pleasure and social connections, something virtually programmed out of the functionalist city of the modern movement. See Manfredo Tafuri, *The Sphere and the Labyrinth: Avant-Gardes and Architecture from Piranesi to the 1970s* (Cambridge: MIT Press, 1987), 152; and Bernardo Secchi.
29. Roland Barthes, *Sade/Fourier/Loyola* (Baltimore: Johns Hopkins University Press, 1976), 112
30. Simon Sadler, *The Situationist City* (Cambridge: MIT Press, 1999), 118.
31. Eleonore Kaufman and Elizabeth Lebas, introduction, in *Henri Lefebvre: Writings On Cities* (Oxford: Blackwell Publishing, 1996), 16–20.

experimented on by a diverse set of authors over time who are continually proposing new forms of "association."

Walter Benjamin's interpretation of Fourier's Phalanstère as a machine for the production of social pleasures is an important example of an interiorized urbanism that complements the capitalist commodity culture he observed in the arcades of Paris. But unlike the arcades and their informal and fragmentary distribution in Paris, Fourier's street-galleries created an urban whole grounded in the social life of the interior and independent of the city—a city within the city. In this way both the Phalanstère and arcades prefigured the future interiorized urbanisms facilitated by global capital at the turn of the twentieth century—the shopping malls, the megastructural projects in Asia, all driven by economic interests and largely absent of an intentional social project.[28]

A Retreat within Which One Moves

> Architecture and urbanism reciprocally withdraw in favor of an overall science of human space, the primary characteristic of which is no longer protection, but movement: the phalanstery is a retreat within which one moves. The greatest concern of this organization is communication.
>
> — Roland Barthes, *Sade-Fourier-Loyola*, 1971

In this description of Fourier's urbanism, Roland Barthes aphoristically describes a key aspect of the Phalanstère and, by extension, the project of the multilevel city. The paradox of "a retreat within which one moves" characterizes the nature of urban space as a fundamentally human sociocultural construct that becomes reified in architecture and urban form.[29] In the 1960s, parallel to the emergence of the megastructure and its continuous interior space as an alternative urban form, there was also a resurgence of the ideas of Charles Fourier. His theory of association became "patterns of association" for Team 10, and his concept of "unitary architecture" became the "unitary urbanism" of the Situationists and Henri Lefebvre.[30]

Lefebvre's lifelong intellectual project on the social implications of space in the city was concerned with the dialectic of modernity and everyday life.[31] Underlying this work was a critique of the functionalism of early CIAM and its impact on the city through an oversimplification and compartmentalization of the urban program. Instead, Lefebvre proposed a "unitary urbanism" that experientially mixed and layered the social and the functional aspects of urban life through Fourier's concept of association.

It is from Fourier that Lefebvre would derive his main concept of the "production of space." Underlying the Phalanstère and the *rue galeries* was the central idea that creating new social relations would require the production of new forms of urban space. Offering an alternative to the austerity model in other socialist projects, the communitarian society envisioned by Fourier was based on pleasure and social connections, something virtually programmed out of the functionalist city in the modern movement. Lefebvre was able to look past the limited forms of the Phalanstère, including those designed by the followers of Fourier, and focus instead on the underlying socio-spatial thinking of the Fourierist city.

The Phalanstère presaged the future interiorized urbanisms of global capital in the manifestations of shopping malls, event centers, and the interiorized skyway cities of North America, which are now proliferating worldwide. It is one of the interesting aspects of Fourier's socialist project, which did find inspiration in the galleries and commerce of the Palais-Royal, that capital would be the principal engine of these transformations of urban space in the twenty-first century.

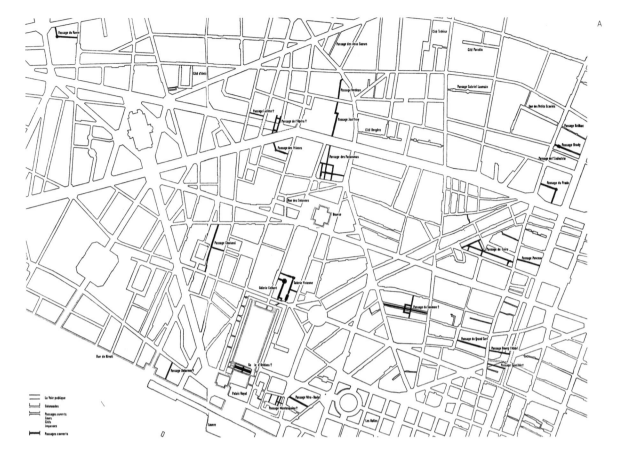

A. Map of the Arcade, Paris,
reprinted courtesy MIT Press from
Johann Friedrich Geist, *Arcades: The
History of a Building Type*, 1983
B. Passage Choiseul, Paris, Cour-
tesy Clicsouris/Wikimedia Commons

137

32.   Jonathan Beecher, *Charles Fourier* (Oakland, California: University of California Press, 1990), 59.
33.   Frampton, *Megaform as Urban Landscape*, 8.
34.   Lukasz Stanek, "Collective Luxury: Architecture and Populism in Charles Fourier," in *Hunch 14: Publicity* (Rotterdam: NAI Publishers/Berlage Institute, 2010), 134–136.
35.   Anthony Vidler, *The Scenes of the Street and Other Essays* (New York: Monacelli Press, 2011), 45–48.
36.   Lukasz Stanek, *Henri Lefebvre on Space: Architecture, Urban Research, and the Production of Theory* (Minneapolis: University of Minnesota Press, 2011), 170.

Fourier first conceived of the ideas of unitary architecture and association in 1822 based on an earlier visit to the commercial arcades of the Palais-Royal, as a way to create a more rational and aesthetic form of social organization.[32] The arcades (Galleries de Bois and D'Orléans) at the Palais-Royal created a complex intermixing of diverse people and activities. Functioning both as a "free-port"and a center of culture and commerce, it was a zone where traditional social boundaries could be ignored.[33] The arcades were a social center as well as a forum for political and philosophical debates. They also provided a space for comingling where the sensory, aesthetic, intellectual, and amorous could be found in an egalitarian setting—an essential characteristic of a liberal society.

Fourier believed that society could be fundamentally reformed through social planning and architecture. In the gallery arcades of Paris, he discovered a concept of "social condensation," the idea that sociopetal architectural spaces would result in new social forms. By replacing the commercial interiors of the arcades with comparable spaces fostering communication and play, human behavior could be changed. What Lefebvre sees as critical in Fourier's project, and why these architectural concepts have been so valuable to the social project of the city, can be found in the adaptability of their forms as "transitional objects."

As such, each form of the Phalanstère represented a stage in its development relative to its use at that particular point in history.[34] This serialism in the concepts of the Phalanstère and the *rue corridor* also allows the model to adapt to different scales and contexts. Fourier's interconnected and ringed megastructure, the Ideal City, was conceived in 1820 and published in 1842 as another in this series of communal interiors organized by elevated pedestrian spaces. Each section of housing in the Ideal City would contain meeting rooms and other communal spaces connected by galleries to the housing components, creating a network of spaces for interaction. By connecting the city both horizontally and vertically, interaction created through the mixing of industry, commerce, and pleasure would coalesce in the arcades. It was, as Benjamin described it, a "city of arcades."[35]

Fourier's concept of collective luxury also fascinated Lefebvre. Although the Phalanstère proposed leisure as a key aspect of urban life, it was also a prescient vision of the consumer-driven culture that would emerge more than a century later.[36] Lucasz Stanek describes the situation in the 1950s as both utopic and dystopian, which positions Lefebvre's ideas firmly within his own decade. In this way, the Fourierist project underlies multilevel speculations, such as La Ville Spatiale by Yona Friedman and Constant's *New Babylon*. It also aligns with the critical provocations of Archizoom's No-Stop City (1969) or Exodus, or the Voluntary Prisoners of Architecture (1972) by Rem Koolhaas and Elia Zenghelis.

The Ever-Expanding Urban Interior

In the first volume of his *Spheres* trilogy, philosopher and cultural theorist Peter Sloterdijk develops the concept of the sphere as a mediating condition necessary to transcend the interior/exterior dichotomy. Tracing the concept through five hundred years of Western globalization, his analysis of socio-spatial relationships is of particular relevance to a project of theorizing the emerging urban interior.

In Benjamin's analysis of the Paris arcades and the social-psychology of capitalism, the exterior is neutralized as all of the processes of capitalist production are externalized to be replaced and represented as commodities on the interior. As Benjamin observed, the emergence of consumer culture in the nineteenth century rendered direct engagement unnecessary, allowing the consumer to withdraw from the world while simultaneously consuming it.

A   Yona Friedman, La Ville Spatiale, Paris, 1960 ©2016 Artists Rights Society (ARS), New York/ADAGP, Paris

B   Yona Friedman, Vertical Clusters, After Minneapolis, 1997 ©2016 Artists Rights Society (ARS), New York ADAGP, Paris

37.   In writing about Chernechevsky's interiorized vision via Dostoevsky's critique, Sloterdijk says, "The visionaries of the nineteenth century (socialist utopians), like the communists of the twentieth, already understood that after the expiry of combatant history, social life could only take place in an expanded interior, a domestically organized and artificially climatized interior space ... a protected shell." Sloterdijk relies on Dostoevesky's Tsarist narrative of the Crystal Palace in *Notes from Underground*, a critique of revolutionary Ceryshevsky's novel aggrandizing the social utopians' Phalanstère through the Crystal Palace. See Peter Sloterdijk, *In the World Interior of Capital* (Cambridge: Polity Press, 2013), 169–176.

B

Sloterdijk offers an alternative analysis in the spectacle of the Crystal Palace (1851), a kind of grand arcade and a social condenser for the imperialistic culture of Victorian England. For Sloterdijk, the Crystal Palace was the quintessential symbol of global capitalism in which the luxuries and curiosities gathered from remote and exotic places were displayed in an immense interiorized social setting. It was a safe substitute for the world at large, made possible through the immunological technologies of the industrial age.[37] As globalization progressed, the arcades and leisure palaces of capitalism began to absorb, symbolically, more and more of the exterior world replacing it with an ever-increasing interiority.

In spaces where capitalism tends to substitute commodities and other cultural assimilations for the exterior world, Sloterdijk sees the morphologies of communal space continually reproducing and evolving, and with population density, increasing in size. The social and physical properties of the interior, not to mention the psychological, are always dependent on the phenomenological concept of the exterior. These relationships are extremely complex. The contemporary shopping mall and its predecessor, the arcades, are interiorized hybrids of the spatial types of the salon and market. The need to

A   Future Systems Architects,
Selfridges, Birmingham, UK
Photo: Wojtek Gurak
B   Foreign Office Architects, John
Lewis Store, Leicester, UK, Courtesy
Peter Jeffree Photography
38. Peter Sloterdijk, "Spheres
Theory: Talking to Myself About the
Poetics of Space," in *Harvard Design
Magazine* (Spring/Summer 2009): 30.

psychologically immunize the interior of capitalism was achieved by creating boundaries to control content and selectively admit others, thereby transforming "immunization" from a biological concept into a phenomenological one.[38] The aggregation of individualized private zones or spheres paradoxically creates a condition of "connected alienation," as Thom Mayne suggests, or a "foam"—an accretion of Sloterdijk's bubbles that act as a continuum of autonomous spaces.

To possibly extend Sloterdijk's metaphor of the immunological sphere, one can examine forms of urban space that are inflected either inward or outward, reinforcing what may be called the communitarian and the cosmopolitan tendencies of urban space. The history of the multilevel city is replete with examples of communitarian projects aimed at reinforcing and, in Sloterdijk's terms, immunizing social space. A corollary to the communitarian tendency may be found in the concept of cosmopolitanism, or the paradoxical necessity for urban forms to open toward and engage an exterior. Sloterdijk's immunological sphere can be seen as the ubiquitous mediator between the two complementary, but ever shifting, characteristics of urban space. In this way, the once oppositional concepts of inside/outside and object/space that are fundamental to our understanding of architecture and the city are forever bound together.

With the urbanization of conflict, architecture has become the pathology of this era.... The surface of the Earth—now increasingly called upon to perform as evidence/witness in political negotiations, international tribunals, and fact-finding missions—has a certain thickness, but it could not be considered a volume. It is not an isolated, distinct, stand-alone object, nor did it ever "replace" the subject; rather, it is a thick fabric of complex relations, associations, and chains of actions between people, environments, and artifices. It inevitably overflows any map that tries to frame it, because there are always more connections to be made.

In this context, architecture is both sensor and agent. Sensor, in what way? We think of architecture as a static thing, but physical structures and built environments are elastic and responsive. Architecture, I once proposed, is "political plastic"—social forces slowing into form.

— Eyal Weizman, "Forensic Architecture: Notes from Fields and Forums," 2015

Why enclave? What types of incentivized urbanism will actually benefit from physically segregated infrastructure—from being separate and even distant from the dense and dynamic central spaces of existing cities? Given that the zone is now generating its own urban programs—aspiring to be a city—what economic and technical benefits can result from constructing what is in effect a double or shadow of the city?

— Keller Easterling, "Zone: The Spatial Softwares of Extrastatecraft," 2014

6. SECTIONAL DEMOGRAPHICS

6. SECTIONAL DEMOGRAPHICS

1.   Frei Otto, *Occupying and Connecting: Thoughts on Territories and Spheres of Influence with Particular Reference to Human Settlement* (Stuttgart: Edition Axel Menges, 2011), 10–14, 50–56, 65.
2.   Peter Sloterdijk, "Foam City," in *LOG 9* (Winter/Spring 2007): 63–76.
3.   Ibid., 63–76.
4.   David Harvey, *Paris: Capital of Modernity* (London: Routledge, 2003), 80–85, 304–308.

Occupying and Connecting

The use of the urban section for the purposes of articulating and regulating human relationships is not new. The evolution of fortified towns and cities, which themselves divide the urban "interior" from the surrounding "exterior" countryside, also encompasses the development of numerous sectional strategies for retreat, surveillance, self-defense, and social articulation. Two principal tendencies can be found in all forms of human settlement, operating simultaneously at different scales relative to the needs and strictures of the communities they define.

Although of enormous complexity in the context of an entire modern city, these tendencies of spatial definition can be described conceptually in the simple dualism of *occupying* and *connecting*, as articulated by Frei Otto in his book of the same title.[1] Otto's concept of spatial development places points of occupation—whether at the scale of the individual, the settlement, or the territory—in an elastic field of synchronous relationships called connections. It could also be said that these two opposed but interdependent characteristics of human settlements have corollaries in sociopolitical concepts such as communitarianism and cosmopolitanism. While this may seem to reduce a complex and highly contested set of sociological concepts to an overly simplistic dichotomy, the pairing may provide a useful way to understand how these two complementary tendencies inform multilevel urbanisms and their spatial dynamics.

For our purposes, the terms communitarian and cosmopolitan simply represent two tendencies of social spatial dynamics that include, respectively, the human need to circumscribe and define their various social forms (occupying) and the complementary need to openly engage the surrounding context to create larger fields of action (connecting). These two distinct ideas of social space operate at many different scales simultaneously and remain in constant flux, even relative to their more permanent reifications in architecture and urban form.

Peter Sloterdijk lays out his spatio-social theory of bubbles, globes, and foam, developing a comprehensive model of the many forms of human relationships defined in spatial terms. In his third book, the concept of "foams" is a metaphor for what he calls the "episodic clusters and enduring symbioses" of social forms, starting with the individual as "always co-isolated islands that are momentarily, or chronically, connected to a network of adjacent islands constituting mid-sized or larger structures."[2] The value of Sloterdijk's metaphor lies in its capacity to model conceptually the complex spatio-temporal relationship of social forms in a way that does not result in reductive concepts, simplistic dichotomies, or fetishizing geometries.

In "Foam City," Sloterdijk details the urgent search for spaces of assembly and expression to house the new sociopolitical forms of the French Revolution. His survey of the revolutionary reoccupation of Versailles Palace in 1789 was followed by the interior and exterior spaces of the aristocracy in Paris. The adaptability of social form to physical circumstances and the alternative malleability of physical forms of urbanity to meet new social demands is demonstrated in the "refunctioning" of the spaces of the monarchy and the appropriation of classical forms of architecture to represent the new French Republic.[3]

The interplay of socio-spatial forms and the plasticity of the urban section is best demonstrated in the repeated physical reconfiguration of Paris throughout the nineteenth century. The opening of the city to capital development and international commerce with the concomitant police and military enforcement of *civility* exemplifies the cosmopolitan tendencies of modernization inherent in Baron von Haussmann's plan for Paris. However, the desire to redesign the city to facilitate commerce, improve hygiene, and provide security and control was inevitably going to collide with the territorial claims of the lower classes being displaced to make room for this transformation.[4]

5. Howard Eiland and Michael W. Jennings, eds., *Walter Benjamin: Selected Writings, Volume 4: 1938–1940* (Cambridge: Harvard University Press, 2003), 6.

6. Joseph Rykwert, "The Street: The Use of Its History," in *On Streets* (Cambridge: MIT Press, 1986), 15–23.

7. Aldo Rossi and Peter Eisenman, *Architecture of the City* (Cambridge: MIT Press, 1982), 156–157.

In the street battles that recurred throughout the century, the continuity of the street-datum would be broken though the erection of barricades. In 1871, the three-dimensional modification of the urban fabric to enclose and protect the Paris Commune from the growing cosmopolitan city was, once again, the most readily available strategy to contest Haussmann's alterations, population displacement, and a host of associated grievances. When Walter Benjamin recalled Baudelaire's description of the barricades of the Commune as "magic cobblestones which rise up to form fortresses," the cobblestones are magic "because Baudelaire's poem says nothing about the hands that set them in motion."[5] By removing overt reference to the agency of the Communards, the plasticity of three-dimensional urban space is foregrounded and the social form of the Commune is made manifest through its absence. As the Versailles troops pushed the rebels back in a series of battles, it seemed that the Commune was retreating into an ever-shrinking walled city as if to finally recover its lost original fortifications. The elastic spatiality evident in this relationship between the communal space of retreat and resistance and the cosmopolitan space of projection and absorption is graphically represented in the battle for Paris.

Partitioning and Compacting

The opportunistic use of the urban section for strategic advantage is also associated with concentrations of wealth and power. As cities grew in density, topographical spatial characteristics described as vantage, prospect, and promontory also took on a symbolic role in class status. In architectural terms such as the *piano nobile* or the belvedere, the codification of social status and privilege through the sectional logic of the city becomes evident. In the Renaissance the sectional expression of social class would reach its apotheosis in the first comprehensive proposal for a multilevel city designed by Leonardo da Vinci. After the plague of 1484 in Milan, he proposed a *strada nobile* for his Ideal City (*Citta, Codex B*, 1490), which provided a hygienic upper-level circulation zone for aristocrats and clergy overlooking a city inhabited by tradesmen and workers. Da Vinci's city was conceived holistically from the point of view of the aristocracy. It was compact, sectionally partitioned, and organized with elevated streets and palazzi above a utilitarian ground level with service buildings, roads, sewers, and canals.

In eighteenth-century London, the multilevel urban design concepts of da Vinci would gain new currency in the Adelphi project designed and built by architect/developer Robert Adam and his brothers in 1772. The mixed-use complex included 24 terrace houses and offices built on elevated streets above vaulted warehouses and service streets that connected to the wharves. Following da Vinci's Ideal City, the Adelphi separated the office and residential level of the city from the spaces of river-based commerce below.[6] The result was the overlaying and compaction of the social and economic program of the capitalist city. The sectional partitioning thus reconciled the class-based spaces of labor with the aestheticized spaces of management, residence, and leisure while providing picturesque views of the River Thames for the enjoyment of the gentry. From the point of view of business interests, the Adelphi offered an ideal form of class-based social organization by simultaneously enabling segregation and proximity in a compact urban development.[7]

Proximal Segregation

A more traditional example better illustrates the complex issues of what could be termed "proximal segregation" in multilevel cities. Ghadames, Libya, an ancient Berber city in the Sahara Desert, was built around an oasis that had been settled since the fourth century BC. Its streets and residential structures

– Leonarda da Vinci, Manuscript B, Pages from a notebook with the plan for a four-level structure (Fol 36R) with various galleries and arcades, 1485–1488 Photo: R. G. Ojeda, Courtesy Bibliotheque de l'Institut de France ©RMN-Grand Palais/Art Resource, NY

– Leonardo da Vinci, *Città Ideale*, 1487–1490, Model, 1955–1956, Courtesy Museo Nazionale della Scienza e della Tecnologia Leonardo da Vinci

8.   Intisar Azzuz, "Contemporary Libyan Architecture: Possibilities vs. Realities," in ArchNet (MIT), 2000, accessed September 10, 2015, http://archnet.org/system/publications/contents/2605/original/DPC0038.pdf?1384765954.

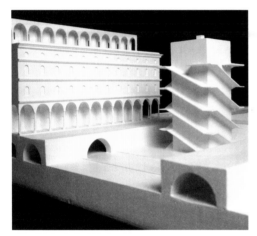

and its compact urban fabric have been occupied for centuries by seven clans that built a key example of environmentally responsive vernacular desert architecture.

While very little historical information of the city exists, it appears that the bi-level pedestrian paths in Ghadames evolved after the influx of Arabs in the seventh century and the conversion of the local community to Islam. The resulting gender-segregated multilevel city provided for the occupation of the shaded lower-level streets and storage areas by men and the rooftops by women; families inhabited the mid-level spaces. Away from public interaction with men on the streets, women used the interconnected rooftops for cooking and socializing, creating a separate and private domain.[8] The potential spatial conflict resulting from the introduction of a gender-based social immiscibility into a highly compressed urban environment was remediated by using strategies of three-dimensional urbanism. The physical structure of Ghadames

144

A   Robert Adam, Adelphi Project,
1768–1772, London
B   The ancient city of Ghadames
was abandoned in 1982 when
modern housing was offered to its
inhabitants. The old city is navigated
by a network of covered adobe
pathways and corridors, and there
are also pathways that connect most
of the rooftop sleeping areas of the
homes. ©George Steinmetz
9.   Stefano Bianco, *Urban Form in
the Arab World*, (London: Thames &
Hudson, 2000).

A

B

simultaneously segregates and connects based on the social mores of the community.

Multilevel pedestrian systems reoccur in the service of diverse social, cultural, and political agendas because they can resolve three-dimensionally the apparent contradictions of two-dimensional plans and their simple territorial definitions. They are also an expression of power precisely in terms of how they control movement and afford connections. Significantly, these systems allow for incremental growth and can be negotiated and renegotiated over time, depending on circumstances.

Urbanists Ismail Serageldin and Stefano Bianca have written about bridges and passageways in Arabic cities, which as an outcome of Sharia law create specific urban morphologies.[9] Serageldin identifies a unique differentiation present—the negotiation between individuals resolving small-scale elements and spaces and the large-scale negotiations between institutions that generate urban space. Islamic law also provides for the negotiation of air

A   Moshe Safdie, Mamilla Masterplan, Mamilla Center pedestrian bridges, *Jerusalem*, 2009 ©Tim Hursley

B   Moshe Safdie, Modi'in New Town, 1989 Photo: Miron Cohen

10.   Ismail Serageldin, "Infrastructure, Technology and the Pattern of Urban Settlement," in *Development and Urban Metamorphosis 1*, Ahmet Evin, ed., Yemen at the Cross-Roads, 27–30. Singapore: Concept Media/ Aga Khan Award for Architecture, 1983.

11.   Jon Calame and Esther Charlesworth, *Divided Cities* (Philadelphia: University of Pennsylvania Press, 2009), 92–95.

rights for private developments as well as private encroachments on the public domain and offers unique solutions for corners and subplots.[10] The model of bi-level gender separation was followed in other Islamic cities in East Africa where upper-level bridges called *wikios* were used to create private and controlled zones for women. Other Islamic cities in the Middle East have used similar sectional devices, including ancient cities like Shibam in Yemen and contemporary cities like Riyadh, Saudi Arabia's main financial center.

The Contested Three-Dimensional Space of Jerusalem

While there are numerous examples of multilevel urban forms driven by cultural and economic forces, the role of three-dimensional urbanisms in contested political contexts has barely begun to emerge. Rather than reviewing the use of new spatial forms in social and political terms, much of the discussion of colonialist architectural and urban form has principally addressed the use of modernism to aesthetically overwrite local cultural histories. In the 1960s, proposals for the multilevel city were central to an ongoing debate in the territorially contested city of Jerusalem. International influences through CIAM and Team 10 shaped proposals for new multilevel typologies as a replacement for more socially integrated, historic accretional urban forms.

After the 1949 armistice between Israel and Jordan, the historically mixed Jewish-Arab commercial district of Mamilla was divided from the Jordanian territories of East Jerusalem and the Old City. As a result of this partition, called the Green Line, Mamilla became a military zone separating the two halves of the city, creating a largely vacant landscape. Immediately following the British Mandate period, proponents of early CIAM modernism advocated new multilevel urban schemes as a strategy for unifying the divided city. The modern planning techniques were ostensibly neutral and capable of addressing the underlying sociopolitical problems of the city.

In 1965, the Israeli government initiated the first experiment using Mamilla as a development site by holding a design competition to reconstruct the district. The successful entry was a proposal by Michael Kuhn for a multilevel system that separated pedestrians and vehicular circulation in a two-level city. The proposal, developed unilaterally, outlined a plan for modernization that would presumably unify Jerusalem by transcending the embedded histories of Israeli and Arabic occupation.[11]

A

B

12. Alona Nitzan-Shiftan, "Frontier Jerusalem: The Holy Land as a Testing Ground for Urban Design," *Frankel Institute Annual*, Jean and Samuel Frankel Center for Judaic Studies, University of Michigan (2008): 46–49.

13. Eyal Weizman, *Hollow Land: Israel's Architecture of Occupation* (London: Verso Books, 2007), 37, 46, 182.

14. Moshe Safdie, "Reviewed Work: The New Jerusalem: Planning and Politics by Arthur Kutcher," in *Journal of the Society of Architectural Historians* 36, no. 2 (May 1977): 130–133.

15. Nitzan-Shiftan, "Frontier Jerusalem," 46–49.

16. The project was unable to be completed earlier because of ongoing political controversy over the site that was located along the armistice line between Israeli- and Jordanian-controlled sectors of Jerusalem. The site was historically a mixed Arab and Jewish neighborhood located near the area of the Old City. Many residents were relocated and the project was redesigned over concerns about historic preservation.

17. Moshe Safdie, *The Harvard Jerusalem Studio: Urban Designs for the Holy City* (Cambridge, MIT Press, 1987), 148–157.

18. "Architect Battles for New Jerusalem," *Financial Times*, August 13, 2007.

The scheme for the Mamilla district reflected a larger ambition for Jerusalem that would connect it economically to the West and to a larger cosmopolitan agenda. The project proposed a complete tabula rasa, erasing the historic city and replacing it with the image of an early CIAM-like modernist city with a continuously elevated podium contiguous with West Jerusalem. Clusters of cubic building elements on a new elevated pedestrian plane would overwrite the contested history at the street level and encourage international investment. The scheme was derided because of its insensitivity to the city's historic fabric, its layered cultural history, and the conflicts around the Green Line, and the proposal was set aside.

In 1969, after Israel claimed East Jerusalem from Jordan in the Six-Day War, Mayor Teddy Kollek revisited the question of a new urban form for Jerusalem. He created a department of planning staffed by a group of young architects recently educated at architectural schools in England and the United States—primarily the Architectural Association (AA), Harvard, and MIT. This group was tasked once again with creating a design for an international city that would attract investment and unify the heterogeneous population of Jerusalem by using modern architectural forms. The department quickly designed another elevated city, this time influenced by the members of Team 10 who had been the teachers and mentors of the planning department's new staff. Architect Yosef Kolodny cited their influences as Candilis-Josic-Woods, the Smithsons, Aldo van Eyck, Kenzo Tange, Theo Crosby, and Jaap Bakema, who were all advocates of a social and cosmopolitan multi-level form of the modern city.[12] The architects who led the new department proposed urban designs referencing the more organic geometric patterns of historic city forms similar to the elevated schemes of the Smithsons. Like earlier CIAM-influenced designs, towers and elevated pedestrian systems would override the ground plane.

At the culmination of this work, Mayor Kollek formed an urban think tank called the Jerusalem Committee. The international team of leading architects was asked to provide advice on the new strategy for the redevelopment of East Jerusalem. Kollek and the municipal architects expected a positive response, as many of the participants (Louis Kahn, R. Buckminster Fuller, Moshe Safdie, and Denys Lasdun) had advocated modernist forms and elevated pedestrian systems in their own work.[13] But the 1968 scheme proposed by city planners was strongly rejected by the committee for its insensitivity to the historic context and its elevated systems.[14] Reacting to the implementation of institutional forms of modernism that were by then becoming ubiquitous in North America, the committee described the municipality's schemes as choosing "problem-solving" over "aspiration."[15]

In 1972, Safdie was selected to design for the district a concept that would be completed after a twenty-five-year pause.[16] His viewpoint was predicated on a belief in the sociability of architecture and urban design. Having refused to build in the settlement areas and lamenting the construction of the wall separating the Palestinian neighborhoods from Jerusalem, he created a bi-level design for Mamilla that applied a more complex understanding of Jerusalem's social and physical terrain in order to foster physical and visual connectivity on all levels.[17]

Safdie's later work while head of the urban design program at Harvard under Josep Lluís Sert included the Jerusalem Studio (1980–1984), a comprehensive analysis of the complex three-dimensional physical and social characteristics of the city. While criticized for its postmodern application of pseudo-historic forms, the work explored sectional shifts in topography and architecture to bridge communities.[18] Linked overhead walkways and rooftops emerging from the hillside vertically connected public areas overlooking social mixing spaces below. Sarah Williams Goldhagen reviewed his Mamilla scheme favorably for its interweaving of infrastructure, landscape, and building,

A.   Michael Kuhn, Winning entry, East Jerusalem competition, 1964, from " 'East Jerusalem,' a symposium with Michael Kuhn, Dan Etan, and Ram Karmi," *Ha'aretz*, September 8, 1967

B.   Jerusalem Municipality Planners, Jerusalem Axonometric Masterplan, 1968, from Arthur Kutcher, *The New Jerusalem*, 1973

19.   Sarah Williams Goldhagen, "Moshe Safdie," in *Design Observer* (January 11, 2010), accessed November 10, 2015, http://designobserver.com/feature/moshe-safdie/12437/.

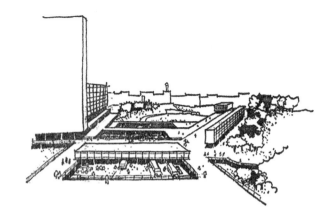

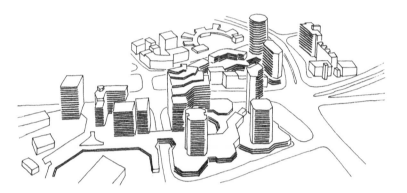

describing it in social terms as a "polynodal, multilevel promenade."[19] While this project is perceived as having an open engagement with its context, many of Safdie's later urban proposals, while socially oriented, create more exclusive and less permeable communal enclaves.

Social Immiscibility

In many cities, elevated walkways and flyover bridges are used to create divided private realms. Israeli architect Eyal Weizman takes a more critical position on their use in the contested city of Jerusalem as part of a complex system of political control in the Palestinian/Israeli conflict. He describes a new fragmented landscape in terms of the processes of its formation: "Cut apart and enclosed by its many barriers, gutted by underground tunnels, threaded together by overpasses and bombed from its militarized skies, the hollow land emerges as the physical embodiment of the many and varied attempts to partition it."

Weizman describes the territorial struggle as a complex "three-dimensional volumetric calculus" rather than a contest of borders simplistically limited to two dimensions. He describes how the 1973 Arab-Israeli war was initially fought with a linear and two-dimensional idea of fronts, with the border as a fixed line. This was then developed by political leaders to become more tactical, incremental, and three-dimensional—a dynamic matrix of events or the use of "deep space." Weizman describes the civilian evolution of settlements in a similar manner, where instead of the legibility of the shifting of borders,

– A reconstruction of the path of the wall around the Tunnel Road   Photo: Daniel Bauer, 2003 Illustration: Eyal Weizman, 2004, Courtesy Eyal Weizman
20.   Eyal Weizman, *Hollow Land*, 15.
21.   Jonathan Rokem, "Politics and Conflict in a Contested City: Urban Planning in Jerusalem under Israeli Rule," in Varias, *Le Bulletin du Centre de recherche français à Jérusalem* 23, January 20, 2013, accessed April 4, 2016, http://bcrfj.revues.org/6895.
22.   Ken Shulman, "Blessed Are the Mapmakers," in *The New Yorker*, April 29, 2013, accessed February 15, 2016, http://www.newyorker.com/news-desk/blessed-are-the-mapmakers.

settlements are more tactically located and the struggle to gain control and territory becomes more about strategies of connecting or disconnecting. In these cases, tunnels and bridges can be used as a geopolitical tool to either create a contiguous or disconnected network of space. As a result, enclaves can be unified by walkways or tunnels or disconnected and alienated by deep "ground barriers." Even archaeology as a thick layer of urban detritus or air-space with its militarized rules can be used to redefine territorial boundaries. The layers of history become politicized as a way of demarking territory in sections. Thus, a "politics of verticality"[20] re-territorializes subterranean or above-ground levels through policy and regulations in order to connect enclaves or strategically divide territories and communities into discontinuous layers.

Describing architecture as a "political plastic" community formed by power relationships and forces, Weizman articulates an evolutionary process in which the hidden social forces shape physical forms. First comes the architecture and then the event that the architecture creates, closely followed by the event that then destroys and reforms the next stage of the architecture. Weizman specifically describes the techniques that have evolved out of the desire to create segregation rather than shared civic space. He cites the example of the complex spirals of new flyovers at the Jerusalem Eastern Ring Road, where connections are no longer simple bridging elements but subdivided by a wall into two paths occupied by either Palestinians or Israelis—the intractable social immiscibilities reflected in the physical form of the infrastructure.[21]

Israeli architect Karen Lee Bar-Sinai, cofounder of SAYA/Design for Change, has developed the notion of "resolution planning" for contested territories, using complex three-dimensional strategies for peacemaking. Seeing the construction of barriers and noticing that design was only seen as an aesthetic and not a spatial activity, Bar-Sinai observed that these barriers could be designed to simultaneously separate and connect, offering a remediating solution as an interim step to better policy.[22]

The Commune and the Enclave

The ghettoization of both Israelis and Palestinians in Israel is often attributed to constructed separations. In a land where two different cultures and religions were once intertwined, the structure of the enclave and the commune, while creating strong centers, abandons the whole by default. Jerusalem's former deputy mayor, Meron Benvenisti, describes this new condition of the Palestinians and Israelis as two three-dimensional worlds, geographically interwoven but disconnected, a six-dimensional space. "Once you accept the premise of separation, you come up with ideas that to ordinary people seem insane, but here begin to seem logical. It is now no longer horizontal division, but vertical as well. Part Arab and part Israeli. And eventually, it will create its own reality."[23]

– *Chungking Express*, Hong Kong, 1994, Directed by Wong Kar-Wai (shown: Wong Faye), Courtesy Miramax Films/Photofest ©Miramax Films

23. Nicolai Ouroussoff, "Architects and Israel's Barrier: A Line in the Sand," *New York Times*, January 1, 2006, accessed January 15, 2015, www.Bloomberg.com.
24. Manuel Castells, *The Rise of the Network Society: The Information Age: Economy, Society, and Culture Volume I* (London: Wiley-Blackwell, 2008), 430–432.

The most complex and elaborate forms of multilevel public space are found in the Asian "economic miracle" cities of Hong Kong and Singapore. These metropolitan areas are also frequently criticized for the disappearance of traditional public space. Manuel Castells describes this phenomenon as less about the development of fixed urban form and more about a process defined principally by patterns of flows of capital and information.[24] While a network is optimally about maintaining connections, when it has a fixed physical form its definition as a network does not ensure that connections are permanently maintained or that barriers are not created. In this way a city like Hong Kong may be understood as a metabolic system reacting constantly to the circulation of capital, information, and people through the ongoing transformation of its physical forms.

The Appropriation of Private Space for Public Use

Hong Kong is frequently used as a case study in the renewed interest in the "right to the city" that began in the 1990s to address the exclusionary tendencies of globalization. Its system of elevated urban spaces has attracted the attention of architects and planners studying individual agency and the informal adaptation of semi-private urban spaces for public use. The creative reappropriation of multilevel space can be seen in recent political confrontations like the widespread occupation of elevated walkways by protestors and their informal occupation by the migrant Filipina domestic workers.

Since the mid-1980s, thousands of these women have gathered in the elevated urban spaces in the Central District on Sundays, changing its intended use from a center of finance and commerce from Monday through Saturday into a temporary zone called "Little Manila" on Sundays—a temporal occupation and reproduction of Filipino culture in the center of Hong Kong. The activities have expanded to include political and social action, including labor rallies and NGOs attracted to the area in support of the workers. The practice of occupying urban space is common in the Philippines, so the act is not consciously one of resistance or rebellion.[25] While the landowners and

A   Sunday appropriation of private elevated walkway space by Filipina domestic workers—Central, Hong Kong, 2010, Courtesy Annelotte Walsh
B   Umbrella Revolution—Occupy Central (bottom) and Mong Kok, Hong Kong, 2014, Courtesy Reuters/Carlos Barria
25.   A. Cuthbert and K. McKinnell, "Ambiguous Space, Ambiguous Rights: Corporate Power and Social Control in Hong Kong," *Cities* 14 (May 1997): 295–311.
26.   Lisa Law, "Defying Disappearance: Cosmopolitan Public Spaces in Hong Kong," in *Urban Studies* 39, no. 9 (August 2002): 1625–1645.

police have tried at times to shift the activity or limit the informal markets, it has become so popular and clearly beneficial that it continues unchecked.

Conversely, the sectional characteristics of the multilevel city were used strategically for police control and surveillance in the three-month occupation of the Central District during the Umbrella Revolution protests that ended in December 2014. These opportunistic occupations, when permitted, selectively act as an extension of or surrogate for the public-assembly function of the street.

From the earliest formation of the elevated system in Hong Kong, its public role was clearly ambiguous and largely controlled by the private sector. In 1972, concurrent with the first elevated extension of the system at the Jardine House, its Deed of Dedication stated clearly its very limited role as public space: "The company shall be entitled to exclude from the dedicated area any persons causing a nuisance or loitering or sleeping therein or hawking or carrying on any business or activity therein, except bona fide use thereof for the purposes of passage."[26]

Within the critique of the global elevated city, assumptions are made about what constitutes legitimate public space. This narrative implies that the familiar colonial forms of public space were created as broadly accessible civic realms or political arenas. Who in the past had access to, for instance, Hong Kong's cricket grounds and gardens that have now been displaced with elevated arcades and public plazas created by banks and shopping malls? Margaret Crawford describes the rigidity of these ideas about public and private space and the conflation of the issues of public space with democracy, citing the familiar narrative in which the "universal consumer" becomes a passive victim to the overwhelming forces of capitalism and its commercial seductions. She questions the ongoing lament of the loss of public space by thinkers such as Michael Sorkin, Jürgen Habermas, and Richard Sennett as

27.   Margaret Crawford, *Everyday Urbanism: Expanded* (New York: Monacelli Press, 2008), 24–29.
28.   Hannah Arendt, *The Human Condition* (Chicago: University of Chicago Press, 1958), 198–199.

focusing on a single, large-scale, and architecturally familiar form of public space (the agora, the town square, the piazza) and the confusion of these forms of monumental public space, which were already spaces of exclusion within a "totality of public space." She proposes recognizing "subaltern" urban spaces, including spaces like sidewalks and empty lots, that through their activation are restructured and redefined as public.[27]

Is the Interiorized Skyway System Public Space?

We use the term "sectional demographics" to describe the tendency for multi-level urban environments to reinforce social and economic divisions. While the reliability of the street as a "space of public appearance,"[28] may be contested in many grade-oriented pedestrian environments, its division into multiple levels only exacerbates problems of social fragmentation, segregation, and political expression. Given the propensity for three-dimensional urban space to stratify populations based on economic class, ethnicity, race, and other factors, it is not difficult to imagine an entire society permanently segregated by caste at various levels of the urban strata.

When the G8 Summit was held in 2000 near Calgary, the city closed down its "public" +15 system to outside users to prevent protests, particularly in the parts of the system connecting the Alberta petroleum industries. While police management of the protests in Calgary was similar to the way street-level protests are typically handled in North American cities, the ease with which the municipality closed down access to the system is indicative of a material difference between traditional streets and grade-separated public space and pedestrian networks. Although written into the system guidelines that the public has ownership and legal right of way in the +15 network, the same municipal guidelines also enable the system to be closed to the public in the interests of the security of private developments.

The degree of control, when and how the systems may be opened to the public, and when they may be closed varies greatly with each city. Within the systems themselves there is additional variability, often creating unpredictable circulation patterns depending on the time of day and local circumstances. Given its public-oriented status, the use of skyways necessitates rules of conduct for both the general public and those responsible for policing such systems. Who is given access or what behaviors are permissible within the system is often left to the discretion of business proprietors and their private security teams. Because the concept of public space in the grade-separated urban interior is difficult to define, it often falls to private entities to make these determinations, sometimes arbitrarily.

With the continued expansion of grade-separated pedestrian systems in North American cities, public and professional criticism began to build in the 1980s and 1990s. These critiques began with the rediscovery of the traditional street championed by critics like Jane Jacobs in the 1960s and the ensuing ideological challenge to modernist urban planning as a whole. Her critique centered, first and foremost, on the degradation of the street as the traditional tableau of urban life. Although Jacobs had supported Victor Gruen's proposal for Fort Worth with its partially elevated pedestrian bridge system, her criticism of the inadequacies of modernist planning and her nuanced sociological analysis of the traditional street, particularly in New York City, would ultimately be brought forward as a critique of the emerging grade-separated pedestrian networks.

In *The Death and Life of Great American Cities*, Jacobs makes a distinction between two characteristics of successful urban spaces that are, from her perspective, fundamental to their success. With the expression "eyes on the street," she established the importance of general security, which she described as freedom from "barbarism." The expectation that strangers

A   Urban Future Organization,
Cloud Citizen, Shenzhen Bay Super
City Competition, 2014, Courtesy
Urban Future Organization with Karin
Hedlund, Lukas Nordström, and
Pedram Seddighzadeh in collabora-
tion with CR-Design, Visualizations:
ExpediteTechnology Co.
B   Cloud Citizen, a continuous
metropolis with programmed public
space suspended in the air (view
from opposite side of Shenzhen Bay)

29. Jane Jacobs, *The Death and Life of Great American Cities* (New York: Vintage Books, 1992), 31–55.

30. Trevor Boddy, "Underground and Overhead: Building the Analogous City," in *Variations on a Theme Park*, Michael Sorkin, ed. (New York: Hill & Wang, 1992), 123–153. See also Jan Gehl and David Dillon on Dallas.

31. Albert Pope, *Ladders*, (New York: Princeton Architectural Press, 1997), 22–24, 61–65.

32. Peter Sloterdijk, *In the World Interior of Capital: Towards a Philosophical Theory of Globalization* (London: Polity Books, 2013), 174–175.

sharing the street would assist in moments of crisis amounts to a kind of *nudum pactum*, an expectation not codified in law but critical to the social institution of the street. For Jacobs, the other essential characteristic of successful cities is the ability to be lost in a crowd, the anonymity available to an individual when surrounded by strangers going about their business. In combination, these key aspects of life in the city offer the possibility of "being together" and "being alone" at the same time, something Jacobs believes makes life in the metropolis more desirable than towns and suburbs. This balance, which of course varies from individual to individual and from culture to culture, may be replaced in the multilevel city by spaces of either overbearing togetherness or complete isolation.[29]

For critics such as journalist Trevor Boddy, the elevated or subterranean pedestrian systems in North America appeared as an invasive and anti-urban phenomenon robbing the street of its role as the great equalizer where daily life is played out on a common plane. Describing such systems as analogous or surrogate cities, critics have also pointed to boarded-up street-level windows, ad hoc patterns of circulation, and the bastardization of historic buildings.[30] Where the new elevated passages and bridges penetrated and linked city blocks, virtually all of the conventions of the traditional city are violated— the dominance of the sidewalk for foot traffic, the facade as the principal expression of identity on the street, and the status of the street as the single most important plane of civic life.

In *Ladders*, Albert Pope theorizes the devolution of the American gridiron city into an anti-urbanism of cul-de-sacs. Using the dichotomy of centrifugal versus centripetal patterns of development, Pope seeks to expose the invisible but powerful generative mechanisms underlying contemporary urbanization and the dissolution of traditional civic space. In comparing the lattice-like logic of open networks exemplified by the gridiron plans of American cities with the dead-ended suburban clustered form, the "ladder" for Pope represents the abandonment of the open, centrifugal city in favor of the centripetal or cul-de-sac. This can be seen as a call for more cosmopolitan urban space as opposed to the communitarian space of the clustered forms that are becoming more and more about retreat and less about engagement.[31]

Typically, proposals for multilevel urbanism are either driven by a desire to extend outward and expand the urban field or by a desire to gather together and circumscribe—integrating systems versus segregating systems. Given the interdependence of these two tendencies, it would be a mistake to treat them as a dichotomy. Urban spaces and territories will always have characteristics of both. However, the propensity for one condition or the other to dominate specific proposals for the multilevel city can be found in both the intentions of its authors and their actual implementation. Cosmopolitan or communitarian ideals have been continually applied to numerous proposals for the multilevel city by social reformers and visionaries alike. A closer analysis reveals both the simultaneity and the irreducibility of these two presumably opposing concepts even under the most contested circumstances.

The communitarian conception of the three-dimensional city assumes that connections are made to facilitate the social, economic, or political intercourse within a limited community. This social pact of exclusivity is analogous to the interiors of Fourier's Phalanstère, where its one thousand six hundred twenty communitarians were to voluntarily coalesce within the domestic and depoliticized interiors of a quasi-urban space. The objective of the communitarian is the cohesion or solidarity of the circumscribed community. Interestingly, the same communitarian logic can be applied to contemporary gathering spaces such as shopping malls and sports stadiums, a point made by Peter Sloterdijk.[32] In the multilevel city, the emerging form of the pedestrian enclave suggests the same interconnected but isolated logic of communitarian space. In this way the self-regulating social behaviors of the urban interior

— London County Council, Greater London Council, Thamesmead,
circa 1965, Courtesy Fox Photos/
Hulton Archive/Getty Images

are not entirely inconsistent with the ways that the traditional street is managed. It is ultimately more dependent, day-to-day, on social consensus and
informal coercion between businesses, developers, and government authority
than on laws and regulations. This point is made numerous times by Jacobs in
her studies of public space and applies equally to the multilevel city, with an
important distinction between exterior and interior urban space. Urban interiors are associated innately with the authority of the building proprietors, their
customers, and their tenants. It is this ambiguity between public space and
private property that problematizes the pedestrian streets of the multilevel
city, particularly its interior spaces.

A cosmopolitan conception of the pedestrian city assumes that circulation is extended outward, opening the system fully to the population at large.
This ambition is consistent with the thinking of visionaries like Dr. Jules-Antoine
Moilin or Harvey Wiley Corbett or even Alison and Peter Smithson, who contributed proposals for systems with indefinite boundaries and the capacity to
be extended in many directions. The cosmopolitan view can also be identified with most of the extant elevated pedestrian systems, like those in North
America or Hong Kong, with the fundamental assumption being that the system will be extended and interconnected in as many ways as possible. Because
of this ambiguity, the complexities of social space in the three-dimensional
city threaten to become almost incomprehensible.

However, reducing urban spatial and territorial issues to simple dichotomies—such as public versus private, open versus closed, interior versus
exterior, connected versus disconnected—tends to obfuscate the real complexity of urban space. Where the relationships of individuals, social groups,

33. Ibid. 149–154,

neighborhoods, and corporate and bureaucratic organizations are in continuous renegotiation, their boundaries and connections are dependent on innumerable social, economic, and political variables, not to mention the resistance offered by the existing architecture and infrastructure.

To better understand this dynamic, it is useful to revisit Sloterdijk's metaphor of the immunological boundary that secures the interior from the exterior but maintains an active interest in mediating the intercourse between the two. This way of understanding the socio-spatial implications of human habitation transcends simplistic dichotomies of interior and exterior without entirely abandoning the significance of the interior and the exterior as concepts.[33] Using this analogy, the complexities of the multilevel city—its proliferating layers, interconnections, and ever-shifting social congregations—may begin to be theorized.

7. THE SYNTHESIZED CITY

We must invent and rebuild the Futurist city like an immense and tumultuous shipyard, agile, mobile and dynamic in every detail. The lifts must no longer be hidden away like tapeworms in the niches of stairwells [but] must scale the lengths of the façades like serpents of steel and glass. It must soar up on the brink of a tumultuous abyss: the street will no longer lie like a doormat at ground level, but will plunge many stories down into the earth, embracing the metropolitan traffic, and will be linked up for necessary interconnections by metal gangways and swift-moving pavements…. Let us overturn monuments, pavements, arcades and flights of steps; let us sink the streets and squares; let us raise the level of the city.

— Antonio Sant'Elia (with Filippo Tommaso Marinetti), "Manifesto dell'architettura futurista," 1914

Another thing that seems indicated for the future is the realization of a wholly new concept of three-dimensional linkage. If we are successful at making meaningful complexes of form and activity near the ground, we are notably successful at going into the air with linked functions…. This type of linkage is necessary because we will be building more high buildings as land in our cities become scarcer. Sant'Elia gave some idea of what the visual residue of such an idea of three-dimensional linkage might be as early as 1913. Ultimately, linking is assembling patterns of experience in the city.

— Fumihiko Maki, *Investigations in Collective Form*, 1964

7. THE SYNTHESIZED CITY

– Antonio Sant'Elia, La Città
Nuova, 1914, Drawing courtesy
Musei Civici de Como

– Architecture Research Office competition entry, City of the Future, (New York City in 100 years), 2007, Courtesy Architecture Research Office

1. Esther Da Costa Meyer, *The Work of Antonio Sant'Elia: Retreat into the Future* (New Haven: Yale University Press, 1995), 112–130.
2. Sanford Kwinter, "La Città Nuova: Modernity and Continuity," in *Zone 1–2* (New York: Urzone, 1986), 81–121.
3. Adam Yarinsky, "Envisioning Radical Futures—New York City 2106: Back to the Future," in *Places*, *20(2)*, 2008, accessed November 8, 2015, http://escholarship.org/uc/item/69f0j5zc.

Expressed with revolutionary fervor, Sant'Elia's futuristic city, La Città Nuova (1912–1914), was a poetic projection in text and images of the three-dimensional metropolis and the synthesis of architecture and infrastructure. Representing a daring new society, he proposed a corresponding set of urban forms that would liberate the historic city for the speed and connectivity of modern life.[1] This fusion of architecture and infrastructure in the urban fabric suggested that programs could be continuously expanded and adapted. Sanford Kwinter describes this process not as "a literal realizable program, [but] as a set of instructions." Growth was foreseen as a plastic process of duplication and recombination, like an endless series of machine parts. This expansion finally achieved a new plasticity of three-dimensional space independent of the traditional boundaries of interior and exterior and the framework of the street, reordering the city into a "multilayered acentric field."[2] Fumihiko Maki's vision of Sant'Elia's utopian Futurist city carries this concept forward and renders this plasticity and replication anew. His version creates a unified city of high-rise towers with podium levels interconnected by bridges and walkways, all multiplied to create an urban-scaled megastructure.

The synthesized city suggests an aggregation of disparate parts, where integration achieves a continuous urban fabric unifying buildings, landscape, and infrastructure. While elevated pedestrian systems were once considered a way to make cities more efficient and adaptable to changing technologies, the contemporary city is faced with new and extreme conditions resulting from rapid urbanization, resource depletion, pollution, and shifting populations. The morphological crisis of the contemporary city, exacerbated by global climate change, is evident in projects such as Architecture Research Office's (ARO) City of the Future, a vision of New York City circa 2106 affected by rising sea levels. Streets become canals and futuristic architectural megastructures, reminiscent of the urban visions of Harvey Wiley Corbett, Raymond Hood, and Hugh Ferriss, extend east and west over the deluged city. ARO's proposed new urban prototype for a series of pierlike mixed-use volumes containing presumably all future development in the city hovers over the flooded streets of Manhattan.[3]

ARO's City of the Future, although a provocation, is just one of a multiplicity of speculative proposals meant to address the looming problems faced by global cities. The range of elevated city ideas is illustrative of the general confusion in the planning and architectural fields where the speed of change outpaces the generation of urban design strategies and architectural prototypes. Clearly a diversity of new concepts will be necessary to address

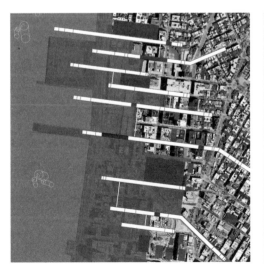

– Steven Holl, World Trade Center Project, New York City, 2002 © The Museum of Modern Art/Licensed by SCALA/Art Resource, NY

the twenty-first century's numerous challenges. But more importantly, a far greater level of intellectual malleability is needed to retheorize urban development under these unpredictable conditions.

Five global cities reveal variable futures about infrastructural urbanism: New York, Shenzhen, Mumbai, Singapore, and London. Although each is imperfect as a holistic urban form, they contain examples of dynamic and changing urban conditions that offer a glimpse of the future synthesized city. In some cases these systems are futuristic, and in others they are highly pragmatic—creating an imaginable laboratory of multilevel urbanism. In their more hopeful forms, these multilevel concepts make cities more interconnected, differentiated, exciting, and potentially more resilient. In their more pessimistic form, they raise larger questions of control and isolation.

New York: Elevating the Latent Program of the Street

By the 1970s, plans for an extensive pedestrian system in New York City were all but abandoned. With the exception of a few New York architects, the

– Steven Holl, Parallax Towers, New York City, 1989, Courtesy Steven Holl Architects

dream of a multilevel level city lay dormant. But in the late 1970s, Steven Holl began proposing multilevel systems for Manhattan, beginning with Bridge of Houses (1979). His Edge City project, a cluster of towers boldly interconnected with irregularly spaced diagonal bridges, was reminiscent of Yona Friedman's earlier proposals for Manhattan. Although Holl's Parallax Towers wasn't an entire renovation of the Manhattan skyline, it was a compelling vision of an interconnected urbanism—a cluster of towers springing out of the Hudson River resonant with twisted abandoned dock structures at the river's edge. This was the predecessor of a number of similar proposals by Holl culminating in his competition scheme for the reconstruction of the World Trade Center site (WTC II) (2002) in collaboration with firms headed by Peter Eisenman, Charles Gwathmey, and Richard Meier. The scheme links a grid of five towers with multiple levels of interior bridges and sky-gardens high above the street.

Other competition entries to rebuild on the World Trade Center site, the former testing ground of Urban Design Manhattan's plan, also explored the concept of the elevated pedestrian city, and the multilevel metropolis was again en vogue. In fact, nearly all of the competition's finalist proposals had made provisions for grade-separated public space within the redevelopment site—including SANAA, Steven Holl, Norman Foster, Daniel Libeskind, and Foreign Office Architects. Imagining public spaces high above the streets of Manhattan, they described their projects in more therapeutic terms as "gardens in the sky," "kissing buildings," or "buildings holding hands." The communitarian impulse seemed right.

Of all the urban schemes proposed in the wake of the 2001 terrorist attack, however, the most provocative—a Dadaesque concept for an "upside down skyscraper"—came from the Office for Metropolitan Architecture (OMA) (Rem Koolhaas, Joshua Prince-Ramus, and Dan Wood). The mirrored inversion of the stepped skyscraper suggested the possibility of a completely

A. Richard Meier & Partners
Architects, Eisenman Architects,
Gwathmey Siegel & Associates,
Steven Holl Architects, World Trade
Center Memorial Square Competition
entry, 2002, DBOX courtesy Richard
Meier & Partners
B. Foster + Partners, World Trade
Center II proposal, 2002, Courtesy
Foster + Partners

new ground plane in the city, an idea that appears to miraculously re-create the city street forty-five stories in the air. It was a scheme that Corbett would likely have approved. The implications of these schemes were significantly different from the pragmatic, delaminated, ground-plane scenarios of previous proposals for lower and midtown Manhattan from the 1960s and 1970s. The public spaces in the WTC II competition proposals produced later by others were similarly thrilling vertiginous spaces of leisure and connection—using reconstruction as an ameliorating symbolic act.

With the construction of the High Line in 2008, the elevated pedestrian street would be reintroduced in New York, but this time with a twist; instead of promising efficiency for busy urbanites, it instead offered a leisurely stroll along its promenade. Aside from some of the quieter villages and Central Park, spaces of urban respite are difficult to find in the busy and densely occupied streets of New York. This industrial relic of an elevated railway-turned-park creates a parallel atmosphere of leisure and recreation above the existing

C. SOM, SANAA, Michael Maltzan, James Corner Field Operations, World Trade Center II proposal, 2002, Courtesy the LMDC

D. United Architects, (Foreign Office Architects, Ltd., Greg Lynn FORM, Imaginary Forces NYC, Kevin Kennon Architect, Reiser + Umemoto, UNStudio), World Trade Center II proposal, 2002, Courtesy the LMDC

– Steven Holl, Bridge of Houses, 1979, New York, Courtesy Steven Holl

4. Adam Sternbergh, "The High Line: It Brings Good Things to Life," in *New York Magazine* (May 7, 2007), accessed November 8, 2015, http://nymag.com/news/features/31273/index1.html.

5. Steven Holl, *Pamphlet Architecture No. 7: Bridge of Houses* (New York: Princeton Architectural Press, 1978), 4–7.

street. The idea had been explored by Steven Holl in 1981 with his proposal for the reuse of the High Line. Working to convince New Yorkers of the abandoned rail bridge's value as elevated public space, he described it later as "a suspended green valley in the Manhattan Alps."[4]

Holl's fascination with synthesized forms of architecture, infrastructure, and landscape can be seen in many of his earliest speculative projects. In the *Pamphlet Architecture* series, he would repeatedly explore ideas for interconnected urban spaces. In his project for Melbourne, Australia, proposed bridges would become "urban arms" and sites for new speculative social programs: a Cultural Bridge; a Bridge of International Trade; a Bridge of Pools and Baths; a Bridge of Piazzas; and a Bridge of Odd Flowers.[5] His poetic urban imagery intentionally conjured an image of the city of pleasure, offering urban social communion, cultural delights, and thrilling spatial experiences. These concepts do not subscribe to the idea of the city as a machine, but suggest a Fourier-esque city of desire.

With the completion of the first phase of the High Line (Field Operations and Diller Scofidio + Renfro) in 2008, it would become Manhattan's most radical elevated pedestrian walkway yet to be realized. The mile-long elevated park was inspired in part by the Promenade Plantée (Jacques Vergely and Philippe Mathieux, 1994) in Paris, a linear park completed on a similar remnant of railroad track. The repurposing of abandoned railroad infrastructure from an industrial to a postindustrial use could be described as a form of *détournement*, if the High Line was not also the driving force in a massive redevelopment and gentrification of the Chelsea neighborhood. The project demonstrates how a precise intervention that introduces an additional level to the ground-plane experience may release the latent social potential of a particular urban condition. With the recent completion of the third and final phase of the High Line (2014), a new era of multilevel urban speculation was sanctioned in

A.   James Corner Field Operations,
Diller Scofidio + Renfro, with Piet
Oudolf, The High Line, 2011–, New
York City, Courtesy Iwan Baan
Photos: Iwan Baan ©2009–2011
B.   View of terminus
C.   Aerial view
D.   Amphitheater

– UNIT, Sky Street, Shenzhen Bay Super City Competition entry, 2014, Courtesy UNIT
6. James S. Russell, "Arts Ban in Stimulus Bill Is Stupid Economics," in *Bloomberg News*, February 13, 2009, accessed January 15, 2015, www.Bloomberg.com.
7. Rem Koolhaas, *Project on the City: Great Leap Forward* (London: Taschen Books, 2002), 248–249.
8. MVRDV, *The Vertical Village: Individual, Informal, Intense* (Rotterdam: nai/010 publishers, 2012), 25–52.

New York City. A public investment of $170 million generated $5 billion in development before the first phase of the park even opened while accelerating construction of another two phases of development.[6] Its success has led a number of other cities to look at elevated parks as a regenerator of urban vitality.

Shenzhen: The Multilevel Laboratory

After Shenzhen became one of China's first Special Economic Zones in the 1980s, it developed into a megalopolis within thirty years.[7] The multilevel conditions in the Futian District (Central Business District) originated from familiar typologies found in many recent Chinese cities, such as the large-scale elevated building podium and the familiar floating walkways. Most interesting in Shenzhen's rapid development, however, are its daring forays into new three-dimensional urbanisms.

The initial plan for the Central Business District, developed through international competitions, resulted in an underutilized and over-scaled monumental podium and gridiron. It contained a series of disconnected towers and public buildings that were severed from complex networks of infrastructural space below street level. The plan replaced an earlier hyper-dense model of informal development referred to as the "urban village" that created inter-related urban centers. While denigrated as outmoded and criticized for its extreme overcrowding, the urban village development was more spatially diverse, flexible, and socially dynamic. Kowloon's Walled City, while an urban anomaly on contested territory, was a well-known example of this kind of dense, informal multilevel settlement. The conceptual Vertical Village study by Dutch architecture firm MVRDV (2011) explored the possibilities of informal three-dimensional urban settlements leveraging the spatial variety possible in these collective forms. Using the interconnected aggregate forms opportunistically, MVRDV proposed communitarian zones on rooftops and bridges with other social amenities such as hanging gardens, open-air cores, and 3-D streets.[8]

While Hong Kong has a long history of employing elevated urban systems, the first important innovation in multilevel urbanism, the Vanke Center by Steven Holl, would be built on the outskirts of Shenzhen in 2006. As a variation of the megastructure raised over a tropical park, the Vanke Center

A. MVRDV and the Why Factory, Welcome to the Vertical Village exhibition, Total Museum of Contemporary Art, Seoul, South Korea, 2012 ©MVRDV

B. Kowloon Walled City (1898–1993), Courtesy Roger Price/ Wikimedia Commons

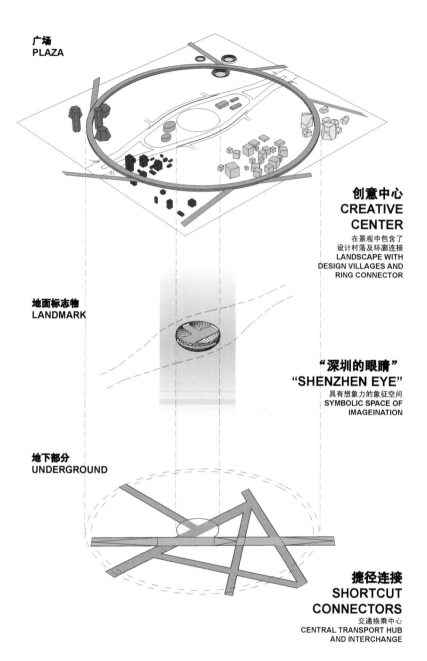

广场
PLAZA

创意中心
**CREATIVE
CENTER**
在景观中包含了
设计村落及环廊连接
LANDSCAPE WITH
DESIGN VILLAGES AND
RING CONNECTOR

地面标志物
LANDMARK

"深圳的眼睛"
"SHENZHEN EYE"
具有想象力的象征空间
SYMBOLIC SPACE OF
IMAGEINATION

地下部分
UNDERGROUND

捷径连接
**SHORTCUT
CONNECTORS**
交通换乘中心
CENTRAL TRANSPORT HUB
AND INTERCHANGE

horizontally interlinks a diverse mixed-use program that includes the offices of Vanke Industries, apartments, and a hotel. A conference center, spa, and parking ramp are located below grade. With its obvious debt to Kiesler's Horizontal Skyscraper project and Constant's *New Babylon*, the Vanke Center contains a variety of spatial innovations, not least the possibility of preserving the ground plane for urban space and gardens in a massive new development. Derived from a set of ad hoc site and programmatic relationships, the design employs a range of inventive sectional strategies that suggest the potentially poetic spatiality of the emerging multilevel city.

In recognition of the success of its ongoing design experimentation, Shenzhen was designated a "City of Design" in 2008 by UNESCO, which

– OMA, Shenzhen Creative
Center, proposal, 2009 ©OMA
9. Neville Mars and Adrian
Hornsby, *The Chinese Dream:
A Society Under Construction*
(Rotterdam: nai/010 publishers,
2008), 252–277.

placed it in the company of Bilbao, Curitiba, Turin, and Helsinki. To promote its new status, Shenzhen held a competition in 2009 for a new Creative Center for the city. The selected entry, Crystal Island by OMA, proposed a multilevel pedestrian scheme to activate "micro urbanisms" and foster the development of small-scale informal building clusters called "design villages." Hovering over Shennan Avenue, the Crystal Island interconnects the Civic Center podium to the north with the Convention and Exhibition Center on the south. Connections are also made with the subterranean transportation hub, public program spaces, meeting areas, and shopping areas. Creating a continuous field of pedestrian spaces, the floating ring reconciles the disjunctive urban forces converging on the site. More importantly, the large circulation hoop creates a foil by confronting the placelessness of the oversized city grid of the Futian District. Designed to strengthen Shenzhen's creative industries, the project provides interconnectivity between the "design villages," thus acting as both an urban branding device and an armature for the development of informal building clusters.

Utopian Form as Critique

Neville Mars's Beijing Boom Tower (2005) is a critique of China's potential future urbanism as projected forward in terms of a Western or American model of development. The shock value of this speculative metropolis, in the spirit of Ludwig Hilberseimer, suggests to Mars "an antidote for severe gratification" and poses the question: "Can the city withstand fifteen more years of this kind of urban expansion?"[9] The project, while formally compelling with its cylindrical towers and interconnected linkages, caricatures a "theoretical

169

– Neville Mars, Beijing Boom
Tower, 2005, Courtesy MARS
Architects/Dynamic City Foundation

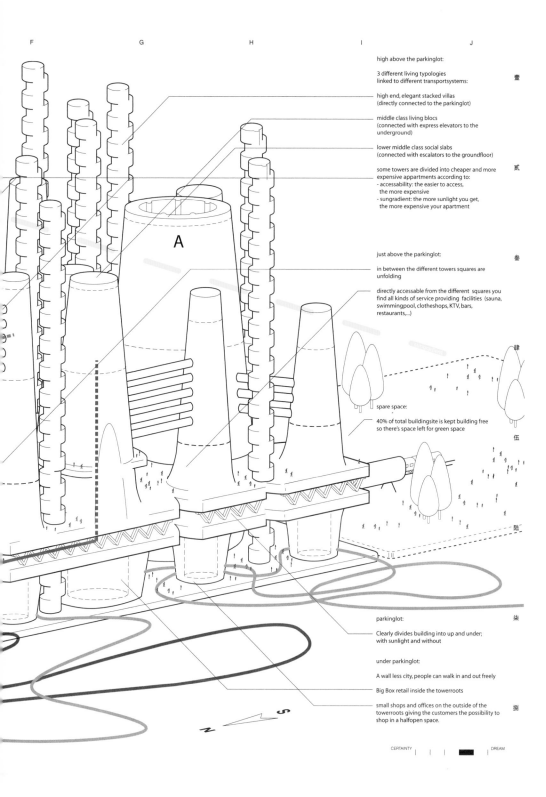

F G H I J

high above the parkinglot:

3 different living typologies
linked to different transportsystems:

high end, elegant stacked villas
(directly connected to the parkinglot)

middle class living blocs
(connected with express elevators to the
underground)

lower middle class social slabs
(connected with escalators to the groundfloor)

some towers are divided into cheaper and more
expensive appartments according to:
- accessability: the easier to access,
  the more expensive
- sungradient: the more sunlight you get,
  the more expensive your apartment

just above the parkinglot:

in between the different towers squares are
unfolding

directly accessable from the different squares you
find all kinds of service providing facilities (sauna,
swimmingpool, clotheshops, KTV, bars,
restaurants,...)

spare space:

40% of total buildingsite is kept building free
so there's space left for green space

parkinglot:

Clearly divides building into up and under;
with sunlight and without

under parkinglot:

A wall less city, people can walk in and out freely

Big Box retail inside the towerroots

small shops and offices on the outside of the
towerroots giving the customers the possibility to
shop in a halfopen space.

CERTAINTY | | | ▬ | DREAM

壹

貳

叄

肆

伍

陸

柒

捌

A

– Rocker-Lange Architects,
HK-SHZ Biennale 2013/2014, The Ideal
City of Refigured Civic Space ©2014
rocker-lange architects, all rights
reserved

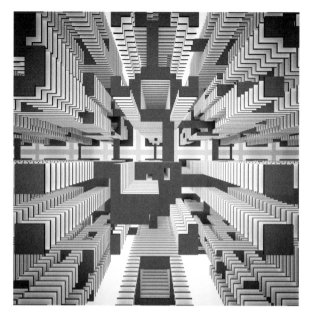

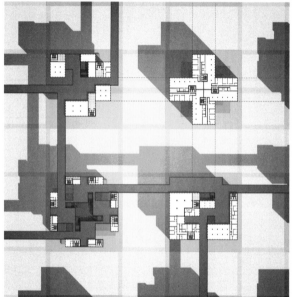

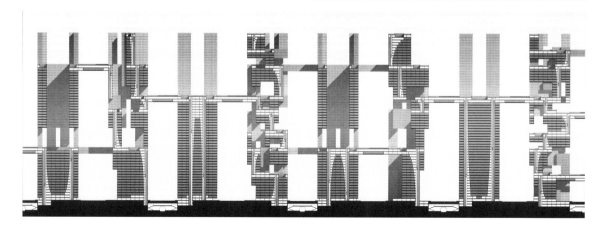

10. The Biennale continues and expands the program held since 2005 by Shenzhen.
11. Fabio Gramazio and Matthias Kohler, eds., "Made by Robots: Challenging Architecture at a Larger Scale," in *AD (Architectural Design)*, Book 229 (June 2014): 131–133.
12. Winy Maas, Alain Guiheaux, et al., *MVRDV Reads* (Rotterdam: nai/010 publishers, 2003), 104–121.

market" by responding to all future market demands. Mars's towers for mainland China are stratified based on class and income, supporting ten times the density of Manhattan and two times the average floor area of a house in suburban Los Angeles. Other architects embrace this density in similar urban forms less critically. A dialogue around the potential of this inevitable three-dimensional urban condition has emerged in both Shenzhen and Hong Kong, with both cities cosponsoring the Bi-City Biennale of Urbanism Architecture (UABB) as an international exhibition focused solely on the topics of urbanism and urbanization. The biennale has become an important venue for experimentation with multilevel city forms.[10]

The Hong Kong-Shenzhen Biennale of 2013/2014 included The Ideal City of Refigured Civic Space by Rocker-Lange. This speculative project critiques what is described as the simplistic regulations that limit public space to horizontal surfaces of streets and plazas, proposing instead a new, more complex vertical condition defined as a ratio of open space to building mass. This geometrically volumetric zoning layers public spaces strategically, distributing public zones throughout to maximize their intersection with pedestrian movement. The irregular geometries, interconnected bridges, and elevated plazas are serialized and computationally controlled. The construction of its volumetrically complex geometries would be achieved robotically through variable customization within a repetitive system.[11]

The 3-D Village

As provocations, MVRDV's many urban proposals draw from both the power and absurdity of real urban conditions in a self-described process of radical pragmatism. Within the context of "systems," Alain Guiheaux explains their work not as a preoccupation with autonomous form but its derivative characteristics that, nonetheless, have the ability to affect things beyond the form itself. He goes on to detail their methods, in comparison to those of the Smithsons, Candilis-Josic-Woods, and Archizoom, as a "utopia of disappearance."[12] Many of these projects play on a fascination with the "real" multilevel and layered urbanisms as found in informalized urban conditions and in the large-scale synthesis of buildings, landscapes, and infrastructure.

MVRDV's 3-D Street proposal for Shenzhen (2009) combines two very different ways of thinking about urbanization: the emerging multilevel city and the traditional street. While typical past forms of the multilevel city have tended to focus on purpose-built spaces with fixed circulation programs, the traditional street form is more ambiguous and less prescribed, allowing for a range of informal activities that reveal latent possibilities for reactivation. MVRDV combines two often oppositional conditions in the master plan for the redevelopment of heavily congested Hua Qiang Bei Street. They propose a set of socially constructed and internally focused building forms (factory, superblock, village, arch, dome, cone) that are arranged informally and connected to each other and to the ground plane by a diagonal system of tubular links. The proposal for an interconnected system of new building typologies that both bypass and connect with the street expands the range of possibilities for pedestrian movement and spontaneous social activities. The interior linkages are intentionally minimal in width, intended for expediency; the programmatic spaces are introduced as new spatial typologies functioning independently of the space in-between.

WORKac's proposal for the same competition explores another version of the three-dimensional street. Instead of interconnected above-ground volumes, a series of multilevel circulation nodes transcends the limitations typically associated with more expedient urban connectors. The horizontal bridge and vertical elevator hub—basic components of an interlinked multilevel city—are enlarged, twisted, and strategically connected to multiple

– WORKac and ZhuBO, Views of
Hua Qiang Bei Road, Shenzhen, 2009
©2009 WORK Architecture Company

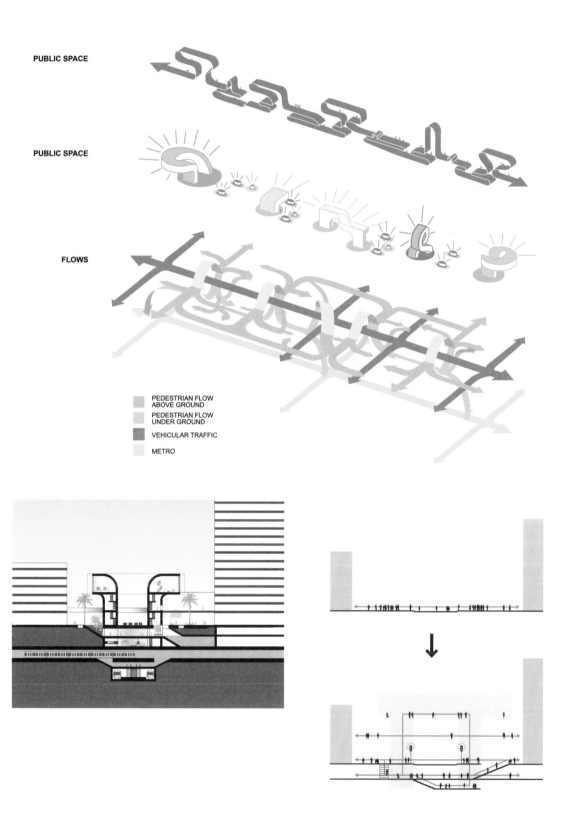

PUBLIC SPACE

PUBLIC SPACE

FLOWS

PEDESTRIAN FLOW
ABOVE GROUND

PEDESTRIAN FLOW
UNDER GROUND

VEHICULAR TRAFFIC

METRO

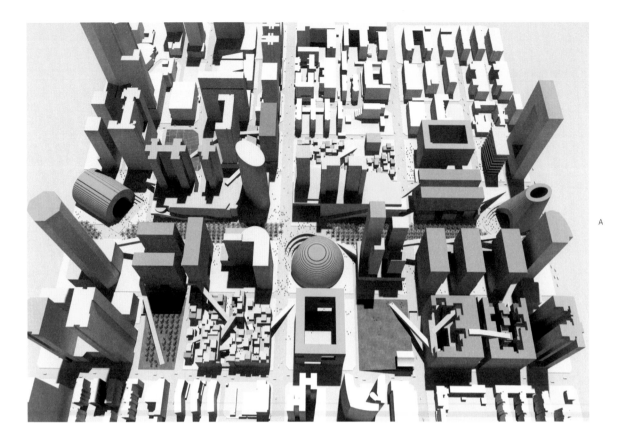

A.   MVRDV, Drawing of Dutch
pavilion, Expo 2000, Hannover,
Germany, 1997–2000 ©MVRDV
B.   MVRDV, Shenzhen 3-D Street,
2009 ©MVRDV

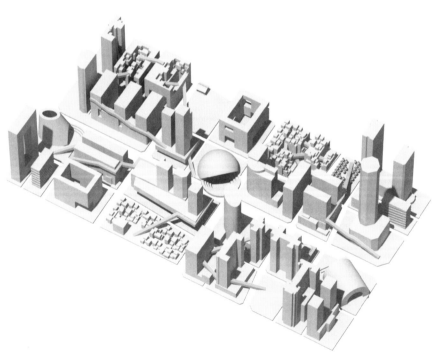

–   Metropolitan Region Development Authority (MMRDA), Skywalk at Grant Road, Mumbai, 2013 ©DNA-Daily News & Analysis

13.   Kenneth Frampton, *Megaform as Urban Landscape* (Champaign-Urbana: University of Illinois, 2010), 13.

14.   Menaka Rao, "Mumbai Skywalks: Are These Elevated Paths 'Ugly Caterpillars' or Precious Public Space?" *The Guardian* (UK), Thursday November 27, 2014, accessed February 14, 2016, http://www.theguardian/com/cities/2015/nov/27/mumbai-skywalks-are-these-elevated-paths-ugly-caterpillars-or-precious-public-space.

levels of program above and below the street. The linkages become volumetric social spaces, tactically intensifying activities at highly visible nodes in the city. Scaled up, these social connectors become building-like icons and representative cross sections through the circulation levels of the city.

Mumbai: Elastic Infrastructures

Barcelonan architect Manuel de Solà-Morales developed the socio-environmental concept of "urban acupuncture," using small-scale interventions to modify a larger urban field.[13] Mumbai's Skywalk system can be seen as an example of this technique, where multiple multilevel connections are made within a larger urban field, creating the potential for a polynodal transformation of the city. Mumbai began developing its skywalk system as a response to extreme traffic and congested streets, employing a series of informal but planned multilevel strategies to alleviate congestion. A densely populated city (at twelve million, a megalopolis) that is largely pedestrian (fifty-two percent), Mumbai uses elevated interventions that are driven by convenience and concerns for safety.[14] The Mumbai Skywalk project is intended to move people from the formally planned spaces of train stations, commercial centers, housing, and offices, bypassing rickshaws, hawkers, vendors, and street festivals. Conceived as an engineering and infrastructure project, the system is not continuously connected, but made up of a network of strategically located elevated bridges.

In response to the ongoing development of Mumbai, Rahul Mehrotra argues against the oppositional relationship of "formal" and "informal" planning. Historically there has been a perceived inequity between formal and informal urbanisms: the former being associated with the more stable colonial British town planning and the latter with a more disordered "native" periphery. In the city center, the architecture created a focus of relative permanence, but at the periphery the attention was on temporal events. Mehrotra's research on the Kinetic City, or Bazaar City, proposes an animated urbanism that is about events, time, and activity, not architectural objects. In the development of architectural and infrastructural space, these urban events can be planned, programming the formal with the informal. He suggests that when planners consider streets they should then look beyond

15.   Rahul Mehrotra, "Negotiating the Static and Kinetic Cities," in *Other Cities, Other Worlds: Urban Imaginaries in a Globalizing Age* (Durham and London: Duke University Press), 2008, 205–218.

16.   Eric Bellman, "Mumbai Builds 'Skywalks,' Elevated Walkways That Let Pedestrians Move Above Crowded Streets," *Wall Street Journal*, January 19, 2010, accessed February 1, 2014, http://www.wsj.com.

17.   Kester Rattenbury, *Cedric Price: Magnet* (London: The Architecture Foundation, 1997), 4–5.

18.   Caitlin Dover, "Architect Neville Mars on His 'Landlink,' " Guggenheim Blogs, November 11, 2013, accessed November 8, 2015 at http://blogs.guggenheim.org/checklist/mondays-in-motion-architect-neville-mars-on-his-landlink/.

congestion to the space of social and commercial exchange—revealing the city as "an elastic urban condition."[15]

Designed and implemented by the Mumbai Metropolitan Region Development Authority (MMRDA) from 2007 to 2009, the Skywalks initially served a minimal program of connection as a standardized trussed and elevated pedestrian overpass requiring stairs at each end. Commuters climb up only to climb down again. While criticized for being underutilized and thus unsafe, the Skywalks exclude the informal layered activities of the bazaar that attract urban life. But because of the shortage of public space for informal use in the city, they have been appropriated for economic and social exchange— they are being used by children for play, by friends for impromptu meetings or walking, or by individuals as a place to read a newspaper or smoke a cigarette.[16] As the system of components has evolved, the Skywalks have also shifted away from the simplistic and seemingly temporary prototype to components that are more elaborate, site-specific and permanent.

Despite the temporal nature of these infrastructures, their use as catalytic elements, deployed to adapt to the flows of the city, may lead to long-lasting modifications to the urban environment. Price's Magnet City (1996–1997) concept for "anticipatory architecture" suggests other applications for this model of elevated infrastructure. Price's Magnets were conceived as a series of temporary urban structures designed as public amenities that would act as architectural attractors to recatalyze the urban field. He also saw them as a counter to the distraction of the "building as object" that "lulls" people into accepting as permanent such adverse urban conditions as infrastructural barriers, congestion, and privatization. Instead, Magnets focus on creating new situations, using promenades, stairways, piers, and arcades to provide points of physical and visual access. Price's site-specific devices proposed around London would leverage their contexts to create new and unanticipated spaces for urban life, afford views into semi-private spaces like zoos, construct a "friendly jungle-gym" of stairs, platforms, and lifts, or insert a public library in the form of a bridge between two gated communities.[17]

Through a series of investigations and discussions on public space in Mumbai, another series of proposals for informally inhabiting elevated urban spaces was developed by the BMW-Guggenheim Lab (2012–2013). These investigations culminated in a public competition for "Rethinking Kala Nagar Traffic Junction," a proposed Skywalk node. Rethinking the project as not merely a bypass, local residents proposed the informal use of urban space, including food courts, gardens, event spaces, and public parks.

Neville Mars's proposal for the Mumbai lab took this work further by studying existing elevated infrastructures as spaces for development called "infra-space." Converting a large-scale water pipeline designated for decommissioning into a site for redevelopment, the Landlink project proposed layering an urban circulation and development program above the pipeline. The project's repurposing of an existing structure intentionally contrasts with the nearby Sea Link Bridge, a costly single-purpose infrastructure serving only automobiles and trucks. The Landlink would be built initially to support pedestrian, bicycle, and rickshaw traffic in an underserved area located between two of Mumbai's larger slumlike settlements. The pedestrian decks are designed to expand informally by first serving as a conduit for traffic, then social space and commerce, and finally as an armature for larger developments—creating a "central business district" as a form of "ad hoc capitalism."[18] Mars also proposed adaptation schemes for existing skywalks, modifying the infrastructure to serve as a water-collection device that uses rooftop structures as rainwater collectors, and mounting the bridges on cisterns to hold and distribute potable water.

Other projects, similar to Price's Magnet City, suggest models for more tactical urban prototypes. Urban-Think Tank's Metro Cable-Car in Caracas, Venezuela, can be seen as another emerging multilevel infrastructural device

19. Andres Lepik, *Small Scale, Big Change: New Architectures of Social Engagement* (New York: Museum of Modern Art, 2010), 123–124.

20. Rem Koolhaas, "Singapore Songlines: Portrait of a Potemkin Metropolis…or Thirty Years of Tabula Rasa," in *S,M,L,XL* (New York: Monacelli Press, 1995), 1011–1055.

21. William Gibson, "Disneyland with the Death Penalty," in *Wired* 1.04 (September/October 1993).

22. Singapore Improvement Trust, *Master Plan* (Singapore: Chip Bee Press, 1955), 6–8.

that operates at a relatively small scale but is designed to impact larger fields of activity.[19] Like Mumbai, Venezuela experienced rapid economic development in the 1970s and 1980s that generated extreme population growth in the city of Caracas, where sixty percent of its inhabitants live in informal settlements—impoverished areas lacking in infrastructure, public space, and amenities. In this case, architects Alfredo Brillembourg and Hubert Klumpner of Urban-Think Tank proposed an elevated cable car system as an alternative to road construction to connect the communities to the city center. Integrating infrastructure with program, the five stations connect Caracas's mountainside communities with the central city's transportation network while vertically integrating social and cultural components within its layered sections. The infrastructural prototypes of both Mumbai and Caracas serve as case studies for ways that three-dimensional urban strategies can be used to catalyze and recharge the urban field. But like any urban interventions, they may also impact property value either positively or negatively, in some cases facilitating gentrification.

Singapore: Scripting the Leisure City

Some of the most radical forms of three-dimensional urbanism to emerge in Asia were first developed in the 1960s and were directly influenced by the work of Team 10 and the Metabolists. New urban prototypes were initially constructed in Singapore, Hong Kong, and then Tokyo. In Singapore, a group of architects, largely educated in the West, created a new form of the linked multilevel city in the late 1960s that was modern and distinctly Asian. Their ideas merged infrastructure with architecture to create communal space and achieve a larger social agenda.

Rem Koolhaas's fascination with Singapore as a "unique ecology of the contemporary" is something that he describes in both political and architectural terms. In 1995, he questioned the results of the city's urban experimentation as a "melting pot that produces blandness and sterility from the most promising ingredients." Koolhaas attributed this to the "social compact" that was struck shortly after the country's independence to create the new society: the success of the collective in exchange for the freedom of the individual. Unlike postcolonial Mumbai, the new city-state of Singapore, created in 1965, reconciled the relation between colonial and "native," or the formal and the informal, by eradicating both.[20] Erasing its history, Singapore created a new city by initially adopting CIAM strategies for constructing a modern urban form completely controlled and managed by its government.

Writer William Gibson describes Singapore as an entire city of infrastructure conceived as a totality, which also required a concise program.[21] In 1959, to counter fears of instability with its emerging independence, the new government of Singapore created the perfect program of development strategies that emphasized leisure and tourism, technology, scientific research, and an export economy. This script for the future city would be run by a centralized government and partially funded by outside multinational financial interests. Despite Singapore's hierarchical structure, its urban form would evolve through a negotiated process.

Social Planning/Social Engineering

Singapore's urbanization process was implemented with very little transparency or public process as the government adopted a large-scale plan to facilitate growth. The plan covered a broad range of areas, effectively monitoring all aspects of its development and the lives of its residents, such as "transportation, employment, communications, education, welfare, community development, public relations, capital investment, and savings."[22] This

A

MAGNET

A.   Cedric Price, Magnet, Platform
St. Gilles Circus, London, 1995,
Cedric Price Fonds, Collection Centre
Canadien d'Architecture/Canadian
Centre for Architecture, Montreal
B.   Neville Mars, Landlink, Mumbai,
2012, Courtesy MARS Architects/
Dynamic City Foundation

B

– Urban-Think Tank, Metro Cable,
Caracas, 2010   Photos courtesy
Iwan Baan

— SPUR, Asian City of Tomorrow, Singapore, 1967, from Koh Seow Chuan, SPUR 65–67

23. Ibid., 6–8.
24. Iain Jackson, "Tropical Architecture and the West Indies: From Military Advances and Tropical Medicine to Robert Gardner-Medwin and the Networks of Tropical Modernism," *The Journal of Architecture* 18, no. 2 (2013): 167–195.
25. Hiang Koon Wee, "An Asian Avant-Garde: A Lexicon of Asian Modernity," *Globalizing Architecture: Flows and Disruptions* (Washington, DC: ACSA Press, 2014), 265–271.
26. Singapore Planning and Urban Research Group, SPUR 65/67 (Singapore: 1967), 2–10.
27. Eric Mumford, the CIAM Discourse on Urbanism, 1928–1960 (Cambridge: MIT Press, 2000), 167.

bureaucratic structure was further empowered by colonial laws, such as the Land Acquisition Act, which allowed the government to acquire private land to promote state interests, even if it was transferred to private developers.

While initially criticizing the low-density garden city plans created by the British Planning Authorities in 1955, Singapore's planners adopted its green-belt ring of new towns and comprehensive development areas and adapted them to the city's anticipated evolution into a dense metropolis, thereby overcoming the space limitations of the island-state.[23] Although critical of some aspects of the British Project Techniques Office (PTO)–influenced master plan, the new government still engaged a group of advisors from the United Nations (UN) and from the LCC and PTO (William Holford) to help them plan for its ongoing development. This process was primarily guided by Otto Koenigsberger, a UN expert and London director of the Architectural Association's (AA) Department of Development and Tropical Studies. Koenigsberger's concept of the "Action Plan" evolved from the British colonial interests in social stability and economic development underpinning "tropical architecture."[24] Using a model of loose guiding concepts instead of a master plan, the local authority implemented and monitored the reconstruction of the island as an urban complex, beginning with the early CIAM-influenced Housing and Development Board (HDB).

Urban renewal flourished in Singapore in the postwar period of the 1950s, as it had in postcolonial cities throughout the world, a counter-critique began to take form in Singapore against the modernist strategy of tabula rasa. At this time a young architect named William Lim cofounded SPUR (Singapore Planning and Urban Research Group) to counter the early CIAM-influenced urbanization strategies that were being rapidly deployed by the new government as a way to accelerate outside investment.[25] Instead, SPUR looked to the Team 10 and the Metabolist models that emphasized the social connectivity of the city.

SPUR envisioned a new synthesized multilevel urban form for Singapore—an "Asian City of Tomorrow."[26] Lim's unique education put him at the intersection of a range of different multilevel urbanisms emerging in the early 1950s. He was present at CIAM 9 in Aix-en-Provence, France, when his teachers at the AA, Alison and Peter Smithson, challenged its principles and presented their cluster cities. After graduation, he was a Fulbright scholar at Harvard's Graduate School of Design (GSD), where he was connected with Fumihiko Maki and attended the first Urban Design Conference organized by Josep Lluís Sert, listening to lectures by Victor Gruen, Vincent Ponte, and Kevin Lynch.[27] Lim also studied with MARS Group member Jacqueline Tyrwhitt at Harvard and learned development economics. This education immersed him in a dialogue around urban reform and public space that bridged CIAM and Team 10.

Lim returned to Singapore at the time of independence and like many young architects who had trained abroad, was excited about creating a modern urbanism that was locally grounded. Following the model of participatory rebellion set by the Smithsons, Lim worked parallel to the efforts of the CIAM-influenced Urban Renewal Group (modeled after the British LCC) while also critiquing their process and tendencies. In a series of publications, SPUR promoted an alternative form of multilevel urbanism based on the Metabolist concepts of Group and Collective Form. SPUR also worked to broaden the conversation, inviting internationally known architects connected with Team 10, the GSD, and the AA to contribute articles and asking that Maki and Tyrwhitt travel to Singapore to promote these concepts. While initially excluded from participating in the development of public policies, Lim and other members of SPUR would influence planning in Singapore a decade later after Tan Jake Hooi (a core member of SPUR) was appointed chief planning officer of the HDB.

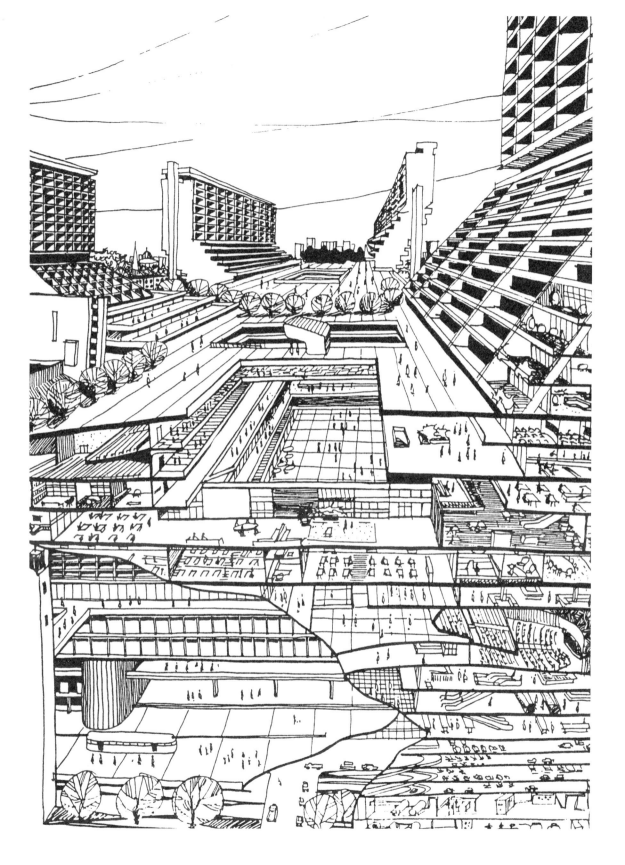

A.   WOHA, PARKROYAL on Pickering, Singapore, 2013, Courtesy Patrick Bingham-Hall
B.   WOHA, Vertical Cities Asia, Singapore, 2011, Courtesy WOHA
28.   Wee, "An Asian Avant-Garde," 270.

The City as a Project

The city-state's first major urban private-public development would be created through a public competition. Lim and Design Partnership (which also included Manchester and MIT graduate Lim Chong Keat), won the competition for the site in 1967 with an elevated version of a new kind of civic urban space centered on leisure.[28] The first privately owned and publically programmed megastructure for Singapore, together with the People's Park Centre (1970) and the Golden Mile Complex (1974), the structure was envisioned as a city within the

185

– ARC Studio Architecture + Urbanism, The Pinnacle@Duxton, Singapore, 2009 Photo ©Philip Oldfield
29. Koolhaas, "Singapore Songlines," 1055–1087.

city containing the first components of an expanded multilevel urban fabric. The projects were a variation on the SPUR vision and an application of Maki's Linked Collective Form. The initial six-story multilevel urban complex (People's Park) contained markets and offices and introduced the idea of a city corridor, which extended interior atria and a series of elevated pedestrian bridges into the future urban fabric.

The success of the People's Park and Golden Mile complexes motivated Singapore to follow with policy changes to promote the construction of skywalk links to encourage economic development throughout the CBD in the 1960s. Architect Alan Choe, who headed the Urban Renewal Group, was an advocate of CIAM 8 and Victor Gruen. He promoted component-based pedestrian systems that would extend throughout the city, including a new typology—the "shopping-cum-bridge"—which integrated market stalls into pedestrian links.[29] As a system it was never completed, and as Singapore developed it adopted a more varied network of nodal systems within the city.

Maki described the completed People's Park project to Lim as the realization of his Metabolist dream. It was the first in a series of interlinked Metabolist-influenced elevated projects in Singapore, followed by the Golden Mile Complex and the multilevel projects on Orchard Road and Marina Centre (Design Partnership, 1986–1997). The People's Park Centre was followed quickly by a very similar project in Hong Kong (Connaught Place, 1973) by MIT-educated architect James Kinoshita—a tower-podium form with open-air pedestrian bridges extending outward to the city. DP Architects has also continued to develop work independently of Lim since the late 1970s, collaborating with architects such as John Portman and Pei Cobb Freed on designs

– Grant Associates with WilkinsonEyre, View of the Supertree Grove at Gardens by the Bay, Singapore, 2012 (Marina Bay Sands Hotel designed by Moshe Safdie, 2010, in the background) ©David Noton Photography/Alamy Stock Photo

30.   Lucy Bullivant, *Masterplanning Futures* (London: Routledge, 2012), 83–84.
31.   The demand by the public for this vertiginous experience of nature concerned private developers, who worried about their inability to compete with this model of a subsidized project. The government assured them this was a unique condition and not part of a new public housing prototype.

that integrate elevated streets to create multilevel shopping and entertainment complexes. Most recently these urban forms have been readapted by Zaha Hadid Architects (ZHA) in a project called Biopolis (2013), a seven-building complex and part of ZHA's two hundred–hectare master plan for One North, a mixed-use urban center for biomedical research to be completed in 2021.[30]

From Horizontal to Vertiginous

By the 1990s development in Singapore had fallen flat and the government ushered in a new element of leisure to transform the shopping program and elevated streets of the 1970s and 1980s. Heightened vertiginous experiences were proposed that included tropical island–themed marina overlooks, elevated entertainment parks with pools and beaches, and other raised communal recreation spaces as links in clusters of public-housing towers.[31] These multilevel prototypes are very different from the communal form of civic leisure space advocated by SPUR. Emphasizing the urban spectacle and the vertiginous over the social space of the elevated street, the city has created a series of recreation-oriented enclaves and parks. Tourist destinations include TreeTop Walk in Singapore's national park (2004), an 820-foot-long elevated walkway enabling visitors to move through the tree canopy suspended 82 feet above the forest floor, or the Supertree Grove at Gardens by the Bay (Grant Associates with WilkinsonEyre, 2012), a vertical garden connected with a 426-foot-long aerial walkway called the OCBC Skyway that incorporates an elevated restaurant with a view of Marina Bay. Designed to promote urban nightlife, these attractions employ solar-powered sculptural lighting effects to illuminate artificial tree canopies. The Marina Bay Sands with its SkyPark Observation Deck (2010), designed by Moshe Safdie, features the world's

32.   Noam Dvir, "Israeli Architecture with Eastern Promise," in *Haaretz*, February 3, 2012, accessed November 8, 2015 at http://www .haaretz.com/israel-news/israeli -architecture-with-eastern-promise -1.410815.

33.   "This Week in Tech: 3-D Modeling Singapore," in *Architect Magazine* (June 2015), accessed November 8, 2015, http://www .architectmagazine.com/technology /this-week-in-tech-3d-modeling -singapore_o.

34.   Kyle Maxey, "Dassault Systèmes and Singapore Team Up to Create 3-D Model of an Entire Country," Engineering.com, accessed November 8, 2015, http://www .engineering.com/DesignerEdge /DesignerEdgeArticles/ArticleID/10303 /Dassault-Systemes-and-Singapore -Team-Up-to-Create-3D-Model-of-an -Entire-Country.aspx.

largest cantilever—a 492-foot-long infinity pool overlooking the city skyline with attractions that include light and water shows and base-jumping.

Safdie claims that the elevated forms of public space reappearing in his work since the late 1960s are inevitable with densification in cities like Singapore: "The principle of using suspended levels was conceived with Habitat." He suggests a new relevance for these ideas: "When you build in the densities of China, you cannot provide public green areas on a reasonable scale on the ground, and so you have to raise them upward. Today the Chinese are in a process of urbanization and densification that is unprecedented in history, and for this you need to invent new urban systems."[32] The recurring idea in this work is that this complex three-dimensional urbanism enables public space and social interaction where it would otherwise be impossible.

The integration of elevated landscape vegetation has become a critical part of Singapore's three-dimensional development in recent years and a familiar element in its architectural vocabulary. WOHA Architects, based in Singapore, has extended the multilevel experimentation in projects like Duxton Plain Public Housing for Singapore's Chinatown competition (2002) and the Park Royal Hotel complex (2013). These projects propose an urbanism of housing, hotels, schools, and public buildings interconnected with gardens and bridges. Their elevated green spaces, described as sky-parks or sky-gardens, allow the landscape to subsume the architecture, projecting forward a futuristic form of a multilevel tropical urbanism that is both visionary and pragmatically real. The new generation of public housing constructed by Singapore's HDB includes the interconnected high-rise project Duxton Plain Pinnacle Housing (2009). Designed by Singapore-based architects ARC Studio Architecture and Urbanism as part of the same competition, seven towers of fifty-story housing are interconnected on upper levels by communal sky-gardens for recreation and exercise.[33]

The power of an elevated private landscape within a dense urban context was first captured in the multi-authored design of Rockefeller Center in the early 1920s. Harvey Wiley Corbett's initial site plan was reminiscent of his visionary proposals of traffic separation, with a two-story commercial mall with arcades and garden plazas bridging adjacent streets. Raymond Hood's proposition for seven acres of interconnected private roof gardens above, which he referred to as the Hanging Gardens of New York, can be seen as a predecessor of the contemporary elevated gardens in cities like Singapore. Hood had argued similarly for the gardens in economic terms, comparing the increase in real estate value with tenant space overlooking Bryant Park.

Smart Cities: Is It Utopia if Everyone Follows the Same Script?

Singapore's success in shifting the majority of its population from low-density private to high-density public housing has accommodated its rapid growth. This achievement has made Singapore a laboratory for China, where Singapore's architects are also employed in China's massive urbanization projects. Singapore's bureaucratic model of continually adaptable and highly controlled urban growth is now being merged with technologies used in cities such as Masdar in the United Arab Emirates to design "smart cities," taking the model of totalizing urbanization to a new level.

In 2015 Singapore's government hired French software developer Dassault Systèmes to create Virtual Singapore, a three-dimensional digital model of the city-state as a tool to collect and consolidate data about "topography, building composition, and demographics...to inform planning about security, disaster management, and infrastructure maintenance."[34] The project is led by architect Ingeborg Rocker, head of the GEOVIA 3DEXPERIENCity project at Dassault Systèmes, a former professor at Harvard's GSD, and

35. Academie Schloss Solitude, accessed February 15, 2016, http://www.akademie-solitude.dc.

36. Online brochure produced by Dassault Systèmes, accessed January 2016, http://www.3ds.com /products-services/geovia/

37. Catherine Bolgar, "Sensing the City of the Future," in Perspectives, October 30, 2014, accessed January 10, 2016, http://perspectives.3ds.com.

previously an architect in Peter Eisenman's practice.[35] Using this technology, Singapore's three-dimensional complexity will now be able to be mapped and comprehensively monitored and optimized.

In a smart city, total urban integration is finally possible where sensors and devices track system performance, comprehensively documenting the physical characteristics of the city and recording in real time the preferences and patterns of behavior of its residents. In the next projected stage of the smart city, sensors will be employed to understand how people use the city, to gauge their emotions and reactions and the effectiveness of their interactions. Proposed initially to optimize environmental performance and resiliency, the sensor-based environment of a smart city will soon require data-mining at an unprecedented scale. Because it is typically a private service, the data also has economic value to a host of primarily non-public entities: the aerospace and defense industries; construction and real estate development; retail, energy, mining, and utilities sectors; environment, gaming, tourism, and transit concerns; and governmental agencies.[36] This information is not guaranteed to flow freely throughout the city, and may in fact simply become another commodity to be traded between system developers and their private and governmental clients in finance and development.

Norman Foster's Masdar City (2007) is the first constructed prototype for a smart city, creating a multilevel, energy-efficient urban environment that integrates transportation optimized for efficiency and performance. According to the city's promotional materials, Masdar will be the "world's largest cluster of high-performance buildings that together create a real-time laboratory to monitor and study how cities use, conserve, and share resources."[37] But the city's data-gathering is designed for very specific interests and implementation goals: resource distribution, space utilization, emissions management, and traffic management. The architect's role is largely limited to questions of style. The smart city model has provoked an open data movement based in Vancouver to push these systems away from solely monitoring efficiency and toward social applications focused on quality-of-life issues, recognizing that in the end it will be those writing the script who will ultimately design the utopian/dystopian city of the future.

London: The Wall, the Bridge, and the Enclave

> Once, a city was divided in two parts. One part became the Good Half, the other part the Bad Half.
> The inhabitants of the Bad Half began to flock to the good part of the divided city, rapidly swelling into an urban exodus. If this situation had been allowed to continue forever, the population of the Good Half would have doubled, while the Bad Half would have turned into a ghost town.
> After all attempts to interrupt this undesirable migration had failed, the authorities of the bad part made desperate and savage use of architecture: they built a wall around the good part of the city, making it completely inaccessible to their subjects.
> The Wall was a masterpiece.

> — Rem Koolhaas, Madelon Vreisendorp, Elia Zenghelis, and Zoe Zenghelis, *Exodus, or the Voluntary Prisoners of Architecture*, 1972

In 1972, Rem Koolhaas's thesis project at the Architectural Association was based on the urban island effect of the Berlin Wall. Inspired, he wrote an ironic proposal for the City of London. It depicts a divided city in which one side is about practicality, the other pleasure, and the occupants choose where they wish to be. Fast-forward to London in the twenty-first century, a global

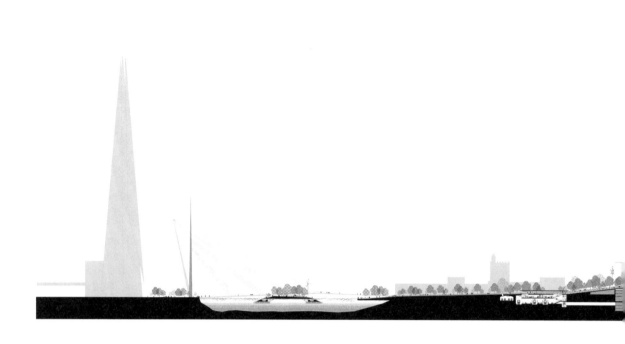

– John Robertson Architects, The Developing City: A Vision for 2050, 2012, Courtesy John Robertson Architects

38. Ian Jack, "Why Is London's Garden Bridge Worth as Much as Five Lancashire Museums?" in the *Guardian*, February 13, 2016, http://www.theguardian.com.

39. Sam Jacobs, "The Garden Bridge is a magic bullet for a certain idea of the contemporary British City," *DEZEEN*: (December 2014), accessed November 8, 2015, http://www.dezeen.com/2014/12/22/sam-jacob-opinion-heatherwick-garden-bridge-social-criticism-london-money-power/.

city competing for international investment, talent, and tourism. By necessity, the city as spectacle must ramp up its multilevel urbanism to compete with other global cities. Just as the London Eye reestablished the previously dormant urban program of the amusement park, the proposed Garden Bridge (Heatherwick Studio, 2013) reintroduced the urban garden as a phantasmagorical othering of nature. In the case of the Garden Bridge, the privately funded, quasi-public park would cross the Thames in the center of London. Using laws based on its status as private leisure space, the green island bridge could limit access, public speech, and any non-jogging activities, and track its users' mobile phone signals.[38]

Sam Jacob's scathing criticism of Thomas Heatherwick's proposal for the Garden Bridge is also a cultural critique of London as a neoliberal city, reframing infrastructure solely as an "experiential promenade rather than a route." Jacob describes Heatherwick's design as the spirit of "copying as a creative act," adding that it is generated through a collage of the elements of the desirable contemporary city, as if you "fused Jan Gehl, Cities for a Small Planet, Capability Brown, psychogeography and Isambard Kingdom Brunel." While noting the project's spectacular engineering, enhanced walkability, and its "faint promise" of sustainability, this new icon for London uses the idea of a garden to "cloak concentrated power and speculative development" solely to generate tourism and attract wealth, not to create the social conditions for a healthy city. "The bridge is an end to real urbanity—the post public city."[39]

A similar mutation of the social project of the city can be seen in more recent applications of multilevel urbanism adapted by firms first working on elevated schemes in the Middle East and Asia and then readapting them in Western cities like London. Many of these concepts appear to be derived from circulation logics more suitable for private or even authoritarian contexts, differing from their more socially driven progenitors by creating internalized enclaves at the tops of office towers. While not portrayed as systems, these are the circumscribed and defensible spaces of the new economic elite

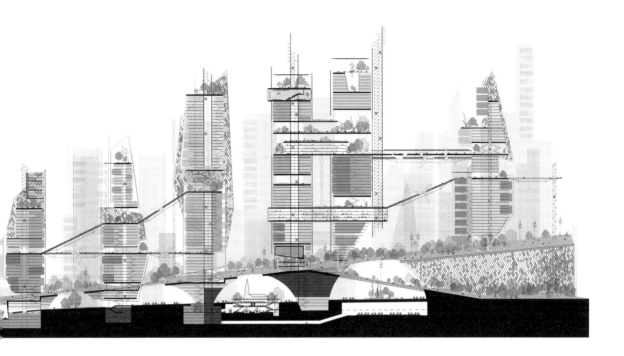

40. Ian Mulcahey, "London 2050:
The First Genuinely Global City," in
Gensler on Cities: (June 20, 2012),
accessed November 8, 2015, http://
www.gensleron.com/cities/2012/6/20
/london-2050-the-first-genuinely
-global-city.html.

defined by interlinked tower clusters sharing amenities, recreational spaces, and privately accessed sky-gardens. In 2012, the exhibition *The Developing City 2050* was held in London at the Walbrook Building in the financial district. Warning of the dangers of being overtaken by the progress of urban development in Hong Kong, Shanghai, Singapore, and New York, a design collective of architects commissioned by the City of London Corporation proposed a new application of elevated urbanism at a scale not attempted since the years after the Blitz.

London's expansionist goals are framed not in terms of need but in terms of growth. This is not an outward extension toward the Commonwealth as in days past, but rather an inward focus on accumulation, densification, and a recolonization of the heart of the city. The plans envision a future London whose urban form is critical to its success and its defense against the rapidly growing BRIC (Brazil, Russia, India, China) economies, making it the de facto capital of the Global Free Trade Zone in 2050.[40] Looking at the City of London's Square Mile and its transformation into a new financial center and work environment, the exhibition featured new towers and development projects that offered an in-depth look at a proposed series of interconnected districts proposed for the Barbican, Aldgate Financial Center, the Thames District, Shoreditch, and the Smithfield Cultural Center.

Emphasizing the city's resiliency through new icons of sustainability and leisure, the projects couple multilevel urban complexes of generic towers with wind turbines and pedestrian bridges. These idealized urban forms envision privatized enclaves to attract investors, not necessarily residents, using walkability and sustainability to increase investment value. Recently completed developments have negotiated with the city to expand their density by providing public-realm amenities, including the public-private sky-garden on floors thirty-four through thirty-seven in the Fenchurch Street tower by Raphael Vinoly. While marked as public spaces, these new forms of quasi-public space have been heavily criticized for their exclusionary tendencies.

41.   Anthony Vidler, "How to Invent Utopia: The Fortunes and Misfortunes of Plato's Polis," Mellon lecture at the Canadian Centre for Architecture, May 17, 2005, accessed October 10, 2014, http://www.cca.qc.ca/en/study-centre/281-anthony-vidler-how-to-invent-utopia-the-fortunes-and.

42.   While Vidler describes the Utopia or Ideal City as beginning with Plato, others describe the Utopian City project in different terms. According to Pier Vittorio Aureli, the project of the city began in the fifteenth century with a renewed interest in Vitruvius (died AD 15) and his "will to systemization" in the conception of architecture. According to Hanno-Walter Kruft, it began with the age of social reform and humanism in the era of the French Enlightenment, because Utopia is inherently social.

The Archive and the Scenario

While none of these cities can be described as ideal, each attempts to respond to the rapidly changing dynamics of urban development, competitive economics, and shifting demographics by applying a range of adaptive and three-dimensional architectural and urban strategies. By appropriating abandoned infrastructure for public space, New York City elevates the pedestrian path to make manifest the latent leisure program of the street. In Mumbai, planners and architects introduce a series of elevated pedestrian walkways that function like "urban stents," enabling circulation links that bypass congested streets and surcharge particular urban precincts. Shenzhen experiments with radical architecture, creating a toolbox of new multilevel prototypes. Singapore transforms itself from CIAM modernism and an incubator of Metabolism into a leisure city-state, taking the "city as spectacle" to new vertiginous heights. London speculates on its own reinvention as a three-dimensional urban enclave—a multilevel commune for global capitalists. Like earlier examples of the multilevel city and its historical antecedents, the implicit utopianisms of many contemporary proposals may seem to offer panaceas for the myriad problems facing the city in the twenty-first century. But is this optimism justified, or is it simply the seduction of the illusory urban spectacle of neoliberal economic development pursued obsessively without consideration for its societal impact?

The social and cultural implications of the multilevel metropolis are too significant to ignore. If, as we argue, the next stage of three-dimensional urbanization is imminent, this phenomenon is deserving of greater attention through both design research and scholarship. The pace of development in various urban centers around the world is difficult to predict, and multilevel urban forms will continue to evolve into new and unexpected physical realities. With exploding populations, climate change, and ensuing conflict, the multilevel metropolis will test the ability of architects, urbanists, sociologists, and others to theorize new urban forms while adapting to such rapid changes.

Utopian speculations, Anthony Vidler argues, can be a necessary obsession in times of crisis. He suggests that "Utopia entails its opposite—our imagined fears of the city."[41] Using this dichotomy, Vidler attempts to reclaim utopia, not as a literal alternative to the real world but as an indispensable discursive tool necessary for the critique of society and the urbanisms engendered in its forms.

But what should be done with the perennial and seemingly quixotic utopian visions of the future city? Vidler's analysis of how a series of radically different ideal cities proffered in Plato's *Republic* is used to evaluate and critique models of both an ideal society and a real city (Athens) is a step toward the rehabilitation of utopia from its often paradoxically dystopian history. Fundamentally, what Vidler is identifying in Plato's use of utopia is not subjugation to a singular formal or fixed image of either human society or the city. It is utopia subsumed within a recursive process through the ongoing production of utopias, a dialectical process acknowledging that every ideal city is interdependent with its real counterparts.

If the recursive models of utopia can be viewed as tools "for thinking"[42] forever locked in a dialectical relationship with the real city and society, they may lead to new and coherent strategies for urban development. Urbanist Bernardo Secchi revisits the social concepts of space and urban form influenced by Henri Lefebvre's *The Right to the City* (1968). His concepts developed with Paola Viganò of La Ville Poreuse (The Porous City) attempt to connect segregated infrastructures and make these rigid and inaccessible urban forms more permeable. Identifying the problematic opposition between the tendencies of contemporary architectural and urban design practices, Secchi offers a warning: "I am providing an extreme version of the two sides of the same

43. Bernardo Secchi, "08-Three Words," in *Planum Magazine*: (September, 2010), accessed August 1, 2015, http://www.planum.net /these-words.
44. Ibid.
45. Ibid.

coin: at one extreme is a possible 'authorial' identity and at the other 'the author's death' and the emergence of a diffuse identity defined by norms and rules that are external to it."[43]

It would seem that the disciplinary polarity between what Secchi describes as "this 'authorial' identity above and beyond all irony and legitimate pretension" and "the planner who has obstinately refused self-referencing" characterizes the current situation. Whether this is simply the result of disciplinary hermeticism or the agnotologies of our current political and economic environment, or both, the resulting void undermines discourses on the future of the city. The same disconnection can be seen in the simultaneous development of utopian visions of the multilevel city and the realization of similar urban concepts in their most banal and bureaucratic forms. The self-referential architect and the urban planner may have felt the necessity to avoid contamination from their counterparts and their unintentional collaborators, causing a memory loss of the motivations and concepts entailed in the original imported models.

The social idealism underlying so many proposals for elevated and interconnected urban space can be contrasted with the compartmentalized and segregated spaces that are more often created. Because of the variability and indeterminacy of its effects on social and political space, a more adaptive mode of exploration seems critical. While not advocating for the application of singular and complete models of utopia, Secchi argues for confronting the problems of the modern metropolis and its indeterminacy in creative and meaningful ways: "Today the rhetoric of uncertainty plays an important role in legitimizing the different forms of relativism. If nothing can be spoken with certainty, if everything appears un-certain, un-reliable, and un-believable, everything can appear speakable and this can cover up substantial redistributions of power."[44]

He offers what he calls "scenarios" and the "archive" as possible antidotes to the disarray of professional discourse on the contemporary city. Scenarios offer the possibility of maintaining both the creative dynamism of ideal models and the critical distance necessary for "the conquest of the possible." As he describes it, "Finally others are true scenarios—attempts at inquiring into 'what would happen if...' If, in an overly-determined field of phenomena, such as urban transformations, some aspects are isolated and we ask what would happen if these phenomena reached their extreme or probable consequences, we obtain images of the future—scenarios that are partially incompatible. And it is just this partial antagonism that makes them interesting."[45]

While contemporary and historic images of "the city of the future" are invariably fascinating, their real value may lie in their incorporation into what Secchi calls "the archive," in both the palimpsests of the real city and through knowledge of historic "authorial models."

Our survey should be seen, hopefully, as an attempt to expand our archives of urban models, to include, within this trajectory of ongoing ideas, the seemingly disparate images and ideas of thinkers who have for centuries followed a sublime civic obsession—the multilevel city.

APPENDIX

ATLANTA: A PATERNALISTIC INTERIOR

The 14-block, 20-building system of the Peachtree Center complex in Atlanta is a result of the single vision of one man, John C. Portman, Jr., an architect, developer, and financier. Envisioned as a new downtown for Atlanta, Peachtree Center began to take shape in the 1960s as a major destination. An insular collection of a convention center, hotels, high-rise offices, and retail, Peachtree Center is a hub-and-spoke network of buildings and structures connected by covered footbridges, while interior walkways surround soaring, sculptural atria. While principally designed by Portman, the system was not the result of a single master plan but developed opportunistically as land and tenants were secured for various components. As a result of the commercial success and downtown economic growth resulting from the system, the new urban form had been developed expediently with little political resistance.

Although Portman invokes the genius of Leonardo da Vinci's La Città Ideale as inspiration for his atria and pedestrian bridge systems, his urban interiors have been passionately criticized by theorists Fredric Jameson, Edward Soja, and Albert Pope as the anti-urban postmodern interiors of late capitalism. Interestingly, Portman's urbanism could also be compared to the paternalistic social utopian proposals of Charles Fourier and Dr. Jules-Antoine Moilin, who proposed similar spaces for their ideal societies, but without the grand spectacle. In the ongoing struggle between the cosmopolitan (open) and communal (bounded) tendencies of urban space, capitalism seems to prefer the depoliticized interior.

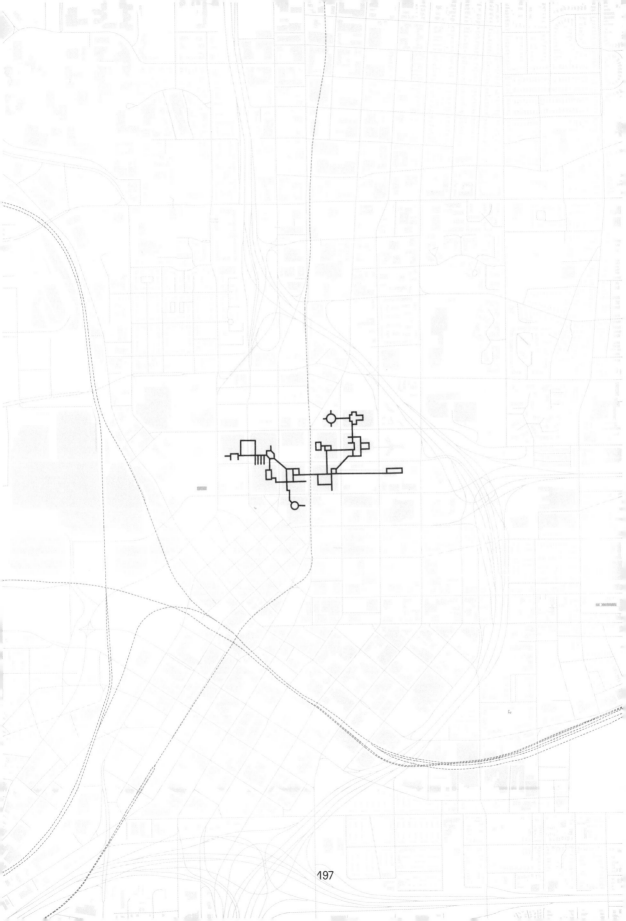

CALGARY: THE SYNTHESIZED CITY

Since its opening in 1970, the +15 system has expanded through the city for a total of 11 miles, making it one of the most extensive grade-separated pedestrian networks in the world. The current network employs 62 footbridges to interlink the meandering paths and atria typically located in the center of the city blocks.

In 1966, a recent Massachusetts Institute of Technology (MIT) graduate, Harold Hanen, began his career as city architect for Calgary, Alberta. A proponent of the urban ideas of Team 10, Hanen developed a plan for a comprehensive network of pedestrian bridges, passageways, and atria to link the entire gridiron city with an elevated pedestrian level that would later be called the +15—a reference to the fact that footbridges are about 15 feet above street level. Having studied under Harvard professor and Team 10 member Jerzy Soltan at MIT, Hanen cited Team 10 and Italian Futurist architect Antonio Sant'Elia as well as Constructivist concepts such as the social condenser as key influences on his proposal.

The +15 is publicly owned and maintained, much like a public street. Developers are mandated to connect to the system, and tax credits and bonus-density incentives are used to facilitate the extension of the system. The +15 is connected to the greater metropolitan area by the city's light rail system that runs east-west through downtown, allowing convenient pedestrian movement into the system. Calgary has begun expanding the network through the addition of a second and third tier of the system—the +30 and +45. The quest to create public space within the system is exemplified by the Devonian Gardens, an elevated 2.5-acre interior city park.

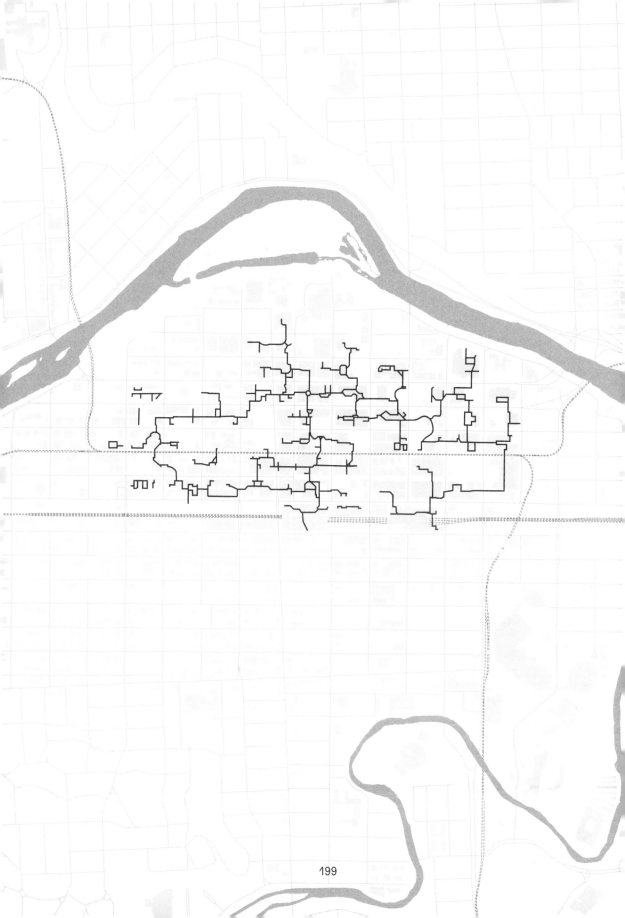

CINCINNATI: THE DISASSEMBLED SYSTEM

Although first suggested in 1957 by city planner Herbert Stevens, Cincinnati's skywalk system was initiated in 1962 by Victor Gruen (the father of the shopping mall) and further developed by RTKL in 1967. Intended to help the downtown compete with suburban shopping centers, the two consecutive master plans led to the creation of an elevated pedestrianized core in 1969 with 15 open-air public bridges. Unlike other North American systems, the original was a publically funded, open-air, deck-access network scheme similar to London's Pedway. Since then 64 additional bridges, including enclosed bridge connections, were constructed by private interests, extending the system to 1.3 miles by 1997. It exists as two separate clusters, technically but ineffectively joined by the pedestrian plaza, Fountain Square.

The deck-access system in Cincinnati suffered from a number of ill-considered and poorly designed conditions that damaged the historic building fabric and the quality of the original sidewalks. As public criticism grew, the city council decided to terminate the system and begin to remove the original bridges. This triggered a counter push from businesses harmed by the reduced pedestrian traffic. Due to lost business, a group of tenants successfully sued the city for removing a bridge, forcing the city to pay a fine of $1,000 a day until the skywalk was replaced. However, by 2002, the city approved a final plan to comprehensively remove the system, and bridges are currently being dismantled as part of a larger effort to increase street-level pedestrian activity and to enliven the downtown core.

Photos: Mark Mascolino

DALLAS: DISJUNCTIVE CITY

The Dallas Pedestrian Network is a 3-mile system employed in alternating clusters of below-ground and overhead walkways. The Dallas Centre development plan (1977) and Phase 1 Tower (1979) by Pei Cobb Freed introduced the first elevated skywalk connecting office towers to the system. Concurrently proposed as a tool to revitalize downtown by increasing shopping and encouraging commercial development, the underground system was the outcome of a comprehensive master plan (1981) by Vincent Ponte, associate of Pei and the designer and promoter of Montreal's Ville Souterraine (Underground City). The nodal components of the Dallas system are largely privately owned and controlled with differing degrees of access, and exterior spaces are primarily corporate plazas. Up until the last 20 years there has been little to no incentive for creating public space or overall coherence within the system. An exception is the little-used Skywalk Park in the center city that is primarily accessible from vertical circulation that leads to a skywalk above. As in most American cities, planning is oriented around automobile circulation and the components of the system are defined by task-oriented circulation—home to office to lunch or shopping and home again. Early critics such as David Dillon and William Whyte described a segregated system divided by race and income with largely white, middle-class office workers above and lower-wage service and retail workers of color below. More recently, the Dallas system has been criticized for robbing the street of urban vitality. The private uses, prioritizing parking over civic spaces and alternating between below-ground and overhead, makes the system discontinuous and underpopulated.

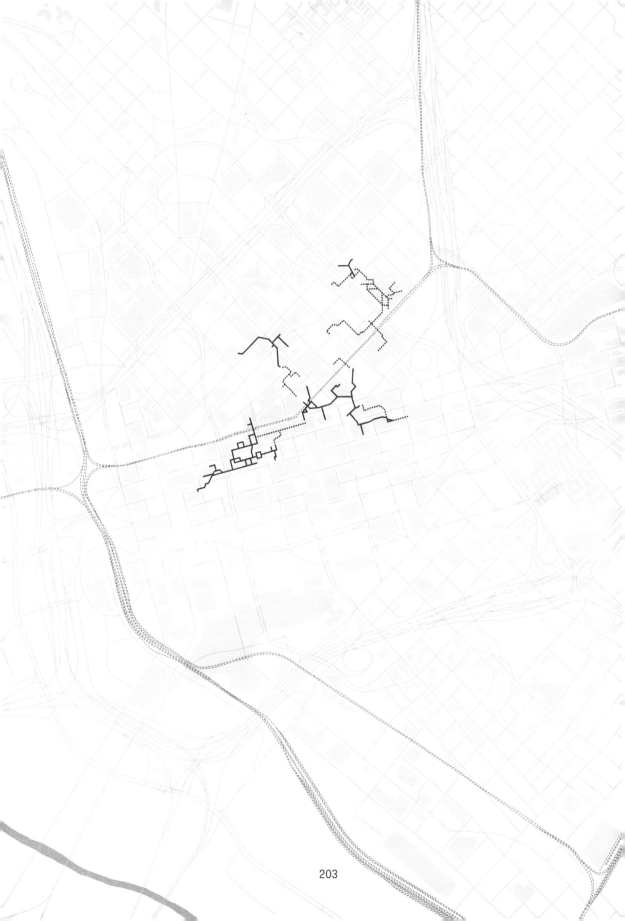

MUMBAI: METABOLIZING GROWTH

Mumbai's rapid urbanization has created extreme congestion and traffic safety issues, particularly at the confluence of the city's major arteries. To remediate these conditions, the Mumbai Metropolitan Region Development Authority proposed in 2007 a series of 58 skywalks designed by the city's engineers to strategically allow pedestrians to bypass crowded streets. Each bridge is constructed on land controlled by the municipality and adapted to the specific needs of multimodal transportation hubs, including buses, trains, rickshaws, and foot traffic. Creating recognizable urban figures, the overpasses convey pedestrians above congested areas to make strategic connections between residential areas, shopping centers, and markets. The largest, a nearly mile-long link that creates the first semblance of a system, Bandra, was completed in 2010 and is used by more than 100,000 pedestrians daily. It has five access points and six stairs and connects to a bus station, the National Library, and a mosque. Most skywalks share a similar design vocabulary of a canopied walkway built on bright yellow supports. Of the original 58 proposed bridges, 37 skywalks have been completed at strategic locations.

In 2013 Dutch architect Neville Mars proposed the Landlink project, an elevated circulation conduit between neighboring slums to facilitate movement and commerce. By repurposing the right-of-way of an abandoned pipeline, his proposal anticipates increased multistory development generated by the release of constrained circulation flows. Mars's proposals for elevated circulation structures in Mumbai also anticipate incremental improvements in modes of transportation that enable neighborhoods to make improvements as resources become available. This is an informal realization of the Metabolists' ideal—the city as process—achievable in this case only through tactical urban interventions.

The incremental and strategic use of multilevel infrastructural components relative to larger circulation flows can be seen in many other modern metropolises, such as the Metro Cable project in Caracas by Urban-Think Tank (2007–2010).

Top: Courtesy ©DNA–Daily News & Analysis
Bottom: Photo: Menaka Rao, 2014

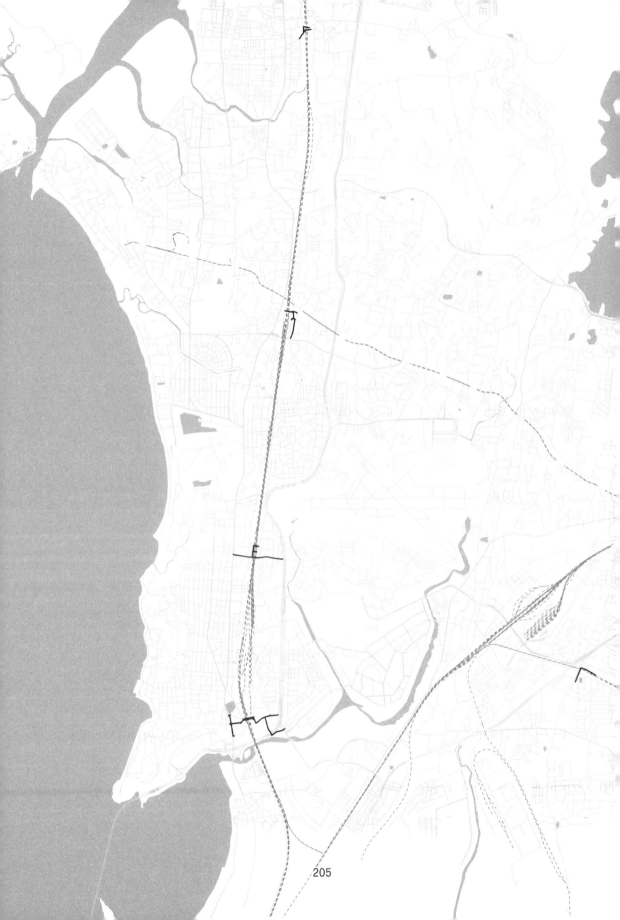

RIYADH: INSTANT CITY

The Saudi Arabian capital of Riyadh is creating a new financial district with a second level of connected circulation via an enclosed, air-conditioned skywalk system—a 3-D oasis, an echo of ancient desert cities like Ghadames in central Libya. The skywalk system was designed as part of an international competition in 2010, with Swedish firm Henning Larsen completing the winning master plan for the district and designing the individual skywalk components. A series of ninety solar-powered bridges will interlink 35,500,000 square feet of retail, residential towers, financial institutions, sports facilities, and cultural amenities into a continuous elevated promenade. Promoted as technically advanced and sustainable, the district was designed as a business and living environment for both local and foreign residents. A cluster of cultural projects and facilities for recreation are incorporated along with connections to housing and retail, creating a self-contained district. The project will also have a retail podium, or raised plaza, that bridges part of the site. Parking is relegated to the periphery of the interiorized district and a monorail connects six different stations. The footbridges are faceted, geometric modules that can be pieced together to construct different lengths of walkway. Ninety-seven bridges are proposed as part of the master plan with 61 being currently constructed in the first phase. They will connect new buildings and towers by a range of Western architects, including Foster + Partners, Zaha Hadid Architects, FX Fowle, Barton Wilmore, Gensler, SOM, and Snøhetta.

Top: Courtesy Henning Larsen Architects
Bottom: Courtesy Ed Reeve

ST. PAUL: THE CONTINUOUS INTERIOR

The construction of St. Paul's downtown skyway system began in 1967, but it was first proposed in 1956 based on Victor Gruen's plan for Fort Worth. Like the one in Minneapolis, the St. Paul skyway system is fully interiorized. The city now has more than fifty footbridges and six miles of continuous skyway circulation space. Because St. Paul has more historic buildings and topographical changes from street to street than Minneapolis, bridges have been designed to adapt to highly complex existing conditions, creating a very circuitous network winding though the city blocks. Urbanist William H. Whyte criticized the system, calling St. Paul the "blank wall capital of the United States"—a reference to the system's disorienting spaces.

St. Paul's skyways were initially federally funded with an urban renewal grant and designed as a publicly owned system using easements to include interior horizontal and vertical circulation for access and control. In this unified complex, bridges were designed based on a single prototype. The skyways identify major city streets below through standardized wayfinding signage, and the overall uniform appearance of the system gives an impression of urban infrastructure. The city has a Skyway Governance Committee that determines approval and the St. Paul Code of Ordinances has a special highly detailed section on "Skyway Conduct" to maintain appropriate behavior in the system. Because downtown Minneapolis has a greater density of people and businesses, the St. Paul system, by comparison, appears underutilized while displacing retail and pedestrians from street level.

SINGAPORE: CITY OF SPECTACLE

After gaining independence in 1965, the city-state of Singapore used a range of infrastructural development strategies to encourage economic growth through outside investment. One of these concepts was also driven by ideas of strengthening community through interconnections, influenced by Team 10 and the Metabolists, and specifically creating an elevated pedestrian system in its commercial district. This development was initially concentrated in a central shopping district, initiated with William Lim and DP Architects' interconnected Peoples Park Complex (1973) and Golden Mile Complex (1974). It was based on a multilevel urbanism that was developed by SPUR (the Asian City of Tomorrow) and expanded by designing policies to promote the construction of additional elevated pedestrian links. From 1986 to 1997, DP Architects developed the region's largest interconnected commercial complex, interweaving Marina Square, Millenia Singapore, and Suntec City and connecting with the Central Business District.

Development in Singapore has shifted away from an extended continuous network to a series of multilevel interconnected mixed use complexes or urban enclaves. While intended for mixed-use, the new developments concentrate on housing and commercial/entertainment. This interlinked and multilevel urban development strategy has also generated a series of spectacular elevated parks, including TreeTop Walk and Supertree Grove, for recreation and to promote tourism.

The Marina Bay Sands, designed by Moshe Safdie, is a unique three-tower design that houses a casino, a hotel, convention and exhibition spaces, retail shops, and entertainment venues, and is capped by the Sands SkyPark. The rooftop park towers are more than 650 feet above the ground and feature the world's largest cantilever, an observatory, and a 492-foot-long infinity pool offering 360-degree views of the city skyline with attractions such as light and water shows and base-jumping. Like many of their urban projects, this $5.7 billion complex was the result of an international competition held by the Singaporean government: the prize was a long-term casino lease for the Las Vegas–based developer. The elevated urban condition continues to develop, incorporating exterior greenspace with elevated circulation in public and private housing and hotels.

Top: Courtesy Sengkang/Wikimedia Commons
Center and bottom: Courtesy Verner C. Petersen

HONG KONG: NEGOTIATED TERRAIN

Hong Kong's multilevel pedestrian system is composed of more than 560 footbridges, making it the most extensive of all global skyway cities. After the first elevated footbridges were constructed in 1963, a more continuous and interconnected system began to take form organically and accelerated with the creation of the successful multilevel development, Connaught Place, in the Central District in 1970. By elevating pedestrian traffic in that area to provide connections across congested streets and roadways, the system enabled a greater development density along the waterfront commercial district. The pedestrian systems have also been used to negotiate the difficult topographical conditions along the hilly coastline.

The Hong Kong pedestrian network is composed of deck-access plazas and podia, flyover bridges, covered elevated walkways, and exterior escalators that climb the steep hillsides.

This patchwork of urban pedestrian strategies is deployed through on-demand techniques, which use data-mapping to develop and refine the system to respond to changing circumstances. Interestingly, the same group of architects that proposed the Pedway system and the utopian MARS Plan for London undertook the planning of post–World War II Hong Kong. Sir Patrick Abercrombie, Arthur Ling, and the London County Council (LCC) architects authored both the Greater London Plan of 1944 and also the Hong Kong Preliminary Planning Report of 1949. The LCC continued to direct the development of Hong Kong parallel to their work on London in the postwar years.

With the shift in governmental control form Great Britain to China in the late 1990s, Hong Kong and its northern neighbor, Shenzhen, are being developed in parallel and integrated into the Hong Kong Special Administrative Region. In Shenzhen, multiple urban centers with the elevated system are being developed similar to Hong Kong's. Concepts for multilevel development have been proposed to radically integrate architecture, urban space, and infrastructure. The new Futian financial district is being developed with a comprehensive master plan that integrates an elevated podium and skywalk system with layers of underground tunnels and commercial space. A series of large-scale landmark components, stacked and composed as iconic geometric figures along a symmetrical axis, include the multilevel City Hall and Train Station, OMA's proposed Crystal Island that creates an elevated ringed walkway system as a monumental connector, a Cultural Centre and Transit Hub, and commercial space. It also includes proposed strategic multilevel components (WORKac) and a new train line interconnected with Hong Kong.

LONDON: THE CRUCIBLE

The allure of three-dimensional urbanisms has long held the interest of London's academic and design circles. The Adelphi project, designed by Robert Adam and his brothers in the City of Westminster in 1768, is one of the most noteworthy examples to presage the multilevel city proposals of Alison and Peter Smithson and other British architects in the twentieth century.

Two centuries later, a system of grade-separate pedestrian walkways began to take hold after the devastation left by the Blitz. In 1938, MARS Group member William Tatton-Brown began promoting a comprehensive pedestrian circulation system as a way to create more active and integrated social centers in the industrial landscapes of London. In postwar London, city planner William Holford put forward a radical proposal called the Pedestrian Ways for the London County Council (LCC, 1947) and by 1963 the plan by Holford had expanded into a proposed 30-mile elevated pedestrian walkway called the Pedway. The full extent of this system is mapped at right, but only a small portion of the network was ever built. The system was to be implemented incrementally, but over time, extensions were limited and eventually blocked by the preservation movement's determination to protect individual buildings.

Alison and Peter Smithson helped articulate new theories of modern urbanism with schemes such as "streets in the sky," a deck-access concept based on the model promoted by the London County Council and Projects Techniques Office. These urban and architectural design strategies came to typify the British housing estates of the 1960s and 1970s, whereby dwellings opened onto wide, external corridors overlooking ambiguously defined parks and social space.

The Pedway scheme seemed to falter from its beginning as it was created in an ad hoc fashion, with nefarious dead-end passageways and a lack of visual continuity and way-finding cues for pedestrians. Retailers resisted occupying the elevated levels and pedestrians were disinclined to walk upstairs to reach elevated plazas. The historic preservation movement in the 1980s, which provided protection to certain buildings, would ensure that the Pedway scheme would never reach completion. Despite its lack of success, London's urban experiments would be decisive in spreading the strategy of the multilevel city around the world.

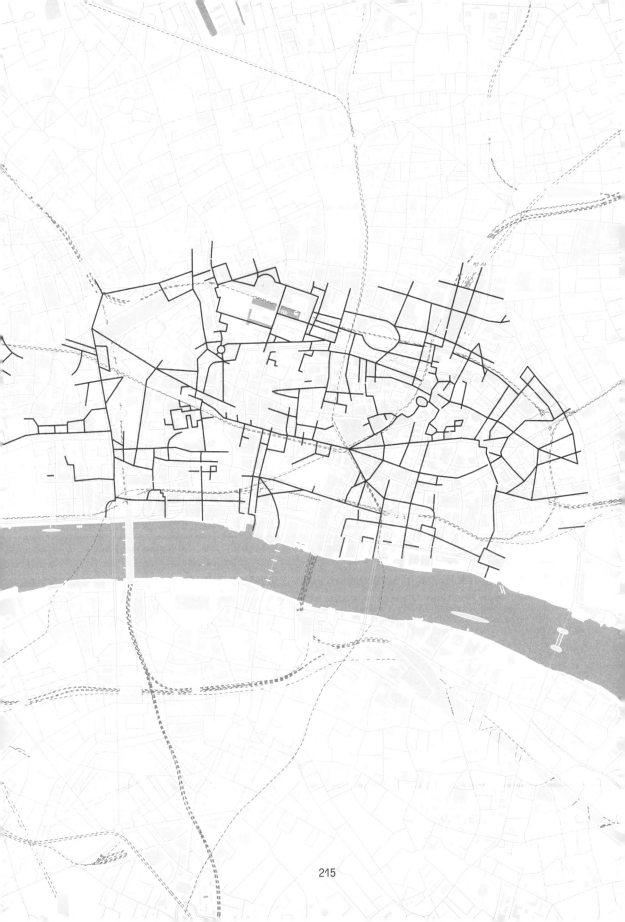

MINNEAPOLIS: SURREPTITIOUS URBANISM

The Minneapolis Skyway System began in 1962 with a few enclosed footbridges connecting downtown department stores. It has since grown to 8 miles, interconnecting nearly the entire downtown core on the second level, creating one of the largest continuous skyway systems in the world. Its growth is driven by the desire of developers to connect to the skyway's second-story level, which can command higher rates per square foot than ground-level retail. The Minneapolis system of skyways was initiated by key business leaders but has now entered a self-perpetuating mode in which future developments must be connected to the network to ensure their success.

The Crystal Court designed by Philip Johnson as part of the IDS Center tower (1972) is a glass-covered public atrium that acts as the central organizing hub for the entire system. The character of the system and design of its component parts is loosely regulated by the Downtown Skyway Advisory Committee, a group composed of building owners or occupants. The advisory committee cannot ensure system continuity, uniform bridge design, consistent and convenient hours of operation, or a comprehensive, understandable way-finding system.

In a region with climatic extremes, 80 urban blocks are interconnected with bridges, providing continuous access to retail spaces with office buildings and parking structures. The chief criticism of the system—that it displaces pedestrian life on grade-level sidewalks—is countered by arguments that with the city's long, cold winters, such street life would be absent for many months of the year. Advocates say the skyway system has succeeded in keeping major offices and retail stores in the downtown core, acting as a bulwark against suburbanization.

Businessman Leslie Park and architect Ed Baker are popularly credited with inventing the idea of the skyway system, but the story is more complex with different actors, including Victor Gruen, architect, urban planner, and inventor of the first enclosed shopping mall (Southdale Shopping Center) in suburban Minneapolis, who also consulted on the St. Paul and Minneapolis master planning efforts; and Athelstan Spilhaus, dean of the Institute of Technology at the University of Minnesota and syndicated author of *Our New Age*, a weekly comic about science and technology.

MONTREAL: UNDERGROUND CITY

Montreal's Ville Souterraine (Underground City) began in the late 1950s with Place Ville Marie by architects Pei Cobb Freed. Its large underground volume of interconnected commercial space and transit connected to street-level public plazas created a new city center for Montreal. The Place Ville Marie project, led by Henry Cobb with urban planner Vincent Ponte, planned for expansion and projected forward a new form of underground urbanism employing large day-lit atria to connect to adjacent outdoor plazas and office tower cores.

After Place Ville Marie's completion in 1962, Montreal hired Ponte to study connections to the new Metro Subway and the systems expansion to other commercial structures. The collaborative work of Cobb and Ponte appeared again in Dallas with the Dallas Centre project and Cobb's work on Fountain Plaza parallel to Ponte's proposals for city's underground system. Based on the success of Montreal, Ponte proposed similar systems for underground pedestrian networks in other North American cities using the integrated superblock concept. Recognized for a long career proselytizing for multilevel pedestrian systems and his grand visions for Montreal and Dallas, Ponte was dubbed the "Multilevel Man" in 1970 by *Time* magazine.

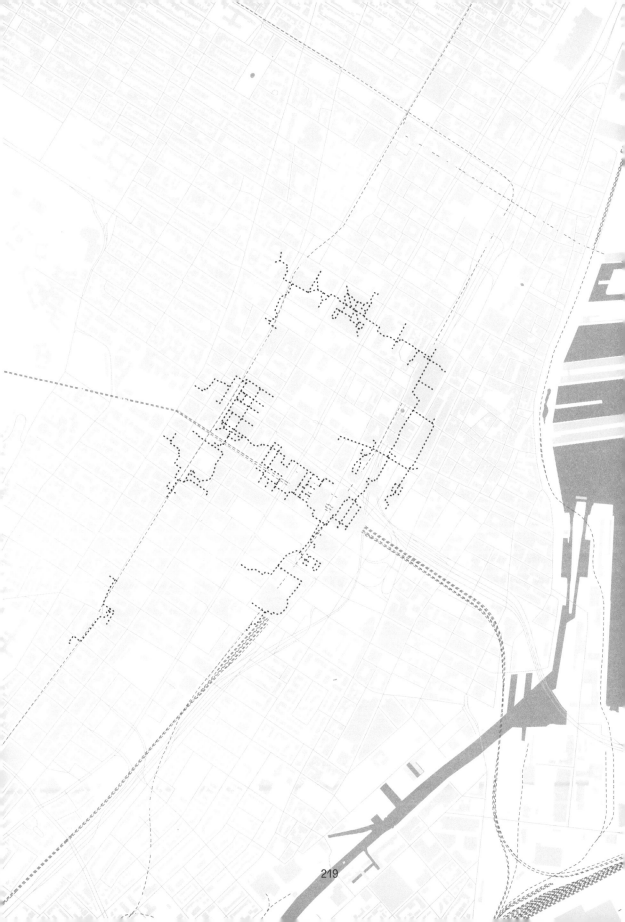

DES MOINES: THE PLANNED CITY

The 3.2-mile system in Des Moines, connecting 35 blocks and the majority of downtown, is arguably one of the most comprehensive in North America. Driven by economic development interests and city planners, the elevated system was initiated in 1969 to facilitate traffic movement and provide climate-controlled pedestrian circulation.

Unlike other systems that have been built incrementally by property owners, the city of Des Moines has planned and financed skywalk locations and bridges in accordance with its comprehensive master plan. This factor, along with clear rules set into place at its conception, has allowed the city to control its development. In response to criticisms of the skywalks taking city life off of the street, the system design provides vertical connections to sidewalks and runs parallel to the streets rather than perpendicularly through the center of blocks.

LEXICON

LEXICON

Aérodromes

The first significant, large-scale utopian urban infrastructure project organized around a social concept was proposed by civil engineer and socialist utopian philosopher Henri Jules Borie and published and distributed widely in Paris between 1865–1867. The infrastructure in Borie's Aérodromes was layered to allow for density without congestion, using multiple levels for ease of circulation above the street and setbacks for better daylighting. Ten-story towers were connected by a network of elevated glass bridges running parallel to the streets on the fifth level. Aérodromes influenced both Eugène Hénard and Le Corbusier in their urban concepts.

Air Streets

If there is one image that captures the optimism of the modern city at the turn of the twentieth century it is the frontispiece of *King's Dream of New York*, published in 1908 by Moses King. It depicts the future metropolis of towering skyscrapers intersected by layers of elevated streets and railways. Again in 1929, with the publication of *Metropolis of Tomorrow*, Hugh Ferriss would depict similar elevated streets and infrastructure called "overhead traffic-ways." Situated on the skyscraper's terraced setbacks, these elevated roadways were aligned between buildings to allow the fluid movement of cars and trucks high above the ground. Ferriss was quick to note that such conditions were "perhaps a paradise for the automobile manufacturer," but offered little relief for the office worker. Other architects and planners such as Harvey Wiley Corbett, Thomas Adams, and Raymond Hood were also speculating on the possibilities of the modern multilevel city with schemes for elevated roadways and railways wrapping and merging into skyscrapers, aerial footbridges connecting towers, and wide, elevated pedestrian promenades spanning city blocks—all deployed to shape the form of the future city. These seductive illustrations heighten the drama of multilayered, vertiginous space with the promise of greater urban efficiency.

Arcade

Typically, a glass-roof-covered walkway formed by a succession of arches on one or both sides of an interiorized street lined with shops. Studied as central to the urban experience of nineteenth-century Parisian consumer culture by philosopher Walter Benjamin in his exhaustive documentation of the Arcades. The first arcade was in the Palais-Royal, which was heavily influential to socialist philosopher Charles Fourier.

Bonus Density System

Bonus density is an incentive strategy that allows developers to increase the size of their projects in exchange for providing connections to the elevated pedestrian system and other public amenities. For instance, Calgary's +15 elevated walkway system requires new development to provide bridges and pedestrian paths fifteen feet above street level that connect into the system. In exchange for providing a public right-of-way through the interior of their buildings, developers may achieve bonus density and substantially increase the allowable floor area ratio (FAR) of their project. If a development pro forma requires an even higher FAR, other urban amenities such as atria or gardens may be offered in exchange. One example of this is the Devonian Gardens, a 2.5-acre indoor park and botanical garden built on top of the Core Shopping Centre in Calgary. The gardens are maintained by the city's parks department and feature a three-block-long skylight, more than five hundred trees, water fountains, and a koi pond.

Central/Mid-Levels Escalator (Hong Kong)

In the film *Chungking Express* (1994), director Wong Kar-wai uses the Hong Kong Central Escalator as a cinematic device to create a sense of social alienation. The immiscible spatial characteristics of the elevated pedestrian system, with its layered and fragmented spaces, are made poignant by the slow-motion glide of the escalator through the dense hillside city. Opening in 1993, the half-mile-long system of covered escalators and elevated walkways connects Hong Kong's central business district with its Mid-Levels residential area and is used by more than 55,000 people each day. The Central/Mid-Levels Escalator ascends 443 feet to overcome the city's steep coastline topography and reverses direction midday to accommodate the predominant travel direction of rush-hour commuters.

City of Bridges

Venice has been a familiar trope for architects attempting to add excitement and romance to their multilevel city proposals. Harvey Wiley Corbett proposed a system of bridges, plazas, and arcades in 1924 to transform Manhattan into what he described as a "modernized Venice." Raymond Hood also knowingly evoked the image of Venice in his proposal for Manhattan called the City of Bridges, but carried the concept to a heroic scale. One scheme proposed a 10,000-foot-long bridge across the Hudson River supported by 50-story residential buildings. In Manhattan 1950, the future city is dramatically represented in an aerial photomontage by a series of bridges spaced at half-mile intervals, subsuming the island. The "Venicification" of elevated pedestrian systems continued into the 1980s as Colin Rowe evoked Byron ("I Stood in Venice on the Bridge of Sighs/A palace and a prison on each hand…") to underscore the indeterminate spatial experience of the Minneapolis Skyway System's footbridges.

Continuous Interior

The concept of the continuous interior has taken on various guises—both utopian and dystopian—in architectural history, most notably in the ironic vision of Archizoom Associati's No-Stop City (1969), where the future is imagined as an endless, artificially lit, and climate-controlled interior city outfitted to perpetuate unfettered mass consumption. The *mise en abyme* of the endless corridor reflects the absurdity of modern industrial society taken to its logical, rational extreme—a critical utopia with an architecture that is all interiority and without exteriority. From 1956 to 1974, artist Constant Nieuwenhuys would develop his project *New Babylon* as a series of speculative proposals for an elevated, interiorized urban superstructure freely traversing both the traditional city and the landscape—a utopic social space of creative free play set apart and above the existing reality. The intensely interiorized spatial characteristics of the continuous interior can be experienced in built systems like the skyways of Minneapolis and St. Paul, which extend for miles in labyrinthine networks.

Deck-Access Scheme

The deck-access scheme became a popular circulation feature of many large-scale postwar public housing estates, particularly in Great Britain, such as Park Hill (Jack Lynn, Ivor Smith, 1961) in Sheffield, Golden Lane Estate (Chamberlin, Powell, and Bon, 1957/1962), and Robin Hood Gardens (Alison and Peter Smithson, 1972) in London. The deck-access scheme allows individual residential units to be reached from a common walkway that may be covered or uncovered but is otherwise open to the elements. Forming a liminal zone that is neither entirely outside nor fully inside, this strategy gained favor over the central interior corridor found in most residential buildings as a way of constructing a more streetlike presence, an equivalent to the neighborhood sidewalk as a shared community space.

Donkey Path Urbanism

In 1889, Camillo Sitte advocated an urbanism that would reinforce the meandering qualities and ad hoc pattern of the historic city, restrict traffic, and favor the pedestrian. The Sitte model was later popularized by Lewis Mumford and conceptually allied with the mid-twentieth-century development of pedestrian malls. Le Corbusier's retort famously argued against Sitte: "Man walks in a straight line because he has a goal and knows where he is going. … The pack-donkey meanders along.… The winding road is the pack-donkey's way, the straight road is man's way." The historical city's accretion of urban strata follows this original, haphazard pattern of the metaphorical donkey, against the rational logic and the orthogonal efficiency of the modern urban planner.

Enclave

An enclave is a clearly bounded territory within a larger territory. Through its desire to create a self-contained community, it creates an area that is separated from the larger whole. Enclaves create definition through physical divisions or methods of control to secure its inhabitants from the exterior. The enclave is often criticized for creating racial, political, and economic segregation in cities.

Endless Bridge

One of the signature features of the Guthrie Theater in Minneapolis designed by Atelier Jean Nouvel (2006) is the Endless Bridge. The 178-foot-long, 30-foot-wide structure is one of the world's longest occupied cantilevers. Functioning as an elevated lobby, the Endless Bridge is also an observatory for the Mississippi River and its surrounding neighborhood. Leveraging the air-rights regulations created for the Minneapolis Skyway System, the Guthrie redefined interior circulation space as public, creating interior space accessible to the public beyond performance hours. The bridge and cantilevered volume above is combined with circulation to function as a privately owned public space, much like the city's skyways, as it is open until midnight daily and free of charge. Although not connected directly to the Minneapolis Skyway System, the Endless Bridge was designed as a skywaylike condition and suggests the incompleteness of any such system. The Guthrie Theater contains another elevated passageway that transports sets and equipment to the main stages from a production facility that sits atop the parking garage across the street.

Festival of Britain

An exposition held in summer 1951 to celebrate Great Britain's postwar recovery and oriented toward the country's future. Centered on London, it focused on the sciences, technology, and the arts and was a demonstration of modern landscape, architecture, and town planning. Influenced by Russian Constructivist architecture and CIAM principles, structures included several iconic and experimental multilevel projects such as the Royal Festival Hall by Leslie Martin and the Sea and Ships Pavilion by Basil Spence. The festival location was seen as a demonstration project to the public for new ideas of town planning. After its demolition, the site became the multilevel Southbank Centre.

Flyover

A flyover bridge, one of the most rudimentary components of a multilevel city, carries pedestrians and/or bicyclists up and over busy streets and congested intersections without impeding vehicular or rail traffic at grade. In Mumbai, the Skywalk system is a nodal network composed of flyovers, which takes pedestrians up and over railway lines and unsafe vehicular traffic so they can efficiently traverse congested neighborhoods to arrive at distant landing points.

Floating City

The Metabolists group of architects in 1960s Japan revisited the possibility of a city floating on air or water in many of their experimental projects. Kenzo Tange presented his Plan for Tokyo: Toward a Structural Reorganization (1960) at the World Design Conference in Tokyo. The proposal built upon an earlier project completed with students at the Massachusetts Institute of Technology (MIT), where Tange had served as a visiting professor. The MIT project explored the possibility of housing 25,000 people over Boston Bay. In his plan, Tange envisioned a linear expansion of the city across Tokyo Bay. His layered, three-dimensional megastructure included a transportation layer organized in a series of cyclical links, which were positioned some forty meters above sea level. The scheme separated major vehicular traffic from pedestrian flows and was designed to handle an estimated five million passengers a day.

Highwalk System

This term is associated with the elevated walkways of the Barbican Estate in London (Chamberlin, Powell, and Bon, 1955–1982). The mixed-use complex of residences, cultural amenities, and educational facilities occupies forty acres in the City of London, an area devastated during World War II. True to its name, which references the gateway in a fortress wall, the Barbican is itself an insular city within a city. The Highwalk system, coupled with the podium level, enabled the architects to create a large area free of traffic and provide space for shared gardens and plazas. Vehicles and other forms of transit are relegated to the original street level below. The Barbican Highwalk scheme was intended to integrate with a separately planned but largely unbuilt network of Pedways extending to the surrounding offices and businesses.

Horizontal Skyscrape

Frederick Kiesler proposed his version of a horizontal skyscraper for Paris in 1925, with a cruciform arrangement of stacked, suspended, and cantilevered residential blocks. For him, the horizontal skyscraper was not simply a spatial inversion of its vertical cousin, but also a programmatic reversal. The horizontal skyscraper avoided a monotonous stacking "like bricks" of urban dwellers by opening individual living units to views, light, and air from various directions. The proposal thus reclaimed ground space for public usage as commons and gardens. El Lissitzky and Mart Stam developed the concept of the Wolkenbügel (Cloud-Iron, 1923–1925), horizontal office buildings lifted high over major intersections in Moscow. Each three-legged, L-shaped structure was perched on top of 164-foot-tall pylons straddling the intersection and intended as a transportation hub with connections to a proposed subway system and shelter for streetcar stations. Envisioned as an eight-structure network, they were sited to mark the major intersections of the boulevard ringing Moscow. The contemporary concept of the horizontal skyscraper would find its ultimate built realization in Steven Holl's Vanke Center project in Shenzhen, China (2009). The mixed-use project contains offices, residences, a hotel, and a conference center.

Kowloon Walled City

An informal walled settlement or vertical village that was located in Kowloon district of Hong Kong. An unregulated urban enclave formed in 1898, it developed into a hyper-dense condition with a population of nearly 40,000 people within a 100-by-200-meter site before it was demolished in 1994. Circulation and open space were reduced within the 14-story structure to extreme minimums, creating impetus for more informal and three-dimensional strategies for public open areas, including terraces, balconies, and rooftops being used to create continuous interconnected urban expanses.

Linear City

This urban model is based on a linear formation and is an alternative to the concentric city. It was first proposed in the nineteenth century by Spanish urban planner Arturo Sora y Mata as Ciudad Lineal. The form is often derived from linear transportation and infrastructure strategies, i.e., rivers, railroads, and highways. Separate zones for housing, industry, greenspace, and agriculture were organized to expand along its length. It was promoted in the 1920s Soviet Union by planner Nikolay Milyutin and developed by Ernst May, Ivan Leonidov, and the May Brigade of German architects in the well-published Magnitogorsk project. These experimental urban projects focused on industry and also incorporated Moisei Ginzburg's social condenser prototypes. The project became a model for experimental linear city forms, including the MARS Plan and Le Corbusier's Plan Obus, Algiers project.

Metabolism

Metabolism as a name for the architectural movement came from the Japanese term *shinchintai-sha*, referring to the exchange of materials and energy between organisms and the physical world, described through a process of growth and renewal. Used to describe society, it was seen as a term applicable to emerging contextual ideas about urban transformation. The group used the English translation of metabolism to describe their movement and concept. This idea of biological growth was merged with Fumihiko Maki's concept of the megastructure, generating large-scale urban proposals based on incremental modules such as Kenzo Tange's Plan for Tokyo (1960), Kikutake Kiyonori's Marine City (1963), Arata Isozaki's City in the Air (1962), and Kisho Kurokawa's Space City. Tange, seen as the group's mentor, described their oeuvre as City as Process. Their work was promoted in conferences, through teaching positions at North American universities, and at the World Expo in Osaka that was curated by Tange in 1970.

On-Demand Planning

A strategy that utilizes the interconnectedness of urban systems and information to help plan cities. By gathering data on urban factors and forces (crime, traffic, economic performance, energy use, pollution), planners can assess real-time areas of concern. Digital modeling, mapping, and "smart" grids are used to monitor data and identify areas to implement reforms. Cities such as Hong Kong use this process to propose and implement planning techniques. Larger concerns about these smart grids and cities are based around issues of privacy, control, and the corporate and governmental use of data. The demand-response system is often validated for its ability to support emerging ideas about the "sharing economy," creating means for efficient distribution of energy, and facilitating the shared use of automated vehicles.

Parametric Urbanism

A technique of generating urban forms based on the use of parameters in computational design. By focusing on the parameter, the digital design of building systems enables the integration of complex variables in the development of varied urban forms. As a movement, parametric urbanism claims the ability to analyze large quantities of data to create new and adaptive architectural forms and critically assess their urban performance. Patrik Schumacher of Zaha Hadid Architects describes parametric urbanism as a new style that uses parametric "versioning" to build up a geometrically complex urban field. It is not yet clear whether the style itself as a dominant parameter for urban design is inherently self-limiting.

The Pedway

The Pedway was the name given to the controversial pedestrian system developed surreptitiously for the reconstruction of London after the Blitz. This ambitious plan to reinvent the center of London as a "modern" multilevel city first emerged in the 1940s as part of the planning work of the London County Council (LCC) and was authored by staff architects who were former members of the CIAM-influenced MARS Group. Architect and planner William Holford participated in the planning for rebuilding postwar London's financial center and was commissioned in 1947 to produce a study called "Pedestrian Ways." The study initially proposed elevated pedestrian systems in select areas around the city. By the 1950s, plans were drawn up for London's Comprehensive Development Areas, including the Barbican, Finsbury, the Southbank, Picadilly Circus, and Paternoster Square. By the late 1960s, the scheme had evolved into a plan for a continuous 30-mile pedestrian walkway that was to be implemented incrementally in London's Square Mile.

Palais-Royal

The Palais-Royal was a palace owned by King Louis XIII and originally constructed for Cardinal Richelieu. It was repurposed by Louis Philippe II in 1780 just prior to the French Revolution to function both as a free port and a center of culture and commerce. In 1784 it was opened to the public as an entertainment and shopping complex. The Palais-Royal created a complex intermixing of diverse activities and attracted a broad range of people to the arcades contained within (Galleries de Bois and D'Orléans). Surrounded by public gardens, a political forum, two theaters, and event space, the arcades themselves contained cafés, reading rooms, markets, and publishers of political pamphlets. They were a social center but also a forum for political and philosophical debates. To Charles Fourier, the social activity he witnessed in the Palais-Royal was the inspiration for ideas he used in the Phalanstère that were key to designing an ideal form of society.

Phalanstère

The Phalanstère was a quasi-urban building complex designed as a model of an ideal community by socialist utopian thinker Charles Fourier. It was structured on a community of 1,620 individuals, based on the concept of a Greek phalanx. The design included an arcadelike *rue corridor* (street gallery) to facilitate movement and create a form of social condensation. Fourier believed that providing the comforts and conveniences of the palace to the community within a choreographed system would create harmony and result in expanded social interactions.

Piano Nobile

The first floor in an Italian Renaissance palazzo containing the main reception rooms, the "nobile floor" was the most prestigious place in the palace. The socialist utopians replicated this spatial idea in their visionary cities, making the noble floor accessible to everyone while elevating everyday experience.

Pilotis and Core

Pilotis was a structural strategy proposed by Le Corbusier to elevate the base of buildings, making the entire ground plane accessible to pedestrians. Kenzo Tange integrated this concept into his Pilotis and Core strategy, combining the elevated building structure for a social purpose (linking public and private space) with a core structure for functional needs (vertical circulation and utilities) into a single architectural-infrastructural concept.

The Plug-In City

Plug-In City, first proposed by Peter Cook of Archigram in 1964, was a constantly evolving megastructure into which various types of programmed units for living, shopping, or working can be inserted using a crane integrated into the existing framework. Archigram reversed traditional hierarchies of building, using modular infrastructure to create multilevel urban form facilitating growth, change, and connectivity. Influenced by an anticipated social nomadism and increased product obsolescence in postwar culture, the project reveals its radical openness and inherent incompleteness through a process of continual change. Archigram's Plug-In and infrastructural concepts were influenced by the technology-focused urban speculations of Cedric Price, Yona Friedman, R. Buckminster Fuller, and the Metabolists.

Podium Level

As the name implies, the podium level raises pedestrians above grade-level traffic and creates vehicular-free city centers. The idea emerged from CIAM's concepts of traffic separation and is exemplified in Le Corbusier's La Ville Radieuse (1924). The podium level is often used in combination with tower structures to create an elevated plaza, a typology that underlies many elevated urban pedestrian schemes, including the Barbican in London. Other examples of podium-level circulation strategies can be found in many new towns in China and have been used in combination with footbridge strategies in Hong Kong since the 1970s. The podium as a continuous surface for pedestrian circulation evolved into the mat-building in the 1960s through the work of Team 10 and was represented by Candilis-Josic-Woods' Free University Berlin (1963) and Le Corbusier's Venice Hospital (1964–1965).

Rue Galeries

Also described as street galleries. An invention of Charles Fourier for an elevated pedestrian street protected from weather for the purpose of "internal communications."

Rue Intérieure

Le Corbusier developed two significant forms of the internalized street. At Unité d'Habitation (1947–1952), the idea of the street is moved inside as the *rue intérieure*, bringing together different populations in shared circulation by connecting housing, an internal shopping arcade, exercise facilities, and a school. Le Corbusier's concept of the promenade architecturale evolved from his work in the 1920s that choreographed the path of people moving through space—typically through the use of ramps and internal bridges—in order to frame vistas, establish spatial orientation, and guide approaches. His use of this technique is epitomized in the plan for the Carpenter Center for Visual Arts at Harvard University (1963) with its ramping bridge. The promenade architecturale was more perceptual than functional, heightening the awareness of building form and social activity.

Sectional Demographics

This is the authors' term to describe the tendency for multilevel urban environments to reinforce social and economic divisions. The capacity of the built environment to normalize, or even concretize, social divisions is well documented by urban theorists such as Henri Lefebvre and David Harvey. Multilevel pedestrian systems problematize one of the most fundamental concepts of public space—the street. While the concept of the street as a functional and accessible public realm can be contested in many circumstances, its division into multiple levels only exacerbates the problems of social segregation and raises concerns about access, movement, public space, and private property rights. Some systems have been criticized for segregating populations along the lines of race, class, or gender.

Skybridge

An elevated horizontal connection for circulation between adjacent spaces or buildings is often referred to as a skybridge. It is typically positioned at great heights between two or more towers to capture dramatic views and the spectacle of vertiginous space. Recent examples include Cesar Pelli's Petronas Twin Towers (1996) in Kuala Lumpur, Malaysia, a walkway between buildings that is more than 550 feet above the ground; and can be found in projects by OMA, MVRDV, Zaha Hadid Architects (ZHA), SHoP, and Diller Scofidio + Renfro. These bridges are useful to developers who wish to create an exciting destination within their towers while also allowing tenants to share upper-floor plates and create connections between adjacent programs. In the World Trade Center II Design Competition, nearly all the competitors proposed the use of skybridges and attributed their designs to needs for security, safety, and connectivity.

Recently, the vertigo-inducing heights of many skybridges have become their own entertainment experience: for instance, the OCBC Skyway, an aerial promenade at Singapore's Gardens by the Bay (2011); the Grand Canyon Skywalk (2007) in Arizona, a glass, U-shaped deck that cantilevers nearly 70 feet out from the edge and more than 700 feet above the canyon floor; and the Zhangjiajie Grand Canyon Bridge (2015), a glass-bottom, 1410-foot-long footbridge suspended between two cliffs with a 984-foot vertical drop.

Sky-Garden

Sky-garden is a term used for elevated exterior or interiorized garden spaces or parks. The concept of a park-in-the-sky has been a recurring motif in urban speculations for the last century. In the early 1920s, New York City architects Raymond Hood and Harvey Wiley Corbett collaborated on Rockefeller Center, proposing seven acres of interconnected roof gardens, which they referred to as the Hanging Gardens of New York. Contemporary examples of elevated parks include Promenade Plantée (1993) in Paris and the High Line (2009/2011/2014) in New York, both of which reused abandoned urban railways as linear gardens. In Calgary, the bonus density system designed to create the +15 was also used to incentivize the creation of an elevated, interiorized urban oasis and public park called the Devonian Gardens (1977/2012).

Skyways

Skyways is the local name given to interiorized, elevated pedestrian walkways located in the central downtown districts of the Twin Cities of Minneapolis and St. Paul. Originally designed to compete with suburban shopping malls by creating a network of covered connections between downtown shops and department stores, their existence is usually attributed to the area's cold winter climate. The Minneapolis Skyway System began in 1962 and now interconnects nearly the entire downtown core on the second level. Public airspace over the streets is leased to building owners to make private bridge connections. The increased lease value of the second level, which often rivals street-level rates, perpetuates the system's growth. An alternative approach was taken in 1972 by the City of St. Paul, where a public system was developed using funds from a federal urban renewal grant. The publicly owned system appropriates private interior space using public easement. Bridges are required to be constructed to the design standards of the city using a single prototype. Other cities have adopted the skyway system model but use names such as skywalk or the +15.

Social Bracket

The social bracket is used by Steven Holl to define an elevated horizontal walkway with double-height or triple-height social spaces that connect multiple residential or office towers. As found in the elevated walkways that connect the towers at Holl's Linked Hybrid in Beijing and his Mixed Porosity Block in Chengdu, the social bracket mixes populations and allows access to public cafeterias, gyms, galleries, and theaters.

Social Condensers

The social condenser arose from Constructivist experiments in Soviet architecture and urban planning in the early twentieth century. Its goal was to influence social behavior by breaking down hierarchies through the creation of more equitable and accessible public spaces. The Social Condenser functions as an interiorized street where various populations converge and can interact, connecting more individual and private arenas with socially driven programs via circulation strategies. The term originated with OSA, the first group of Constructivist architects, and was representative of their interest in social and functional ideas in design. They were led by Moisei Ginzburg, the Vesnin Brothers, and El Lissitzky and were the counterpart of the Berlin group, Der Ring, and through this association and others, highly influential with the early MARS Group in London. The idea of the social condenser has been referenced by the MARS Group's Plan for London, the London County Council, Le Corbusier, Kisho Kurokawa, and Rem Koolhaas/OMA.

Span-over Blocks

Span-over Blocks (circa 1957) are a technical expression of Yona Friedman's principles of mobile architecture. They were deployed in his project La Ville Spatiale begun in the late 1950s—a speculative proposal for an elevated city defined by a loose and mobile framework occupied informally by its population. In La Ville Spatiale, large bridges containing all of the functions of the city are supported on pillars that contain elevators and stairs as well as utility services. Friedman's images of large hovering superstructures suggested the possibility of completely independent urban systems spanning existing historic cities and countryside—an urbanism of spatial detachment similar to *New Babylon*.

Stem and Web

Two interrelated concepts of urban space developed by Candilis-Josic-Woods. The stem (1960) is a basic spine for the public realm, defined as an urban space by the forms around it and used to create a new focus for collective urban activities. In the work of Team 10, the stem is often elevated, as in streets-in-the-sky, and used as a component of the cluster. The stem relies on redefining the role of the traditional street as an urban fragment that both captures and connects with existing spatial practices. The concept of web was based on the idea that urban fabric was complex and capable of change and regeneration, illustrated by the Frankfurt-Römerberg in Germany (1963) and its network of decks, open spaces, and traces. Alison Smithson reframed the concept of web-building as mat-building (also termed the "groundscraper"), using the example of Candilis-Josic-Woods's Free University Berlin. Thomas Avermaete describes the web as a "mesh of traces and open spaces into which programmatic elements can be woven and an alternative for vertical density."

Streets in the Sky

Alison and Peter Smithson created the poetic expression "streets in the sky" as an alternative to the more pragmatic "deck-access system." Intended to reestablish the street and a sense of community, their proposals for elevated walkways in postwar British housing estates such as Golden Lane Housing project (1952) and Robin Hood Gardens (1971) were alternatives to the simple but isolated high-rise tower block in a park. The Smithsons exhibited these concepts along with the Urban Re-identification Grid at CIAM 9 (1953), which featured photographs of children playing in the streets of postwar London—metaphors for social cohesion and urban connection.

The Smithsons and other young architects who had been recruited as the next generation of the MARS Group and CIAM were interested in the idea of "urbanisme"—the interconnection of different programs in the city, the continuity of urban fabric (above and on the street), and the importance of movement patterns and people in shaping the city. Their influence can be seen in the many "cluster" projects proposed in the 1950s and 1960s by various architects that combined diverse programs with multilevel walkways.

The Street as Object

Questioning the CIAM doctrine of rational zoning and Le Corbusier's internalization of the street,

Team 10 began by inverting previous urban models. They reversed the conventional figure-ground relationship of building to street, objectifying it as an elevated superstructure. This figural treatment eventually reimagined the street as the building itself in various urban proposals, such as the reconstruction of Frankfurt-Romerberg (1963) by Candilis-Josic-Woods or in the Berlin Haupstadt (1957) proposal by Alison and Peter Smithson. Team 10 viewed the street as an occupiable space facilitating a free play of programs, social interaction, and movement. Shadrach Woods referred to these low-slung megastructures as "groundscrapers."

Strada Nobile

After the plague of Milan, Leonardo da Vinci proposed his Ideal City (*Citta*, *Codex B*, 1490), which provided an upper-level circulation zone for aristocrats and clergy called the *strada nobile* (nobile streets) overlooking a city inhabited by tradesmen and workers, with sanitation functions hidden below grade. Using various arguments ostensibly promoting hygiene, efficiency, and security, pedestrian systems that were vertically segregated by class and power also appeared in fifteenth- and sixteenth-century Rome, Florence, and Venice. Giorgio Vasari's half-mile-long elevated Corridorio (1565) in Florence was intended to create discreet passage for royalty and protection from assassins. In eighteenth-century London, these ideas would again gain currency as the mercantile class reinforced social hierarchies to maintain their status and security while also retaining close proximity to their waterfront business interests.

Street Bridges

The idea of the first multilevel pedestrian system for a modern city originated in France in the late 1860s with utopian socialist Dr. Jules-Antoine Moilin. He developed a scheme for new buildings in Paris to be interconnected with covered street bridges (*rues galleries*), hoping to eventually connect all of Paris with a weatherproof, upper-level network. In the early 1900s, Paris' city planner, Eugène Hénard, became interested in traffic separation and refined Moilin's idea. In turn, Hénard's proposals for Paris influenced Le Corbusier. Inspired by the traffic separation ideas of Le Corbusier in the 1920s, Richard Neutra proposed Rush City Reformed (1928). In response, Le Corbusier suggested the inhabitants would blow up Neutra's catwalks: "This is a picture of anti-reason itself, of error, of thoughtlessness. Madness ... the pedestrian, from now on, will be confined to raised walks built up above the street, while traffic lanes remain at their present ground level. Madness."

Street Hierarchy

In response to the growing congestion of European and American cities, Ludwig Hilberseimer first defined the term "street hierarchy" in his book, *City Plan* (1927) as a technique for creating road networks with different orders or levels of connectivity that can also exclude automobile traffic from more developed areas. Advanced to enhance the safety of pedestrians as well as facilitate higher speed movement through the city, Hilberseimer's ideas underscored the functionalist notion of the city as a machinelike instrument. His work was the first in a series of CIAM projects that advocated traffic separation in cities and influenced future endeavors by Le Corbusier and others.

Surreptitious Urbanism

The authors' term for an overall urban form that is created incrementally by stealth. It is a method of informal development that is self-organized yet directed toward a specific outcome that may not be clear or as intended at its outset.

hree-Dimensional Town Planning

In 1941 and 1942, William and Aileen Tatton-Brown published the article "3-D Town Planning" along with an elevated pedestrian network study for Finsbury (an early part of the 30-mile Pedway plan), in *Architectural Review*. It included a summary of their strategies for three-dimensional pedestrian systems from the first MARS Group exhibition of 1938. They also reinterpreted the Constructivist idea of the social condenser as the Theory of Contacts to include the intentional overlapping of programs within circulation spaces. Accordingly, shared circulation nodes would create areas of intersection with potential for otherwise dispersed social communities to interact. These ideas were combined to propose a system of elevated public spaces integrated into the historic city center that were conceived of in three dimensions and built incrementally.

Upside Down Skyscraper

Based on the belief that the skyscraper had become an uninteresting vertical extrusion of two-dimensional form with simplistically formed public programs at its base, Rem Koolhaas in 2003 proposed to "Kill the Skyscraper." He has since completed a number of projects that invert the skyscraper typology, using the public program at the base to create varying forms that leverage elevated public spaces or "sky lobbies" and interconnect multiple tower forms. Projects include the CCTV tower in Beijing, OMA's proposal for an Upside Down Skyscraper for post–9/11 New York, and De Rotterdam Tower.

Vertiginous Cities

Giovanni Battista Piranesi's drawings of the *Carceri* (*Prisons*) (1720–1778) prefigured both the futuristic and dystopian aspects of three-dimensional urban environments made up of catwalks, stairways, and ambiguously layered architectural space. Although proffered by Tafuri as a "negative utopia" warning about the future of cities, the *Carceri* also exploits the sublime spectacle of the grand continuous interior for effect—a strategy well known to contemporary developers like architect John Portman.

Ville-Pilotis

A city conceived of by Le Corbusier elevated on pilotis (or concrete piles). The ground plane would be raised 16 to 20 feet, heavy traffic and utilities would be located below with pedestrians and light traffic above. It would allow for a continuous spatial experience on the ground plane of the city, privileging light, air, and greenspace.

Wikio

Wikio are defined as overhead circulation bridges in Islamic cities in North Africa and can be found in Lamu, Kenya, and Zanzibar, Tanzania. They were likely developed in the Omani period (1700s–1800s) and intended to connect related households, allowing people passage without exposure to the street. One of the earliest examples of the bi-level city is 12th-century Islamic Ghadames in Libya, where men and women were segregated from each other on two levels. This model was followed in other Islamic cities in East Africa and the Middle East where upper-level bridges were used to create private and controlled zones for women. These city forms were radically different from earlier models, with specific strategies for controlled movement between levels and with each level of the new city programmed for different uses.

WALKER ART CENTER BOARD OF TRUSTEES 2015–2016

Executive Director
—————————
Olga Viso

President
—————
Patrick J. Denzer

Vice Presidents
—————————
John Christakos
Monica Nassif

Treasurer
—————
John P. Whaley

Secretary
—————
Donna Pohlad

Public Members
—————————
Christopher Askew
Jan Breyer
James Dayton
Andrew S. Duff
Sima Griffith
Julie Guggemos
Nina Hale
Karen Heithoff
Ben Hirst
Andrew Humphrey
Bill Jonason
Matthew Knopf
Anne Labovitz
Martha (Muffy)
    MacMillan
Alfredo Martel
Jennifer Martin
Aedie McEvoy
Dave Moore, Jr.
James Murphy
Dick Payne
Michael Peterman
Patrick Peyton
Dean Phillips
Brian Pietsch
Rebecca Pohlad
Teresa Rasmussen
Elizabeth G. Redleaf
Peter Remes
Joel Ronning
Lynn Carlson Schell
Jesse Singh
Gregory Stenmoe
Wim Stocks

Carol Surface
Laura Taft
Greta Warren
Susan White
Thomas Wicka
Audrey Wilf
D. Ellen Wilson
Wayne Zink

Walker Family Members
—————————————
Ann W. Cadwalader
Ann Hatch
Jean K. Walker Lowell
Gil Roeder
Adrian Walker
Elaine B. Walker
Lindsey Walker

Honorary Trustees
—————————
H. B. Atwater, Jr.
Ralph Burnet
Julia W. Dayton
Roger Hale
Erwin Kelen
Larry Perlman
C. Angus Wurtele

National Advisory Board
—————————————
Gayle and Mike Ahearn
Ann Birks
Gloria Bumsted
David Colburn
Arlene and John Dayton
Lyn De Logi
Martha and John
    Gabbert
Pamela Kramlich
Jeanne and Richard
    Levitt
Barry Murphy and
    Rosemary Dunbar
Mary and John
    Pappajohn
Lois and John Rogers
Judith and Stephen
    Shank
Mike and Elizabeth
    Sweeney

INDEX

235